I0881411

Rome and Barbaricum

Rome and Barbaricum

Contributions to the archaeology and history of interaction in European protohistory

edited by

Roxana-Gabriela Curcă, Alexander Rubel,
Robin P. Symonds and Hans-Ulrich Voß

Archaeopress Roman Archaeology 67

ARCHAEOPRESS PUBLISHING LTD
Summertown Pavilion
18-24 Middle Way
Summertown
Oxford OX2 7LG

www.archaeopress.com

ISBN 978-1-78969-103-0
ISBN 978-1-78969-104-7 (e-Pdf)

Cover image: Waldgirmes. Life-size gilded bronze horse's head with phalerae depicting Victory and Mars

Printed in England by Severn, Gloucester
This book is available direct from Archaeopress or from our website www.archaeopress.com

Contents

List of Figures

M. Martins *et al.*: **Constructing identities within the periphery of the Roman Empire: north-western Hispania**

Foreword

How did the 'Barbarians' influence Roman culture? What did 'Roman-ness' mean in the context of Empire? What did it mean to be Roman *and/or* 'Barbarian' in different contexts? These are only a few guiding questions of the present volume which gathers most of the papers delivered at the *European Association of Archaeologists Annual Meeting*, Istanbul, 10-14 September 2014, organized within the framework of the project PN-II-ID-PCE-2012-4-0490, *'The Other' in Action: The Barbarization of Rome and the Romanisation of the World*. With the concept of *'the other' in action* it is argued that the receptiveness of Roman culture is the basis and thus the key concept for understanding the empire and the provincial system. The concept manifests Rome's unique capacity to creatively adapt elements of foreign cultures, of 'the other', within the framework of Roman rule and to make them part of an integration process.

These conference proceedings explore the concepts of Romanisation and of the Barbaricum from a multi-disciplinary comparative perspective, covering Germania, Dacia, Moesia Inferior, Hispania, and other regions of the Roman Empire. The papers deal with issues including the conceptual analysis of the term 'barbarian', military and administrative organization, inter-cultural and linguistic relations, numismatics, religion, economy, prosopographic investigations, the construction of identities, and reflections on the theoretical framework for a new model of Romanisation. Traditional and inter-disciplinary approaches as well as the re-evaluation of old and new records are emphasized in the papers of this volume.

The first study provides a multifaceted analysis of the term 'barbarian' as employed by the Romans throughout history. G. Rasbach argues that the site Waldgirmes, deep in Germania Magna, is the key to understanding elite control under Roman hegemony as a necessary condition for administrative integration. The paper of D. Burger-Völlmecke deals with the Gallo-Roman 'Auf dem Spätzrech' temple in the civitas Treverorum of Gallia Belgica in relation to the nearby *oppidum* 'Hunnenring', and the nature of the late Roman archaeological remains. Hans-Ulrich Voß identifies an extensive and long-lasting network between barbarian elites in the area outside the Roman frontier of the second century AD; this influenced the spread of both Roman material goods in the Central European Barbaricum and Roman influence on intra-Germanic affairs. The paper by I. Dumitrache and R.-G. Curcă deals with the cultural activity and interactions between the Roman settlers and the natives of Moesia Inferior in light of the epigraphic evidence. The contribution of L. Mihailescu-Bîrliba, a prosopographic study of Roman magistrate of Troesmis is also based on epigraphic sources. L. Munteanu attempts to establish in his study a pattern of the coin finds from Dacia. The paper delivered by A. Popa deconstructs the historiographical 'myth' of the 'Romanisation of the ancestors of the Romanian people' as found in Romanian and Moldovan school textbooks. M.

Martins *et al.* analyse the particular interactions and developments occurring in north-western Iberia when the area became part of Hispania Tarraconensis.

We would like to thank those authors who did not attend the conference but have chosen to publish the results of their research in this volume.

This work was supported by a grant from the Romanian National Authority for Scientific Research, CNCS-UEFISCDI, project number PN-III-P4-ID-PCE-2016-0669, Beyond the fringes of empire. Roman influence and power north of the Danube and east of the Rhine — arheo.ro/ romaninfluence.

What the Romans really meant when using the word 'Barbarian'. Some thoughts on 'Romans and Barbarians'

Alexander Rubel

Institute of Archaeology of Iași

Abstract

This article presents a notional analysis of the term 'barbarian', as employed by the Romans from the moment it was borrowed from Greek until Late Antiquity. It finds that the Romans used this term in a much different manner than the moderns, thus dismissing the classical dichotomy associated with it. The term's shifting semantics always crossed beyond the basic civilisational pigeonholing we employ today, and was contingent on factors as varied as psychological (including Roman self-consciousness), political and juridical status, ideological aims, and geographical needs.

Keywords: Greco-Roman culture, barbarians, alterity, Romanisation

As part of my involvement since 2013 in a research project entitled "The 'Other' in Action. The Barbarization of Rome and the Romanisation of the World" at the behest of the Romanian Research Council, there is a set of ideas that I would like to address here. It seems to me that modern historical and archaeological studies have treated the concept of 'barbarian' a little superficially. Works from recent years bear titles such as: 'Romans and Barbarians' (Williams 1998), 'Rome and the Barbarians' (Burns 2004), 'Romans, Barbarians, and the Transformation of the Roman World' (Mathiesen and Shanzer 2011), 'Romani e barbari' (Giorcelli and Bersani 2004) – and others. Peter Heather does not deem it necessary in his 'Empires and Barbarians', to mention anything at all about the conceptual aspects of the term Barbarian. The Barbarians simply happened to be there in his book and formed the natural opposition to the Romans as well as inhabiting 'Barbarian Europe'[1] (Heather 2009: 21). All of these titles suggest that their authors know precisely who is a Barbarian and how his barbarity is expressed. A look at the sources may well reveal that the Romans themselves were not quite so sure.

The basic underlying and schematised generic term of barbarian is, however, a strictly modern working concept which we extensively and unquestioningly use to divide up the ancient world – as the majority of titles suggest – into an antithetic Hegelianist dichotomy in which the Barbarians definitely need the Romans, in order, above all else, to exist. The Barbarians are in this sense, first and foremost, the non-Romans – the ones who are not part of the Roman Empire.

[1] Cited after German edition 2011.

The analytically modern concept of historians and archaeologists of a barbarian also conveys, just like that of the ancient world, the idea of a cultural gap. Our non-Roman barbarians are also understood in adjectival terms in their existence and in accordance with their behaviour as being barbaric and inclined to barbarity. The mention of barbaric behaviour or of barbarity has once again a modern connotation at a time when the anti-cultural acts of the so-called Islamic State are being denounced. The barbarian, which is the term we generally use for him, as well as being the one that is used when referring to him in scientific tracts on 'Romans and Barbarians', is stuck with this as something that is static and immovable; he is and he remains a barbarian and as such represents the 'otherness'. In our general imagination, the barbarian is not and cannot be one of 'us' and he remains as the enemy of civilisation and – something that is crucial for our modern presentation of the ancient barbarian – he is ethnically alien, is even part of another race, if one is allowed to make use of this rather outmoded piece of terminology. He is essentially externally and phenotypically separate from 'us'. In everyday speech, the word actually only emerges when used in an adjectival form. When we travel in distant countries, we do not talk about visiting the 'barbarians'. Nor do we refer to the inhabitants of other countries in that way. However, to a great extent we do tend to call uncivilised behaviour 'barbaric'. 'Duden', which is the most commonly-used dictionary used by Germans, has the following entry under 'Barbar' or 'Barbarian' (as we would say in English): 1. Rough, insensitive person without culture, 2. [In a specific field] Completely uneducated person, 3. [For the ancient Greeks and Romans] Member of a foreign nation.

Thus, generally when we talk about barbarians, we only have in mind as a secondary consideration those ancient foreign nations, i.e. those that were not part of the Greco-Roman cultural order and of its civilisation; we are referring, therefore, to uneducated ruffians of whatever provenance.

However, we are staying within the concept that we are using if we mean ancient nations and the two opposing parties of 'Romans and Barbarians' that emerge frequently in a variety of literary texts. Without citing any particular cases, there do seem to be significant numbers of modern scientific projects and many valuable studies where the use of the modern concept of 'barbarian' is certainly widespread and consistently used in a somewhat superficial manner even by specialists who are researching the contact areas of the Roman Empire.

The Romans did not have a genuine Latin term of their own which would have fully conveyed the meaning of the original Greek word. If we refer to barbarians in the sense of their being foreign nations, Latin has the descriptive term for this which is *externae gentes*. In addition, foreign nations were classified according to their relationship with Rome and placed in different categories – mostly legally related – with designations such as *amici populi Romani* (friends of the Roman people), *Foederati* (nations to whom ancient Rome provided benefits in exchange for military assistance) or even *hostes* (enemies). The Romans thus used the term Barbarians as a foreign word that they had adopted in a rather more careful and differentiated manner than we generally do, as well as at different times in conceivably differing contexts and meanings. 'The Barbarians' as a concept of the Romans do not exist. There are a number of reasons for this and I would like to briefly describe these and the change that the concept of barbarians underwent. Furthermore, I would also make reference to the peculiarities of Roman citizenship law, and the related extensive granting of freedom to slaves as contradicting a rigid concept of 'barbarians'. Hopefully it will be clear at the end that as far as from a Roman point of view the Barbarians were quite different from the current concept of them.

In the first place, we have to ask the question, who is a Barbarian? To define this from the Roman viewpoint is not simple, since it is a matter of interpreting what was an original Greek concept. The fact is that the split between Greeks (Hellenes) and Barbarians (Barbaroi) cannot be directly converted into a Roman context. On the one hand, the Romans created differences by legal classification within the Empire and their categorisations of neighbours into *amici populi romani*, *foederati* or *hostes*. Also, as Gerold Walser has said, their 'belief in the superiority of their own order constantly prevented the Romans from adopting a position of comparison and contrast within their environment' (Walser 1951: 68). On the other hand, the adopting of the Greek concept was for the Romans always tinged with some uncertainty since they could not exclude the idea that they themselves might also be Barbarians, since that was part of the logic of the Greek concept (Walbank 1972: 159).

Most Greek authors of the Hellenistic period did consider the Romans to be Barbarians. Later Greek writers of the Roman Empire have been forced either to avoid this impression altogether or to contradict it. Dionysius of Halikarnassos was quite inventive in this respect: the Romans were, in his view, proper Greeks, and always had been, simply by virtue of their bold deeds. This point of view offered the advantage that the Greeks could feel secure, from 146 BC onwards, since they were being governed by people like themselves, in other words by Greeks and not by Barbarians.[2] The genesis of the Greek concept of Barbarians must be disregarded here,[3] suffice to say that in the 5th Century BC, and above all through the writings of Isocrates in the 4th Century BC, the concept of Barbaros became a derogatory term for foreigners. The Barbarian is no longer just someone who speaks in an unmistakably non-Greek way, but is primarily inferior from a moral viewpoint, with this relating in particular to the decadent Persian.

A basic premise for the development of the concept was also the initially clear geographic separation of East and West, which Herodotus – admittedly without expressing discriminatory views against the Orient – had made. Edward Said starts the structural-historical-geographic part of his *Orientalism* with this negative Greek image of the Persians, which has remained the predominant view into modern times (Said 1978: 49-73, specifically 56-58).

By way of a small selection, here are a few of the descriptive adjectives frequently used for describing the stereotyped form of barbarian: uncouth, rough, uneducated, brutal, dumb, unscrupulous and prone to violence, which were used as basic descriptions of the natural characteristics of the Barbarians.[4] It seems that the dichotomous division of the world into

[2] See also Gabba 1991: 190-216, and Walbank 1972: 159.
[3] In particular Dihle 1994, Dihle 1962 and Harrison 2002.
[4] See also Christ 1959: 275 and Speyer s.v. Barbarus I, in: *RAC* Suppl 1 (2001): 837-841. Particularly on the vocabulary of barbarian characteristics, cf. Dauge 1981: 413-466, tables and lists 437f, 459. The most common concepts in the description of the Barbarians are: *feritas*, *vanitas*, *ferocia*, *belli furor*, *discordia*.

'Hellenes and Barbaroi' has come about on this basis. But also linguistically speaking, the Greek world was split in two parts, 'we and the others', on the basis of a citizenship law that was much simpler than its Roman equivalent. All other languages were considered to be barbaric ways of speaking and as such not the same as Greek. The concept of the Barbarian was used initially by the Romans in a way that was not likely to be considered offensive. In the prologue of Trinummus (19), Plautus mentions that he had translated an original Greek comedy into 'Barbarian', meaning that he translated it from Greek into Latin: *Philemo scripsit, Plautus vortit barbare.* This usage in Plautus, who calls his predecessor Naevius, the pioneer of the Roman comedies and of the history epics, a *poeta barbarus* (*Mil.* 213, *poetae .... barbaro*), shows clearly that the concept of the Barbarian as initially used by the Romans was not used in a derogatory sense[5] (Wiele 1973: 108).

After Rome became a Mediterranean super-power this naive early self-designation dissolves into a certain irritation about being referred to as Barbarians by the Greeks, as Cato has most clearly formulated (in Plinius, *Nat. Hist.* 29, 14). This is accompanied by the perception that the Barbarian is not only the same thing as non-Greek, but that the concept includes an ethical value and thus denies the one being called a Barbarian any civilising capabilities. From the Roman viewpoint he is now not only the foreigner, but also someone 'plainly uncultured and incapable of being civilised' (Heitz 2009: 26),[6] and who is characterised by his barbaric way of behaving. Quite naturally Roman self-awareness could not see this concept as pertaining to itself, even if later writers do identify the misconduct of Romans as being barbaric, or in the way that Cicero described his opponents, for instance Verres or Antonius, as Barbarians.[7] Verres was even worse than a barbarian, because such a person is a Barbarian only according to provenance and language, whereas he was actually labelled as a Barbarian on the basis of his character (*natura et moribus*).

Hence, the three proper nouns 'Greeks, Romans and Barbarians' became more common in Roman use for the categorisation of the *oecumene.*[8] A certain uneasiness remains, however, and the famous quotation from Horace, according to which 'Greece, once conquered, in turn conquered its uncivilized conqueror, and brought the arts to rustic Latium', was a literary reflex of this unresolved inferiority complex: *Graecia capta ferum victorem cepit et artes intulit agresti Latio* (*Hor. Epist.* 2, 1, 156) (Vogt-Spira 1999).

This uncertainty is also expressed in the writings of Cicero about the State in a conversation between Laelius and Scipio, where it is made clear by Cicero that the important thing when labelling someone as a Barbarian (or not) is not language (*lingua)* or tribal roots (*gens*) but customs (*mores*) and character (*ingenium*) (or the lack of it). The way the Greeks resolve this – and according to which there are only Greeks and Barbarians – is no longer valid

[5] Speyer cites these adoptions of the concept as being 'totally naive', s.v. Barbarus I, in: *RAC* Suppl. 1 (2001), 829, differing from Rüger 1965: 12, who recognises the irony and the usage of *barbarus* for 'Roman' by Plautus and suggests that this is an overstretched joke that has thus become rather bland. An overall discussion of the question of what could be hidden in this context behind the concept of Barbarian, is in McElduff 2013: 66-72, which advocates the view that for Plautus the concept is a device that permits the spectators to see the Greek perspective from which they are now viewing a Greek play.

[6] 'der Kulturlose und Unkultivierbare schlechthin'.

[7] Cic. *Phil.* 3, 15: On Antonius: *quam barbarus! Quam rudis!*; Cic. *Verr.* 4, 112.

[8] Cic. fin. 2, 49, div. 1, 84; 2, 82; Lucil. 615. Cicero is the first to introduce this three-way split: Rüger 1965: 12f.

and the persons or groups in question must be given an individual assessment, as is made clear in the question of whether or not Romulus was a barbarian king: *'Cedo, num' Scipio, 'barbarorum Romulus rex fuit?' (Lael.) 'Si ut Graeci dicunt omnis aut Graios esse aut barbaros, vereor ne barbarorum rex fuerit, sin id nomen moribus dandum est, non linguis, non Graecos minus barbaros quam Romanos* puto.*' Et Scipio: 'Atqui ad hoc de quo agitur non quaerimus gentem, ingenia quaerimus'* (Cic. *De Rep.* 1, 58).

Even though, the cliché-laden concept of Barbarians with its ethically derogative connotation is mostly used by the writers of the golden Latinitas in its pejorative meaning to vilify groups as well as individuals as uncivilised and ignominious, the view of foreign nations remains ambivalent. The concept of the Barbarian finds differing uses in complex contexts, where the precarious situation of the Roman himself remains a matter for consideration in the analysis of the Greek concept. Michel Dubuisson confirms consistently: 'Le mot barbarus n'avaitjamais pris racine a Rome' (2001: 9).

On this point I am limiting myself to investigating two classical authors, whom I have examined in some depth with a complete text search of 'barbarian'-related references. The 'Barbarian' book *par excellence* is undoubtedly *Germania* by Tacitus. Here, one would expect to find considerable usage of the word 'barbarian', since this is the standard ancient work on ethnography. However, the Germanic tribes are described throughout as '*gentes*', with the word *gens* (with its derivatives) appearing 43 times in the small text. The term *barbarus* and its derivatives appear only three times. In Chapter 18 the Germans are the only ones amongst all of the Barbarians – here the neutral and unbiased concept for all foreign nations is meant – who are supposed only to take one wife in line with strict matrimonial rules. *Nam prope soli barbarorum singulis uxoribus contenti sunt.* In this case the concept is still being used in a neutral sense.

The two further mentions in Tacitus refer to the cultural gap and describe negative characteristics of the Germans. The brutal human sacrifice of the Semnones is branded by the quivering Roman as a barbaric rite[9] and the evidently interesting question for Tacitus on the origin and spread of amber, over which the Northern Germans exercised control as an important traded commodity, does not interest the Germans *ut barbaris*, because they are merely Barbarians.[10]

As the few examples from Tacitus have already revealed, he actually wanted to present the Germans as noble savages, in contrast to the decadent Romans who had distanced themselves from the *mos maiorum*, referring to the 'barbarian' attributes principally as uncivilised behaviour and displaying a lack of education. The infrequent use of the term when describing the German nations remains significant. The malicious 'B-word' is used to describe a characteristic, but not as an overall term that applies to foreign nations and, in that case, the more commonly found word *gens* is used, by means of which Tacitus is limiting the use of the word in its pejorative sense to a minimum.

[9] Tac. *Ger.* 39: *Stato tempore in silvam auguriis patrum et prisca formidine sacram omnes eiusdem sanguinis populi legationibus coeunt caesoque publice homine celebrant barbari ritus horrenda primordia.*

[10] Tac. *Ger.* 45: *Nec, quae natura, quaeve ratio gignat, ut barbaris, quaesitum compertumve; diu quin etiam inter cetera eiectamenta maris iacebat, donec luxuria nostra dedit nomen.*

I have found 70 mentions of derivations of the word Barbarian in all of the available books of Livy. It is used for the invading Gauls of 390 BC, but also for the Carthaginians and naturally the Germans.[11] The term is, however, predominantly used as a synonym for enemies,[12] almost exclusively ethnic and mainly in the form of a proper noun.[13] But Roman writers, and occasionally even Livy, make use of a whole catalogue of stereotyped characteristics which apply as being typically barbarian, and *feritas*, *vanitas*, *furor*, and other bad habits are typical descriptions of the Barbarians.[14]

In this respect, the Roman concept comes closer to our everyday understanding of it. But there is a differentiation made consistently in the literature of the Romans and Greeks (of the Roman period) in respect to a simple national psychology. A differentiation is made between Germans, Gauls, Africans, Spaniards, etc., who each have differing characteristics in terms of the classification of their barbarian or barbaric bad habits. Their differing visual appearances and qualities are stereotyped but are for the most part, pseudo-scientifically based and attributed to the influence of the natural environment (too much sun, too cold, etc.). The classification of the nations by Vitruvius in accordance with Lebensraum or living space (Beginning of Book 6) is part of this. Just the climate and rays of the sun in different countries also have significant effects on the outlooks and appearance of the inhabitants according to the information from ancient ethnographers and writers. Diodor emphasises that the extreme cold in Northern Scythia and the heat in lands to the south of Egypt are the cause of the quite different ways of life and of physical aspects that are different from those of the inhabitants of Mediterranean countries (Diod. 3, 84, 7-8). A similar type of classification can be found in the works of Strabo, who in addition to the characteristic Lebensraum also refers to the way of life (nomadic, etc.) (Gracianskaya 1996: 483-487, with quotes).

From the overall viewpoint, it is established that the perception of the 'barbaric' world by the Romans was made in the context of the "dualism of 'us' and 'them'" (Ohnacker 2003: 62),[15] that is to say, in line with the classical sociological theory of 'otherness'. In that way, the concept has a semantic breadth, which extends from the completely neutral designation of the enemy down to the clearly negative view of their being recognised cultural underdogs due to their intemperance and uncivilised savagery.

[11] In particular in the following locations, where the root word 'barbarian' can be found in total 70 times: Book 5: 36, 38, 39. Book 6: 18, 42; Book 7: 24; Book 10: 10; Book 21: 2, 23, 34, 35, 60; Book 22: 22, 59; Book 23: 18; Book 24: 47, 48, 49; Book 25: 33; Book 26: 43; Book 27: 17, 19, 33; Book 28: 1, 3, 13, 17, 18, 21, 33; Book 29: 2, 23, 25; Book 30: 11, 28; Book 31: 29, 30, 33, 34; Book 34: 14, 16, 21, 24; Book 37: 55; Book 38: 37, 40, 49; Book 39: 28, 35, 53; Book 40: 3, 35, 36, 39, 48; Book 41: 3, 11; Book 43: 20; Book 44: 27; Book 45: 29, 30.

[12] Liv. 6, 42: *Nec dubia nec difficilis Romanis, quamquam ingentem* ***Galli*** *terrorem memoria pristinae cladis attulerant, victoria fuit. Multa milia* ***barbarorum*** *in acie, multa captis castris caesa; palati alii Apuliam maxime petentes cum fuga [se] longinqua tum quod passim eos simul pavor errorque distulerant, ab* ***hoste*** *sese tutati sunt.* Ohnacker 2003: 42-47, has indicated the close connection of the concepts of *barbarus* and *hostis* in the historical sources.

[13] 7, 24: *His adhortationibus iterum coorti pellunt loco primos manipulos* ***Gallorum****; cuneis deinde in medium agmen perrumpunt. Inde* ***barbari*** *dissipati, quibus nec certa imperia nec duces essent, vertunt impetum in suos.*

[14] But for example, Livy on 'barbaric infidelity': 22, 22: *Eo uinculo Hispaniam uir unus sollerti magis quam fideli consilio exsoluit. Abelux erat Sagunti nobilis Hispanus, fidus ante Poenis; tum, qualia plerumque sunt barbarorum ingenia, cum fortuna mutauerat fidem.* Dauge 1981 has summarised all of the material. But more precise is Speyer s.v. Barbarus I, in: *RAC* Suppl. 1 (2001): 838-839.

[15] "Dualismus von 'eigen' und 'fremd'".

The Barbarian is both the enemy, as well as the culturally inferior being, the 'Other' and the foreigner, in addition to being viewed with a deliberately satirical bias, as, for example, in Juvenal. The reference to the uncivilised savagery, the lack of emotional control and the further stereotyped characteristics of these 'Others' is accordingly predominant in literary discourse. In this way the moving of the concept away from the Greek idea is a clear and conscious choice.

Possibly Caesar represents an exception. Indeed Mommsen has said that Caesar was one of the few Romans, 'who understood that the so-called barbarians should not be scoffed at'.[16] Individuals are identified in person, but the word barbarian is almost exclusively used in the plural and almost never with respect to the Gauls. Rüger recognises a 'curious reticence in the use of the word and concept of *barbarus*'. Caesar possibly wished to 'give an unprejudiced view of Non-Romans' (Rüger 1965: 107).[17] The term *externae (gentes)* in any case is predominantly being used in the historical discourse of Roman literature much more frequently than the term Barbarian, and it remains – in a typically Roman way – 'a rational, geographic term' (Walser 1951: 67).[18]

One of the most important differences between the Greek concept of barbarian and what the Romans meant by it, comes to light in the astonishing fact that, contrary to modern expectations, that Barbarians could become Romans without any major problem. The fact that the *Imperium Romanum* was in the first place a community of 'nations' bound by a common legal system (the German term 'Rechtsraum' would be more appropriate here) and that Roman citizenship was comparatively easy to obtain, leads to quite different parameters being needed for evaluating the Roman concept of barbarian status[19] (Mathiesen 2006).

The dynamics which brought about the practice of liberation from slavery and the possibility of upward social mobility for those who had been given their freedom, at least from the second generation onward, and the effects of the Romanisation process which had already enabled the integration of members of the Gallic upper-class into the Senate within 100 years of the conquest, made the customary Greek concept of a division between 'us and the barbarians' appear in the case of Rome to be no longer applicable.[20] Local elites in the country towns of the Empire, the *decuriones*, who could also scale the ladder into the ranks of knights or senators – and who served as a reservoir for the elite of the Empire – were recruited principally from non-Roman inhabitants of the provinces and prosperous descendants of freedmen. They were, furthermore, the real backbone of the Empire, which had to be managed to a significant degree without institutionalised administrative structures. Many towns during the earlier days of the Empire owed their

[16] Mommsen, *Roman Hist.* Sect. 3, 299 (Vol. 4, 290 of the latest edition), 'die es verstanden, die sogenannten Barbaren nicht zu verachten'.

[17] '[Eigentümliche] Zurückhaltung im Gebrauch von Wort und Begriff barbarus [...] ein vorurteilsfreies Bild von Nichtrömern geben.'

[18] '[Ein] nüchterner, geographischer Begriff.'

[19] Exhaustively on this subject, see Sherwin White 1973. A useful overview by Coşkun 2009 summarises the recent specialist literature.

[20] On granting of freedom: Gaius, *Inst.* 1, 17-19. But see the discussion on this in Suetonius, where it is mentioned that Augustus had wanted to keep the Roman people '*peregrini ac servilis sanguinis incorruptum*' (Suet. *Aug.* 40, 3) and therefore put limits to *manumissio*. See also Mouritsen 2011.

economic growth directly to freedmen, the *liberti*, and their descendants[21] (Alföldy 1984: 109-114).

Highly symbolic of this mobility is the remarkable career of P. Helvius Pertinax. Pertinax, who was born in AD 126, was the son of a freedman, that is to say of a former slave, and who, in a meteoric rise, reached the rank of Emperor in AD 193. We are told about this quite extraordinary career, which can be compared with the proverbial jump from dishwasher to millionaire of the 'American dream', thanks to detailed sources (in addition to the *Historia Augusta*, we also have an important inscription, which relates to his *cursus honorum*, *AE* 1963: 52). Pertinax, on his way to becoming Emperor, rose from the very lowest ranks in terms of his birth and worked initially as a teacher (*grammaticus*), before he found employment in the army as a centurion, with the help of some well-placed connections. Once there, he furthered his career through his outstanding performance and also thanks to the approval of important people who recognised his talent for leadership. As a member of the *ordo equester*, and later member of the senatorial class, he made his reputation as a skilled trouble-shooter who succeeded in calming a number of potentially explosive situations around the empire on behalf of Antoninus Pius, Marcus Aurelius and Commodus, proving to be an outstanding organiser and administrator in civil and military posts in Syria, Britain, Italy, Dacia, Pannonia and many other places. During his career, he saw service in more or less every part of the great Empire and knew the whole of the *Imperium Romanum* from his own experience better than almost anyone else. His career coincided with the Marcomannic wars, during which the Empire was stretched to breaking point, so that increasingly officers from the lower ranks of the social order were able to significantly advance their careers based on their performance.[22] But the career of Pertinax demonstrates, in all its uniqueness, the fundamentally highly permeable Roman social structure of the Imperial era. Even more significant are the many examples of dignitaries from the towns in the Roman provinces and the economic success stories of rich former slaves and their successors.

Such highly stellar careers still remained a rarity, but the practice of granting freedom represented an enormously dynamic economic factor which enabled people of differing provenance to succeed in the context of the Roman system of values. As a consequence of the Romans' social fluidity, today's barbarian became tomorrow's fellow citizen, or at least his descendants did. Thousands of people of foreign nationality became Roman citizens upon their retirement from the army, as illustrated by the more than 800 Roman military diplomas that have been found. In this way, Mogetissa, from the tribe of the Boii, who was of Celtic origin, and his wife Verecunda, from the Sequani, were given hereditary citizenship rights after this common soldier (*gregalis*) had served for 25 years. His descendants, born after the diploma had been issued, would automatically become Roman citizens, and their daughter Matrulla, who was also named in the certificate, acquired citizenship jointly with her parents.[23] This fact on its own shows the impracticality of the concept of 'barbarian' in the Roman conceptual system, not to mention the possibilities of easily changing one's legal status. It would be frankly absurd to assume that prior to receiving his right of

[21] Also Garnsey 1975; see also specifically Alföldy 1987a and 1999, and Vittinghoff 1994.

[22] On his career in detail, cf. Alfoldy 1987b.

[23] *CIL* 16, 55 from Weißenburg/Bavaria from AD 107. Generally referring to military diplomas, see Eck/Wolff 1986.

citizenship at the end of his career, Mogetissa would have been a 'barbarian', during his 25 years of service in the Army, and would no longer be one only after the legal enactment. This underlines that the present-day concept of a Barbarian could not really have played a genuine role in the Roman world.

The consequences of granting freedom and awarding of citizenship rights can only be roughly evaluated because there are no further census counts available after AD 45. During the time around 90 BC, when the Italian allies of the Romans were fighting for the right of citizenship, there were some 500,000 Roman citizens, and under Augustus this figure had grown to around five million, of whom about a million were under his governance. The census-related counts of AD 45 show that after just 150 years there were already around seven million Roman citizens.[24]

These numbers strongly devalued the concept of Barbarian and added mobility to the social classes to a significant degree. One must, however, refrain from claiming that the Romans, on the basis of rather easily granted citizenship, were pro european humanists, who cared for integration politics. The fundamental absence of any kind of racism characterised by biological perceptions (see below) and the comparatively liberal system of granting citizenship (mostly after usefulness assessments had been made) does not mean that the Roman Empire should be seen as having an 'open society'. The basis of the practice of granting freedom, which incidentally incorporated many advantages (motivation of slaves, as an aid to discipline and reducing the risk of absconding) was the institution of slavery itself, which was a fact of life that would never be called into question. Granting of citizenship was also used as a political tool and was mainly awarded to those foreigners whom the Romans recognised as being useful and loyal (Coşkun 2009: 20-22). Furthermore, the liberal practice of granting citizenship was unique in the ancient world. Thus, this custom played a decisive role for the demographic and cultural adaptability, as well as for the stability of the Empire. Against this background, it is important to establish the fact that the differentiation between Romans and Barbarians was not defined predominantly within the Roman world of ideas by language and origin, but much more by education and moral values (Timpe 2000).[25] The basis for this is the idea that 'barbarity' is a cultural and not a biological concept: 'The *humanitas* of the Roman order was supposed to overcome and transform the *feritas* and *immanitas* of the barbarians and therefore assumes that they are not only able to be conquered in war, but also capable of being transformed' (Timpe 2000: 225).

Let us take Saint Paul as a specific example. The Jewish Paul was brought before Herod Agrippa and Berenice by the hapless *praefectus* (Procurator) Porcius Festus (*Acts of the Apostles* 25, 1-26, 32). Festus did not know where to start with Paul, who had been reported by his own Jewish co-religionists. He could not send him to Jerusalem for trial by the Jews – which would have been the simplest solution – because the accused, as a Roman citizen,

[24] The census counts at Brunt 1971, passim, in summary. The last time we have information on a census of Roman citizens was under the reign of Claudius in AD 45 (6,964,000), see in Hieronymus Ol. 206.1 (Migne *PL* 27: 449).

[25] See also Müller 2009, 5f. Furthermore, it is reported anecdotally, that Emperor Claudius had deprived a delegation from Lycia from their citizenship, because these Greek socialised citizens did not know Latin (Cass. Dio 60, 17, 4).

had exercised his right of appeal to be heard by the Emperor. In addition, the Roman Festus considered the religious accusations as legally trivial and could find no reason as to why Paul should be punished by death.

While in the eyes of many Romans the Jews were the most disliked, intractable and least welcoming of any foreigners[26] (see, for example, the disdainful comments of Juvenal),[27] the trial of Paul shows that as a Greek-speaker, and a Roman citizen of modest means, he not only enjoyed the protection of the law, but despite being a Jew with a rather odd religious zeal – Festus considered him, due to his messianic resurrection story, to be completely demented – he was in no way perceived as a Barbarian. His legal status was the decisive factor and ethnic or indeed racial characteristics played no part in the legal decisions.

These facts show that the concept of Barbarian, which we use to distinguish Romans from foreign nations, with whom they interacted and who they partially integrated, is a modern concept that does not correspond to the Roman concept. Origin and provenance *could* play a role in social status, but were secondary, as can easily be seen in accounts of the advances made by the provincial aristocracy. In this context, a further aspect must be mentioned, which indicates a major difference with modern concepts, and which is the different importance of biological explanatory models and the absence of racial prejudice. If we read Sallust's *Jugurtha*, we can at no point conclude from the text that this book is actually about a North African with a rather black skin (Heubner 2004). The future king of Numidia spent time in his youth serving in the Roman Army and fought in the siege of Numantia; he also had influential friends in Rome and received senatorial support in the struggle for the succession to the throne, since he was a 'peer', like many foreign kings who were counted as *amici poluli Romani* (Marbodius, the Germanic 'Archbarbarian' was also initially an *amicus et socius* of the Romans).

Roman literary sources clearly indicate that dark-skinned persons were not judged on the basis of their appearance. The colour of their skin or where they came from was unlikely to make them any less worthy.[28] Black skin provoked the interest and curiosity of the beholder,

[26] The Jews formed the only nation that remained totally opposed to Roman customs and would not allow themselves to be integrated; they provoked the continuous suspicion of the Romans with their exclusivist religious rules. There is extensive literature on this subject, but see only: Yavetz 1997 and Schäfer 1997, cf. Watts 1976.

[27] Esp. the third satire. The literature is exhaustively summarised in Kißel 2013.

[28] This debate has been summarised in Gruen 2011: 197-220; see also Snowden 1970 and 1983, whose fundamental research results I still consider to be the most appropriate. There are still attempts to attribute racism to the Romans, if not entirely, then at least a kind of proto-racism perhaps springing from the modern lack of understanding with regard to a non-biologically defined perspective on humans, but evidence for such a view is lacking: differences were defined, socially (hierarchically and culturally) – and not by origin, colour of skin, or appearance. A critical approach to this issue, insisting on Roman racism, is most recently – following Thompson 1989 – in Isaac 2004, to be studied only with the reviews by F. Millar 2005 and D. Richter 2006. Somewhat curiously, Isaac (2004: 49f) forgoes any independent discussion about black people in antiquity. He confines his study of an ancient racism to Carthaginians, Gauls and Germans, and above all the Jews. Aside from Snowden, a convincing treatise of the problem of ancient 'racism' (concentrating on the Greeks) was published by Lefkowitz 1996, who is convinced (and I concur) that for the people of the ancient world "culture was a far more important factor in human behaviour than skin colour or other 'racial' characteristics" (p. 9). Lefkowitz also makes critical reference to the absurd subjugation of American university education under the domination of 'political correctness' that are of little benefit, and which are increasingly dominating the routine course of studies in the USA. Thus

and people sometimes became amused about the appearance of black people, above all pygmies, as a few caricatures show. In the case of portraits and other representational forms of black people[29] in artworks, in which true phenotypical features such as black skin-colour, distinctive lips and the occasional prognathism, as well as a wide nose, are seen, the intention was never caricature as such, as modern commentators sometimes suggest (Snowden 1990: 545 sq.).

With Snowden we can conclude the following in accordance with the sources: 'It is important to emphasise that the overall – but especially the more detailed Greco-Roman – view of blacks was highly positive. Initial, favourable impressions were not altered, in spite of later accounts of wild tribes in the far South and even after encounters with blacks had become more frequent' (Snowden 1983: 58 sq.).

This aspect of social differences separates the ancient world's perspective from the modern, post-19th-century imperial approach to the subject of 'racism', which makes it difficult for us to distance ourselves from racially related categories, linked mainly to the colour of the skin. Snowden asserts that the slaves of the Greeks and Romans were predominantly white-skinned people. The majority of the dark-skinned people with negroid features who Roman senators and generals encountered would have belonged to the upper-class or the warrior caste of their respective cultures and thereby were not regarded as inferiors, but rather as 'peers'. In early modern times and during the Age of Imperialism in the 19th century, contacts were established the other way round: colonialist approaches by the European masters towards the indigenous people, often considered to be 'Untermenschen' (or a lower form of humanity) can explain our prejudice or self-consciousness, to which recently 'political correctness' has been added, with the latter unfortunately having a seriously detrimental effect on scholarship.[30] Sources from the Middle Ages, who report on Ethiopian pilgrims arriving in the Western world, are also still significantly free from racially motivated prejudices in relation to skin colour of and provenance. They were considered by the European church dignitaries as envoys of Prester John[31] and had been welcomed by both noblemen and church leaders.

The actual dividing social differences in the ancient world were accordingly more strongly contoured by other factors, and provenance was not a biological or racial category, but first and foremost a social one, which cemented the rank or class differences. In this way the Emperor Claudius could give good advice to the Parthian Prince Meherdates, who was brought up in Rome, for his future office as a ruler about caring for 'the Barbarians with kindness and correctness'. The 'King of the Barbarians', was himself not actually one of

she laments that political correctness makes out Cleopatra as being the proven result of Greco-Macedonian interbreeding – counterfactually – a black African. See also Dench 2005: 122-297, who writes about the Romans on this subject in a well-balanced manner.

[29] See the summaries of the plates section and illustrations in Snowden 1970: 33-99 and 2 to 1-254 and Snowden 1983: 108 sqq.

[30] On the problem of European racism and its relation to slavery and colonialism see the definitive book by Jordan (1968), and on racist ideology, Fredrickson 1971.

[31] Martin 2001: 90ff. and above all Lowe 2005 and 2007. For these useful references I must thank Verena Krebs, whose monograph *Material Diplomacy: Culture Contact and Western Christian Art in Ethiopia 1440-1550* (forthcoming) also covers aspects of this subject.

them.[32] Aelius Aristides also referred to the fact that the Romans divided their subjects into two groups: the nobles, educated and the powerful of the conquered nations who could become citizens (even kinsmen), and the rest as subjects (Ael. Arist. in Romam 59).

Foreigners, either labelled as *externae* or Barbarians, were considered inferior by the Romans and there was a xenophobic tendency which was, in particular, spread by satire; the Romans considered that they were naturally superior to foreign nations. However, these were Barbarians based on their savagery, intemperance and their rough customs, explicable in part by the influence of climate and their lifestyle and not as a consequence of their biological disposition or skin-colour.

Following these observations on the concept of Barbarians, I should like to touch briefly on two further subjects.

On the one hand, there were Barbarians throughout the Roman Empire: not only the 'foreigners' in the capital city of Rome, who are discussed in Juvenal,[33] but also those in the provinces when the Roman Empire was at its peak. Thus, for example, there were in what is today called Spain, not that distant from highly 'romanised' towns, Iron Age settlements, the inhabitants of which fully followed the 'barbarian way of life', as the archaeologist Felix Teichner (2006) has pointed out.

On the other hand, the granting of citizenship to all inhabitants of the Empire as a consequence of the *Constitutia Antoniniana* in 212 reveals the internal ambiguities which also accompany the subject of ethnic identities. In the Rhineland, three Roman soldiers describe themselves as Roman citizens and men, by ancestry originating from the German Taunus region, in an inscription from the year 230: *c. R. et Taunenses ex origine patris* (Riese 1914: 3.1176). We know also about the *cives Romani et Bessi consistentes*, Roman citizens and natives from the tribe of the Bessi, who jointly made offerings in the same place – a *vicus* linked to Histria on the Black Sea.[34]

These examples may be sufficient to illustrate how boundaries become blurred within the Empire. We often find such legally and even culturally differing groups alongside each other. The parameters changed increasingly during Late Antiquity. The colonisation of ethnically homogenous groups *en bloc* in the territory of the Empire brought with it for the new settlers an inferior legal status (*dedictii* or *foederati*), while only the leadership contingent of 'Imperial Barbarians' were given citizenship (see the later 'Reichsgermanen'); this was for the maintenance of, or to cultivate ethnic identities further within Imperial territory, especially since *foederati* (like the Goths after 382) received the right to maintain their cultural and hierarchic customs, thus developing a 'state within a state'. However, these later developments are not a matter for consideration here.[35]

[32] Tac. *Ann.* 12, 11, 2. *addidit praecepta – etenim aderat Meherdates –, ut non dominationem et servos, sed rectorem et cives cogitaret, clementiamque ac iustitiam, quanto ignota barbaris, tanto laetiora capesseret*. See Walser 1951: 70.
[33] There is an abundance of literature on 'foreigners' in Rome and their status, and for this see: Balsdon 1979, Noy 2000 and Donati Giacomini/Poma 1996. See also Coşkun 2014 (very clearly presented with the latest literature). On Juvenal's xenophobia, see the research survey by Kißel 2013, in particular 98-99.
[34] *AE* 1924 1420148 (CIL.III 3505, 7533, 14214). 1st half of the 3rd century. On the *cives Romani consistentes* in the Western Pontus region, see Avram 2007, and with a summarised list of inscriptions.
[35] On this subject, see Schipp 2014. See also Ohnacker 2003, on the concept of barbarian at that time.

Figure 1. 'The Dying Gaul'. Hellenistic sculpture for the Pergamon Altar (Capitoline Museum); photo: Anthony Mayanlahti (antmoos), Wikicommons.

The ambivalence in the notion of 'barbarian' foreign nations, which was most pronounced during the Imperial period, is also mirrored in public art and architecture in Rome, in which representations of 'barbarians' continue to play a role. From the time of Augustus, the classic representation of the Barbarian in art is as the 'loser', the defeated, who delivers glory and honour to the shining victor, the Emperor, and to the Roman Empire. The best-known representation of this type is perhaps the famous large statue sculptured after a Late-Hellenistic model of a dying Gaul (Figure 1).[36] But above all, Roman coin designs featuring representations of conquered people are relevant in this context (Heitz 2006).

The captured and shackled German with his Suebian-knot hairstyle, as represented in a silver figure from Romanian Gherla, presents the typical gesture of subjugation (see Figure 2). This gesture of subjugation also defines in general the representations of barbarians in the art of the earlier Imperial period. The foreigners depicted on the coin designs and other representations from the time of Augustus are to be understood as 'bit players in Augustan unity', whose significance and expressiveness is limited to the gesture of their subjugation (Heitz 2009: 84-90). They are the conquered, but the fact that they are perhaps also Barbarians – or rather *externae* – plays no part in the intended meaning of such pieces of art.

The great triumphal arches built to honour the Emperors also convey this characteristic perspective of the subjugation of the conquered during the period of the Principate. Interestingly, the one-sided representation of foreign nations as enemies and 'losers' changes fundamentally at the time of Trajan and Hadrian (Hölscher 1999 and Heitz 2009, passim, esp. 95-113). In the representations on the triumphal arch of Benevento (Southern

[36] Generally on the pictorial representation of foreigners, see R. M. Schneider s.v. Barbar II, *RAC* Suppl. I (2001): 895-962.

Figure 2. Germanic 'Barbarian' in a gesture of submission, Gherla (Romania); photo: Sigurd Rubel.

Italy), for example, as well as on Trajan's column in Rome, foreign nationals are depicted as military allies and receive generally a more positive representation. Trajan's column depicts both *auxilia* integrated into the Roman army and supporting indigenous troops from different (mostly Germanic) tribes, who fight in the Roman style and are as highly regarded by the Emperor as the already assimilated Dacians, who were evidently enjoying the blessings of Roman civilisation (stone-built towns for example; Heitz 2009: 102-105). As part of the iconographic programme in the arch of Benevento, apart from the defeated enemies and the opponents still to be fought, northern Barbarians appear as allies and an integral part of the Roman army. In particular, a person wearing a sheepskin coat construed earlier as a *signifer* (standard-bearer) has been convincingly identified by Hölscher as an irregular auxiliary troop leader, who is honoured as an associate by the Emperor, surrounded by his lictors (Hölscher 1999: 283-284, also Heitz 2005 and 2009: 107-108). The reliefs of the Trajanic arch of Benevento also specifically 'recognise the role which the provinces and the newly integrated nations play in promoting the well-being of the whole Empire, by strengthening both the army and citizenship' (Heitz 2009: 112).

Thus the Imperial pictorial agenda no longer focuses solely on the subjugation of foreign enemies, but increasingly also includes the trusted collaboration of associated nations beyond the boundaries, and the integration of other tribes within the Empire's territory (Hölscher 1999: 289). This takes place within the framework of developing a conscious Imperial policy, which in pictorial form recognises the role played by loyal foreign allies and underlines the claim to global rule of the Roman Emperor, while emphasising the importance of 'harnessing external forces for the good of the Empire' (Heitz 2005: 222). This fact alone, which is presented in detail by Tonio Hölscher, punctuates the ambivalence of the Roman representations of the Barbarian.[37]

[37] On this in particular, see Hölscher 1999; see also Heitz 2005. A brief observation is worthwhile here: after the partnership-related emphasis in official art and architecture under Trajan and Hadrian, there follows the extremely brutal political turnaround in the representation of the (primarily) hostile Barbarians on the Column of Marcus Aurelius. The scenes in which even captured women are being brutally slaughtered and prisoners executed *en masse* are of a brutality that is without parallel in Roman art. With respect to the Marcus Aurelius Column: see,

Further aspects can be extrapolated. For example the question of whether the representatives of the advanced civilisations in the East, with whom the Romans were not on good terms, such as the Sassanian Dynasty in Persia, were considered to be Barbarians (McDonough 2011 and Drijvers 2011).[38] Or the Egyptians, perhaps, whose Queen Cleopatra was presented as a Barbarian within the propaganda battle of the Civil Wars.[39] Asking this question implies the attribution of modern categories in an unprofessional manner to Roman realities. In the minds of the Romans, foreign nations or tribes are Barbarians only if one wants to disavow them and emphasise the hostility towards them. It is then that the word becomes a verbal weapon or a polemical term and is significantly narrowed down, so that it is virtually devoid of explanatory power.

In Late Antiquity change occurred as the Empire became defined geographically, citizenship was granted to everyone and, beginning in the 3rd century, the term 'Barbaricum' emerges as a territorial concept.[40] In Late Antiquity, Barbarians also become recognisable as 'barbarians' through emerging ethnic identity, marked by dress and customs. In this context, they took part in the affairs of the Empire as leading Roman officials and performed in the military sphere with much success (the best example is Stilicho), but the social distance from the leading Romans became at the same time somewhat greater, since the clearly marked cultural differences remained and were even accentuated by a certain *habitus* with which the Germanic dominated the new barbarian elite and developed their own ideology as a warrior caste (von Rummel 2007). The Roman upper-class accepted the military prowess of the Germans and gave them access to positions, but personal interactions and closer relations were not part of the equation and distance dominated relationships between the new Imperial elite of German origin and the Romans (Goltz 2002: 300).

The *Missorium* of Theodosius, probably crafted in the year AD 388, might serve as an example (Figure 3).[41]

This famous ceremonial silver dish shows in one section Arcadius, the son of Theodosius, who rose to the rank of Augustus in AD 383 at the age of seven. Behind the (then) 11-year-

together with the further literature, Beckmann 2011 and Coarelli 2008, and a discussion of the scenes of violence in Müller 2009: 19-127. The excessive violence is assessed in literature as being a message of Rome's power, which was meant as a signal to the Germans and all other unruly nations that any resistance against Rome is futile. Heitz (2009: 124 sq.) makes reference to the fact that Barbarians are also fighting on the side of the Romans in the Marcus Aurelius Column. But their role is however not so pronounced as on Trajan's column. In addition, Müller (2009: 174-181) recognises in scenes depicting the trusting relationship between Emperor and representatives of foreign nations, a pictorial agenda that supports Roman external policy during the Danube wars, and that incorporates formerly hostile nations as members of an alliance (p. 174). According to Ulrich Gotter (pers. comm.) the excessive brutality of the representation of the subjugated peoples on the Marcus Aurelius column is due to the internal political problems of the Emperor, who needed to depict himself as a hard and hands-on ruler who knew how to take drastic action. The brilliant victory of Lucius Verus in the East had damaged the image of the 'Philosopher-Emperor'. The fact that the border defence in the North – now under the general responsibility of Marcus Aurelius – led to a disaster (the plundering of Aquileia), explains the need of the *princeps* to show hardness as a military leader and to communicate this using propaganda. This explicitly presented brutality in the Marcus column is unique in Roman art and found no echo in any later works.

[38] For the visual representations, see Landskron 2005.

[39] Particularly with Horace, *Carm.* 37.

[40] See also more on the epigraphical record in Sarnowski 1991.

[41] For discussion and relevant literature on this silver plate, which was probably a gift offered by the Emperor, see Beyeler 2011: 316-319.

Figure 3. The *Missorium* of Theodosius, copy at the Museum of Roman Art, Merida (Spain); photo: Manuel de Corselas, Wikicommons.

old boy there are soldiers of the Emperor's bodyguard who are depicted as Germans, clearly recognisable by their weapons and their non-Roman clothing, notably a neck-ring (torc). Germanity is apparently being illustrated here as a hallmark of quality and, specifically, military capability.

The fact remains that the concept of 'Barbarian' was often used by Roman writers only when they wished to complain about something, and for the most part as a projection for the reflection of 'otherness', and not for describing external political realities. Diplomacy, trade, exchange and the use of 'barbarian' soldiers in military service characterise the actual relationship between Romans and their neighbouring 'Barbarians' significantly more than do conflict and warfare. Cooperation was as valid as confrontation. 'The 'normal' Barbarian represents the no-man's land between neighbours whom one needs and one knows and with whom a limited symbiosis is unavoidable just as it is/was with 'migrant workers', a symbiosis which is both desirable as well as being something to aim at' (Timpe 2000: 228). Their capacity for assimilation is guaranteed indirectly, because they can participate in the Roman form of the Paideia, which was conditioned by legal status (for example citizenship, or military engagement). Because of this, the concept of the 'Barbarian' is avoided by Roman writers in neutral descriptions of external relationships. It has no explanatory power in the context of the Roman legal system and of the Roman understanding of citizens' rights. It can only be used for describing culturally very distinct peoples, the 'other', the vanquished, and as an insulting word for describing a cultural gap.

Whether it is the now negative, stereotyped barbarian discourse or the idealisation of the 'noble savage' à la *Germania* (Tacitus), or the brutal suppression of unruly marginal nations, leading sometimes to complete extermination, or the concept of the useful *externae gentes*, characterised by cooperation and military integration of auxiliary troops of foreign origin within the framework of a new Imperial policy under Trajan and Hadrian, the image of the Barbarian is highly differentiated. The Romans do not commit themselves to any fixed view, owing to the possibility of being themselves considered to be Barbarians in the original Greek meaning of the term. But one aspect seems decisive and which separates the Roman perspective sustainably from a modern viewpoint: in the eyes of the Romans, regardless of how uncivilised his behaviour might be, the Barbarian was not defined by ethnicity or skin colour, since these were subsidiary and minor classifications.

Lifestyle and culture are the decisive factors. A Barbarian does not have to remain a Barbarian forever. This was the basis on which the principle of the citizenship system, the adoption principle and the liberal practice of granting freedom was firmly established. In Sallust's account, there was no mention of Jugurtha's skin-colour.

Acknowledgements

This work was supported by a grant of the Romanian National Authority for Scientific Research, CNCS-UEFISCDI, project number PN-III-P4-ID-PCE-2016-0669, *Beyond the fringes of empire. Roman influence and power north of the Danube and east of the Rhine* — arheo.ro/ romaninfluence.

Translation from the German original provided by Jeremy Wheeler.

References

Alföldy, G. 1984. *Römische Sozialgeschichte*, 3rd ed. Stuttgart, Franz Steiner.

Alföldy, G. 1987 (1987a). *Römisches Städtewesen auf der neukastilischen Hochebene. Ein Testfall für die Romanisierung*. Heidelberg, Winter.

Alföldy, G. 1987. P. Helvius Pertinax und M. Valerius Maximianus. In G. Alföldy, *Römische Heeresgeschichte. Beiträge 1962-1985*: 326-348. Amsterdam, Brill.

Alföldy, G. 1999. *Städte, Eliten und Gesellschaft in der Gallia Cisalpina. Epigraphisch-historische Untersuchungen*. Stuttgart, Franz Steiner.

Avram, A. 2007. Les ciues Romani consistentes de Skythie Mineure: état de la question. In R. Compatangelo-Soussignan and C.-G. Schwentzel (eds), *Étrangers dans la cité romaine*: 91-109. Rennes, Presses Universitaires de Rennes.

Balsdon, J. P. V. D. 1979. *Romans and Aliens*. London, Duckworth.

Beckmann, M. 2011. *The Column of Marcus Aurelius. The Genesis and Meaning of a Roman Imperial Monument*. Chapel Hill, University of North Carolina Press.

Beyeler, M. 2011. *Geschenke des Kaisers. Studien zur Chronologie, zu den Empfängern und zu den Gegenständen der kaiserlichen Vergabungen im 4. Jahrhundert n. Chr.* Berlin, Akademie Verlag.

Brunt, P. A. 1971. *Italian Manpower 225 BC - AD 14*. Oxford (2. Aufl. 1987), The Clarendon Press.

Burns, T. S. 2004. *Rome and the Barbarians 100 B.C. - A.D. 400*. Baltimore, Johns Hopkins University Press.

Christ, K. 1959. Römer und Barbaren in der hohen Kaiserzeit. *Saeculum* 10: 273-288.

Coarelli, F. 2008. *La colonna di Marco Aurelio*. Rome, Colombo.

Coşkun, A. 2009. *Großzügige Praxis der Bürgerrechtsvergabe in Rom? Zwischen Mythos und Wirklichkeit*. Stuttgart, Franz Steiner.

Coşkun, A. 2014. Griechische Polis und römisches Reich. Die politische und rechtliche Stellung Fremder in der Antike. In A. Coşkun and L. Raphael (eds), *Fremd und rechtlos? Zugehörigkeitsrechte Fremder von der Antike bis zur Gegenwart; ein Handbuch*: 85-120. Köln, Weimar u. Wien, Böhlau.

Dauge, Y. A. 1981. *Le Barbare. Recherches sur la conception romaine de la barbarie et de la civilization*. Brüssel, Latomus.

Dench, E. 2005. *Romulus' Asylum. Roman Identities from the Age of Alexander to the Age of Hadrian*. Oxford, Oxford University Press.

Dihle, A. (ed.) 1962. *Grecs et barbares*. Fondation Hardt, Entretiens VIII. Genf.

Dihle, A. 1994. *Die Griechen und die Fremden*. München, Beck.

Donati Giacomini, P. and Poma, G. (eds) 1996. *Cittadini e non cittadini nel Mondo Romano: Guida ai testi e ai documenti*. Bologna, CLUEB.

Drijvers, J. D. 2011. A Roman Image of the 'Barbarian' Sasanians. In R. W. Mathiesen and D. Shanzer (eds), *Romans, Barbarians, and the Transformation of the Roman World*: 67-76. Farnham and Burlington, Ashgate.

Dubuisson, M. 2001. Barbares et la barbarie dans le monde gréco-romain. *Antiquité Classique* 70: 1-16.

Eck, W. and Wolff, H. (eds) 1986. *Heer und Integrationspolitik. Die römischen Militärdiplome als historische Quelle*. Köln, Weimar und Wien, Böhlau.

Fredrickson, G. M. 1971. *The Black Image in the White Mind. The Debate on Afro-American Character and Destiny, 1817-1914*. New York, Harper & Row.

Gabba, E. 1991. *Dionysius and The History of Archaic Rome*. Berkeley, Los Angeles, London, University of California Press.

Garnsey, P. 1975. Descendants of Freedmen in Local Politics. Some Criteria. In B. Levick (ed.), *The Ancient Historian and his Materials. Essays in Honour of C. E.* Stevens on his Seventieth Birthday: 167-180. Farnborough, Gregg.

Giorcelli Bersan, S. and Baldini, A. (eds) 2004. *Romani e Barbari. Incontro e scontro di culture*; atti del convegno, Bari, 11-13 aprile 2003. Torino, CELID.

Goltz, A. 2002. Gelehrte Barbaren? Antike Bildung und germanische Oberschicht in der Spätantike. In A. Goltz, A. Luther and H. Schlange-Schöningen (eds), *Gelehrte in der Antike. Alexander Demandt zum 65. Geburtstag*: 297-316. Köln, Weimar, Wien, Böhlau.

Gracianskaya, L. I. 1996. Zentrum und Peripherie: Der ethnopsychologische Befund und seine Widerspiegelung in der Literatur. In B. Funck (ed.), *Hellenismus. Beiträge zur Erforschung von Akkulturation und politischer Ordnung in den Staaten des hellenistischen Zeitalters. Akten des Internationalen Hellenismus-Kolloquiums 8.-14. März 1994 in Berlin*: 475-490. Tübingen, J. C. B. Mohr.

Gruen, E. S. 2011. *Rethinking the Other in Antiquity*. Princeton and Oxford, Princeton University Press.

Harrison, T. (ed.) 2002. *Greeks and Barbarians*. New York, Routledge.

Heather, P. 2009. *Empires and Barbarians. Migration, Development and the Birth of Europe*. London. (German ed. 2011: Invasion der Barbaren. Die Entstehung Europas im ersten Jahrtausend nach Christus, Stuttgart), Macmillan.

Heitz, C. (2005/6). Des Kaisers neue Kleider. Romanitas und Barbarentum am Trajansbogen von Benevent. *Mitteilungen des Deutschen Archäologischen Instituts* 112: 207-224.

Heitz, C. 2006. Alles bare Münze? Fremdendarstellungen auf römischem Geld. *Bonner Jahrbücher des rheinischen Landesmuseums in Bonn und des Vereins von Altertumsfreunden im Rheinlande* 206: 159-230.

Heitz, C. 2009. *Die Guten, die Bösen und die Hässlichen. Nördliche 'Barbaren' in der römischen Bildkunst*. Hamburg, Dr. Kovac.

Heubner, F. 2004. Die Fremden in Sallusts Afrika-Exkurs (Sall. Jug. 17-19). In J. Dummer and M. Vielberg (eds), *Der Fremde - Freund oder Feind? Überlegungen zu dem Bild des Fremden als Leitbild*: 93-111. Stuttgart, Franz Steiner.

Hölscher, T. 1999. Alle Welt für Trajan. Beobachtungen zur Darstellung von Fremdvölkern an traianischen Staatsdenkmälern. In N. Blanc and A. Buisson (eds), *IMAGO ANTIQVITATIS, Religions et iconographie du monde romain. Mélanges offerts à Robert Turcan*: 281-289. Paris, De Boccard.

Isaac, B. 2004. *The Invention of Racism in Classical Antiquity*. Princeton, Princeton University Press.

Jordan, W. 1968. *White over Black. American Attitudes toward the Negro, 1550-1812*. Chapel Hill, University of North Carolina Press.

Kißel, W. 2013. Juvenal (1962-2011). *Lustrum* 55: 7-416.

Krebs, V. *Material Diplomacy: Culture Contact and Western Christian Art in Ethiopia in the late Middle Ages* (in Vorbereitung).

Landskron, A. 2005. *Parther und Sasaniden. Das Bild der Orientalen in der römischen Kaiserzeit*. Wien, Phoibos.

Lefkowitz, M. 1996. *Not out of Africa. How Afrocentrism Became an Excuse to teach Myth as History*. New York, Basic Books.

Lowe, K. 2005. Introduction: The Black African Presence in Renaissance Europe. In T. F. Earle and K. Lowe (eds), *Black Africans in Renaissance Europe*: 1-14. Cambridge, Cambridge University Press.

Lowe, K. 2007. 'Representing' Africa: Ambassadors and Princes from Christian Africa to Renaissance Italy and Portugal, 1402-1608. *Transactions of the Royal Historical Society* 17: 101-128.

Martin, P. 2001. *Schwarze Teufel, Edle Mohren. Afrikaner in Geschichte und Bewusstsein der Deutschen*. Hamburg, Junius.

Mathiesen, R. W. 2006. Peregrini, Barbari, and Cives Romani: Concepts of Citizenship and the Legal Identity of Barbarians in the Later Roman Empire. *American Historical Review* 111: 1011-1040.

Mathiesen, R. W. and Shanzer, D. (eds) 2011. *Romans, Barbarians, and the Transformation of the Roman World*. Farnham and Burlington, Ashgate

McDonough, S. 2011. Were the Sassanians Barbarians? Roman Writers on the 'Empire of the Persians'. In R. W. Mathiesen and D. Shanzer (eds), *Romans, Barbarians, and the Transformation of the Roman World*: 55-65. Farnham and Burlington, Ashgate.

McElduff, S. 2013. *Roman Theories of Translation. Surpassing the Source*. New York, Routledge.

Millar, F. 2005. Review Article: The Invention of Racism in Antiquity. *The International History Review* 27: 85-99.

Mommsen, Th. 1976. *Römische Geschichte. Vollständige Ausgabe in acht Bänden*. München (layout according to Auflage 1874), Deutscher Taschenbuch.

Mouritsen, H. 2011. *The Freedman in the Roman World*. Cambridge, Cambridge University Press.

Müller, Ch. 2009. *Barbarus quid significaverit. Vom Umgang mit Fremdvölkern an Traians- und Marcussäule*. Dissertation Erlangen (online).
Noy, D. 2000. *Foreigners at Rome: Citizens and Strangers*. London, Duckworth with The Classical Press of Wales.
Ohnacker, E. 2003. *Die spätantike und frühmittelalterliche Entwicklung des Begriffs barbarus. Ein interdisziplinärer Versuch der Beschribung distinktiver und integrativer gesellschaftlicher Konzepte*. Münster, Hamburg, London, Lit.
RAC 1950 to the present. *Reallexikon für Antike und Christentum*, Theodor Klauser *et al.* (eds), Stuttgart (27 volumes to date), Hiersemann.
Richter, D. 2006. Review: *The Invention of Racism in Classical Antiquity* by Benjamin Isaac. *Classical Philology* 101: 287-290.
Riese, A. 1914. *Das rheinische Germanien in den antiken Inschriften*. Berlin, Teubner.
Rüger, J. 1965. *Barbarus. Wort und Begriff bei Cicero, Livius, Caesar*. Diss. Göttingen.
Rummel, P. v. 2007. *Habitus barbarus. Kleidung und Repräsentation spätantiker Eliten im 4. und 5. Jahrhundert* (=Ergänzungsbände zum Reallexikon der Germanischen Altertumskunde; Bd. 55). Berlin, De Gruyter.
Said, E. W. 1978. *Orientalism*. New York, Pantheon (25th anniversary edition with a new preface by the author, New York 2003).
Sarnowski, T. 1991. Barbaricum und ein bellum Bosporanum in einer Inschrift aus Preslav. *Zeitschrift für Papyrologie und Epigraphik* 87: 137-144.
Schäfer, P. 1997. *Judeophobia. Attitudes towards the Jews in the Ancient World*. Cambridge, Mass. und London, Harvard University Press.
Schipp, O. 2014. Römer und Barbaren: Fremde in der Spätantike und im Frühmittelalter. In A. Coşkun and L. Raphael (eds), *Fremd und Rechtlos? Zugehörigkeitsrechte Fremder von der Antike bis zur Gegenwart; ein Handbuch*: 121-151. Köln, Weimar u. Wien, Böhlau.
Schneider, R. M. 2001. s. v. *Barbar* II. *RAC* Suppl. I: 895-962.
Sherwin-White, A. N. 1973. *The Roman Citizenship*. 2nd ed. Oxford, Clarendon Press.
Snowden, F. M. 1970. *Blacks in Antiquity. Ethiopians in the Greco-Roman Experience*. Cambridge/ Mass., Harvard University Press.
Snowden, F. M. 1983. *Before Colour Prejudice. The Ancient View on Blacks*. Cambridge, Mass., Harvard University Press.
Snowden, F. M. 1990. Romans and Blacks: A Review Article (Review on Thompson 1989). *American Journal of Philology* 111: 543-557.
Speyer, W. 2001. s.v. *Barbarus* I. *RAC* Suppl. 1, 814-895.
Teichner, F. 2006. Romanisierung und keltische Resistenz? Die 'kleinen' Städte im Nordwesten Hispaniens. In E. Walde and B. Kainrath (ed.), *Die Selbstdarstellung der römischen Gesellschaft in den Provinzen im Spiegel der Steindenkmäler*. Akten des IX. Internationalen Kolloquiums über provinzialrömisches Kunstschaffen - Innsbruck 2005, IKARUS 2: 202-216. Innsbruck, Innsbruck University Press.
Thompson, L. A. 1989. *Romans and Blacks*. London and Oklahoma, Routledge and Oklahoma University Press.
Timpe, D. 2000. der Barbar als Nachbar. In C. Ulf (ed.), *Ideologie - Sport - Außenseiter. Aktuelle Aspekte einer Beschäftigung mit der antiken Gesellschaft*: 203-230. Innsbruck, Die Innsbrucker Beiträge zur Kulturwissenschaft.
Vittinghoff, F. 1994. *Civitas Romana. Stadt und politisch-soziale Integration im Imperium Romanum der Kaiserzeit*, hrsg. von W. Eck. Stuttgart, Klett-Cotta.

Vogt-Spira, G. 1999. Literarische Imitatio und kulturelle Identität. Die Rezeption griechischer Muster in der Selbstwahrnehmung römischer Literatur. In G. Vogt-Spira and B. Rommel (eds), *Rezeption und Identität. Die kulturelle Auseinandersetzung Roms mit Griechenland als europäisches Paradigma*: 22-36. Stuttgart, Franz Steiner.

Walbank, F. 1972. Nationality as a Factor in Roman History. *Harvard Studies in Classical Philology* 76: 145-168.

Walser, G. 1951. *Rom, das Reich und die fremden Völker in der Geschichtsschreibung der frühen Kaiserzeit*. Basel, Helbing & Lichtenhahn.

Watts, W. J. 1976. Race Prejudice in Juvenal. *Acta Classica* 19: 83-104.

Wiele, B. 1973. Der Aspektwandel des Barbarenbegriffs bei den Römern als Ausdruck wachsender Wertschätzung des patrius sermo. In H. Scheel (ed.), *Altertumswissenschaft mit Zukunft. Dem Wirken Werner Hartkes gewidmet*: 106-115. Berlin, Akademie Verlag.

Williams, D. 1998. *Romans and Barbarians. Four views from the Empire's edge, 1st century AD.* London, Constable.

Yavetz, Z. 1997. *Judenfeindschaft in der Antike*. München, Beck.

Germany East of the Rhine, 12 BC – AD 16. The first step to becoming a Roman province

Gabriele Rasbach

Römisch-Germanische Kommission des Deutschen Archäologischen Instituts, Frankfurt am Main

Abstract

A number of new Roman sites have been discovered in Germany which shed light on the period of the Roman occupation of Germany. These include new military camps and various archaeological sites like the battlefield of Kalkriese or the civilian Roman site of Waldgirmes. Especially Waldgirmes is a key to understanding the process of creating a new elite compliant with Roman political structures and thus the establishment of Roman provincial structures works. A larger vision of Roman Germany known as Germania Magna ultimately failed, but west and south-east of the Rhine, Roman military power established provincial structures that survived until the end of 4th century AD.

Keywords: Foundation of a Roman province; Romanisation; Germania; Augustan occupation; Waldgirmes; Roman military camps

In the last twenty years a number of new Roman sites have been discovered in Germany which shed new light on the Augustan period and the period of the Roman occupation of Germany (Figure 1).

These include new military camps and at the battlefield of Kalkriese (the battle in the Teutoburg Forest led by Varus AD 9), but we have much less information on indigenous Germanic sites. Two recent excavations near Hedemünden and at the civilian Roman site of Waldgirmes have furnished new evidence to help understand the complexity of Romano-Germanic affairs. In particular the evidence at Waldgirmes shows that the territory beyond the Rhine was included in the first steps towards the creation of a Roman province. A larger vision of Roman Germany known as Germania Magna ultimately failed, but west and south-east of the Rhine, Roman military power established provincial structures that survived until the end of 4th century AD.

In Caesar's description of the geopolitical situation in Gaul, the Rhine was the dividing line between Celtic and Germanic tribes, but the actual situation was really much more complicated, as we now know from the archaeological data. Caesar himself even drew attention to the problem when he described some inhabitants on the west bank of the Rhine as 'Germani Cisrhenani'. North of the Middle Rhine Valley the river was the Roman frontier until the end of the *Limes* in the late 4th century AD. But in the area north of Koblenz (Confluentes), where the Mosel flows into the Rhine, the

Figure 1. Map of Roman sites in Caesarian and Augustan times in Germany.

frontier was once again advanced across the Rhine at the end of the 1st century AD. The *Limes* left the Rhine and turned eastwards along the ridge of the Taunus mountains, incorporating the Rhine-Main region around Frankfurt and continuing south to the Danube Valley.

With the region south of the Taunus mountains the Romans incorporated an area inhabited by a mixed Gallo-Germanic population, and into which Germanic groups had migrated from the 2nd century BC. The native Gallo-Germanic societies were based on economic structures characterised by central settlements, the beginnings of coin-use and coin production, in other words a situation comparable to the social and economic structures in Gaul, which Caesar had conquered between 58 and 50 BC. Between the northern edge of the low mountain range and the North Sea – the German Northern plain – the circumstances were completely different. There small rural settlements shaped the lifestyle, and the economy, which was based on agriculture and cattle breeding, was only enough to enable self-sufficiency. We find no coin-production or coin-use in the archaeological record.

These circumstances are in contrast with the situation in Gaul when Augustus started his campaigns across the Rhine into Germania Magna in 12 BC. The first buildings of the Augustan period in Germany are to be found on the Petrisberg above Trier (Löhr 2004 (2005): 36-39; Löhr 2003: 21-35).

On the Petrisberg, parts of a military camp were excavated and dated to 30 BC by dendrochronology. Surprisingly, traces of very large buildings were uncovered that are modelled on Mediterranean patterns. The Romans built houses with an atrium or peristyle, like those found in southern Gaul (Gallia Narbonnensis) or in Italy. But in contrast to the more southern examples, on the Petrisberg the houses were erected not from stone but timber. The military camp was used for an unknown legion for only a few years.

The temporary military camps near Limburg east of the Rhine, discovered in 2013, can be dated only by the presence of a particular type of hobnail from the military boots, which are typical for the late Caesarian and early Augustan period. Probably the camps are connected with Agrippa's campaigns, in 39/38 BC, when he resettled the tribe of the Ubii from the east to the west bank of the Rhine.

According to dendrochronological evidence the military camp at Oberaden on the Lippe was established in 11 BC and probably abandoned in 8/7 BC (Figure 2) (Hollstein, 1979: 315-318; Kühlborn 2008).

While the troops were accommodated in tents or barracks, south of the large *principia* luxurious residences were built, similar to atrium houses, with an attached peristyle of Mediterranean type. The atrium of the largest building (which was more than 1800 m^2) was equipped with a wood-panelled *impluvium*, and the peristyle (which was larger than 600 m^2) was provided with an *exedra* and a fountain.

The military camp at Roedgen near Frankfurt-am-Main can be dated to the same period; but in contrast with Oberaden it is an unusual installation with three huge granaries and only a few barracks for a small garrison – an unknown *vexillatio* (Figure 3) (Schönberger and Simon 1976). The camp demonstrates that the Rhein-Main region was strictly under Roman control, and tribute from the fertile area could be collected to fill the granaries and supply the Roman forces during Drusus' campaigns.

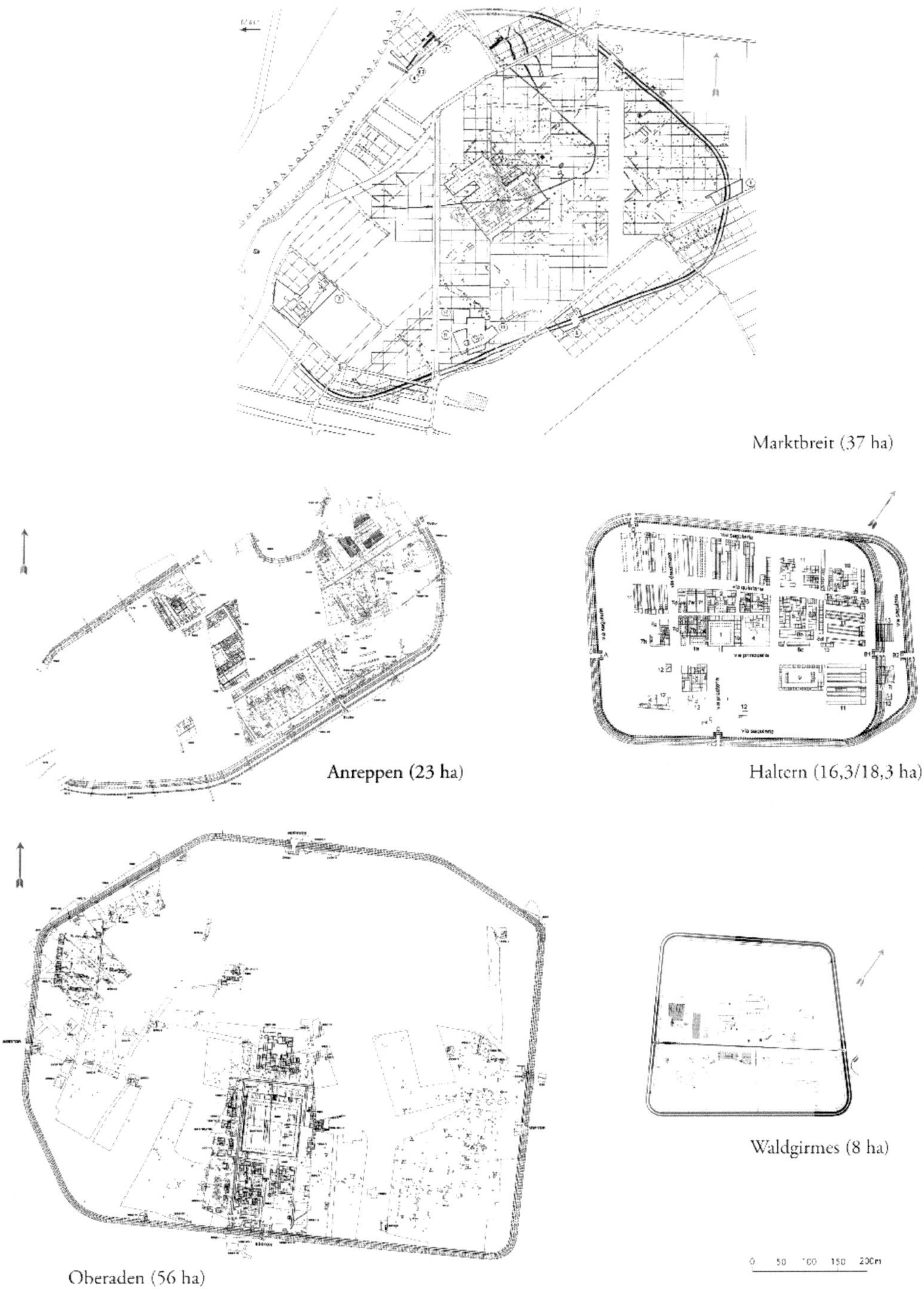

Figure 2. Comparison by size of different military camps of Augustan times and the civil site of Waldgirmes.

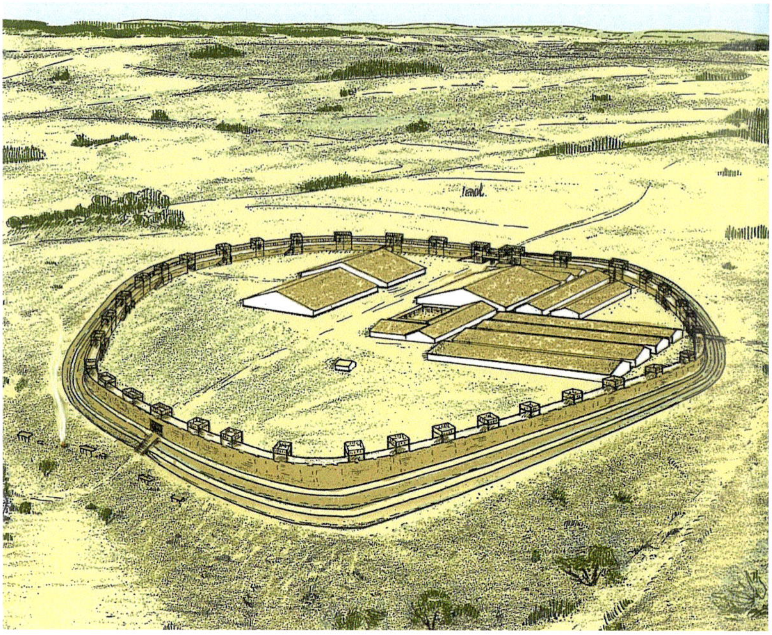

Figure 3. Rödgen. Reconstruction of the military camp.

Another recently discovered site also dates to the period of Drusus' campaigns between 12 and 9 BC: Hedemünden on the river Werra – at the moment one of the most controversial Roman archaeological sites in Germany (Figure 4) (Grote 2015: 191-223; Grote 2012; Review articles: Baatz 2014: 229-238; S. v. Schnurbein 2014).

The coins include mostly *asses* from Nemaussus which are typical for the Drusus period. A circular rampart of uncertain date encloses the top of the wooded hill. Under the embankment, Roman tools came to light (for example nine *dolabrae*) and inside the enclosure complete Roman weapons were found, covered by stone slabs (among them a *pugio*).

Beneath the circular rampart, traces of what is probably a Roman camp were detected by geophysical survey, but until now no excavations have been conducted. The excavators interpreted the enclosure on top of the hill as a Roman military camp, althought there is no evidence in the archaeological record (no trace of barracks, or a *Principia*, for example). The situation also is not typical for a temporary military camp, but reminiscent of Germanic sacred sites such as Illerup Ådal, where military equipment, captured after victories, was deposited as a votive offering to the gods (Ilkjær 1989: 54-61; Ilkjær 2006). Furthermore, at Hedemünden none of the Roman finds show any traces of damage, but were perfectly preserved.

Soon after Oberaden was abandoned the military camp at Haltern was built, probably in 7/5 BC. This Roman camp has been excavated from the late 19th century onwards and has served to characterise our picture of what a Roman legionary camp looks like (Figure 2). On the basis of the later addition of a number of residential houses in the original streets

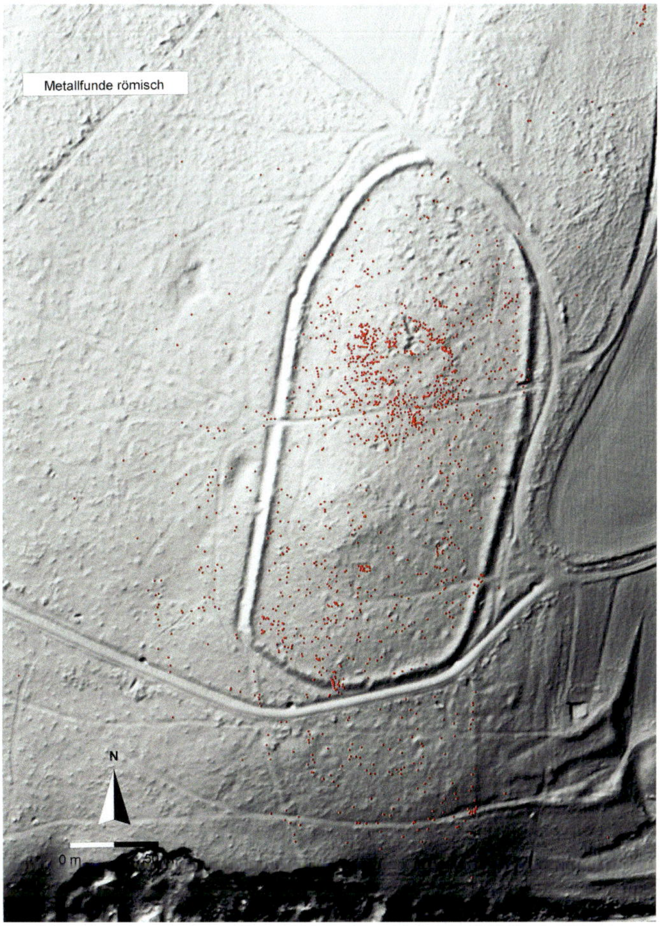

Figure 4. Hedemünden. LiDAR-scan of the archaeological site (Grote 2012).

of the camp, as well as, in a later annexe, the development of a pottery industry and the construction of a water pipeline, it should be concluded that the camp of Haltern took on additional civil administrative and logistic responsibilities until its abandonment sometime between AD 9 and AD 16 (Schnurbein 2013: 91-98; Berke 2013: 58-92; Aßkamp 2010.

The Augustan strategy in Germania Magna, in particular Drusus' campaigns between 12 and 9 BC, had the aim of reorganising northern Gaul in order to protect the province against those eastern Germanic tribes that had periodically crossed the Rhine. The limitation of the ceremonial acts on the occasion of Drusus' death to the tribes 'this side of the Rhine' (*civitates cis Rhenum*), as the Tabula Siarensis reports, suggests that the Romans did not intend to build a province across the Rhine at this time (*Année Épigr.* 1984: 137-145 Nr. 508 [P. Le Roux]; Sánchez-Ostiz 1999). But two years later, following the first campaigns of Tiberius, for which he celebrated a triumph in Rome in 7 BC, and the *pomerium* (at Rome) was expanded, Germanic tribes entreated Augustus for peace. Velleius Paterculus described the area between the Rhine and Elbe as now being nearly a tributary province. Nevertheless warfare with Germanic groups continued; but following further campaigns by Tiberius until AD 7, the region between the Rhine and the Elbe was placed under the civilian administration of Publius Quinctilius Varus, whose main duty was to set up provincial administrative structures and to enforce Roman law.

More than 100 years of research on Roman Germany, and in particular research on the Augustan occupation, has been aimed at military history. Thus when archaeological research began in Waldgirmes in 1993, we expected to find the remains of wooden military

Figure 5. View across the village of Waldgirmes towards the conical Dünsberg.

architecture (such as barracks). Instead what we found has completely changed our view of what took place in Germania under Augustus. Unlike any other site in Germania magna, Waldgirmes was a civilian settlement. The site has a few military elements, but mostly reflects various aspects of civil and rural communities.

Waldgirmes is located on the river Lahn and about 7km southwest of the late Iron Age *oppidum* on the Dünsberg (Schulze-Forster 2014/2015; Schulze-Forster 2005: 159-181) (Figure 5). At the current state of research this pre-Roman settlement ended around 30/15 BC, a few years before the Roman occupation in Germania.

The Roman site of Waldgirmes covers almost 8 acres, and dendrochronological data indicates that it was founded no later than 4 BC (Becker and Rasbach 2015). Surprisingly the settlement was not abandoned immediately after the defeat of Varus in AD 9, but probably continued in use until AD 16, when Tiberius ordered a permanent withdrawal from Germania Magna.

The Romans themselves destroyed the settlement of Waldgirmes by fire, and dismantled the buildings – a typical military course of action that we know of, for example, from the camp at Inchtuthill in Scotland.

From the outside Waldgirmes must have looked like an early military camp, with a timber and earth fortification and two v-shaped ditches in front of it (Figure 6). But inside the fortification walls the wooden architecture includes atrium houses and buildings that look like strip-houses along the streets, while in the centre of the settlement there was a civilian forum, although without a temple.

The very first structure erected at Waldgirmes was a rectangular enclosure with two pits in the centre (Figure 7). The enclosure was built before 4 BC, and was destroyed by

Figure 6. Reconstruction of Roman Waldgirmes on the basis of archaeological data.

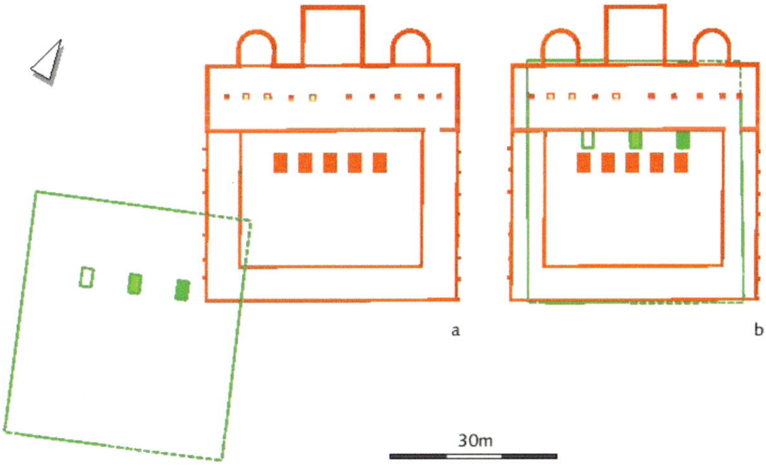

Figure 7. Waldgirmes. Plan of the first constructions, dated before 4 BC.

a street of the later settlement. In the eastern pit a massive foundation of stone and plaster was detected, which indicates the impressive level of Roman control in this area even before 4 BC. The Romans planned to erect a monument, possibly a *tropaion* for Drusus, as Tacitus reports, but the plan was abandoned, and the foundation remained unfinished. No archaeological finds were made that might specify the function of the enclosure.

In 4 BC a small Roman military garrison arrived to survey and prepare the area for the construction of the Roman settlement. The fortification, two wells – to ensure the supply of water *intra muros* – and the streets were built first. But only very few traces of the military garrison have been found – just a single block of barracks with separate officers' quarters (Figure 8). These have a ground plan typical of an early type of military barracks that we know from the military camps such as those at in Rödgen and Oberaden. Small finds of a military character are very rare, and most of them had been broken up in order to recycle the iron, like the small fragments of a *pugio*. The military unit left Waldgirmes a short time later. The officer's quarters were demolished and a small palisade was erected to separate the area around the western gate.

After this initial phase, the settlement was developed further with the construction of storage buildings and granaries in its north-western quarter, which was separated from the rest of the town by a palisade (Figure 9). In the southern part of Waldgirmes houses

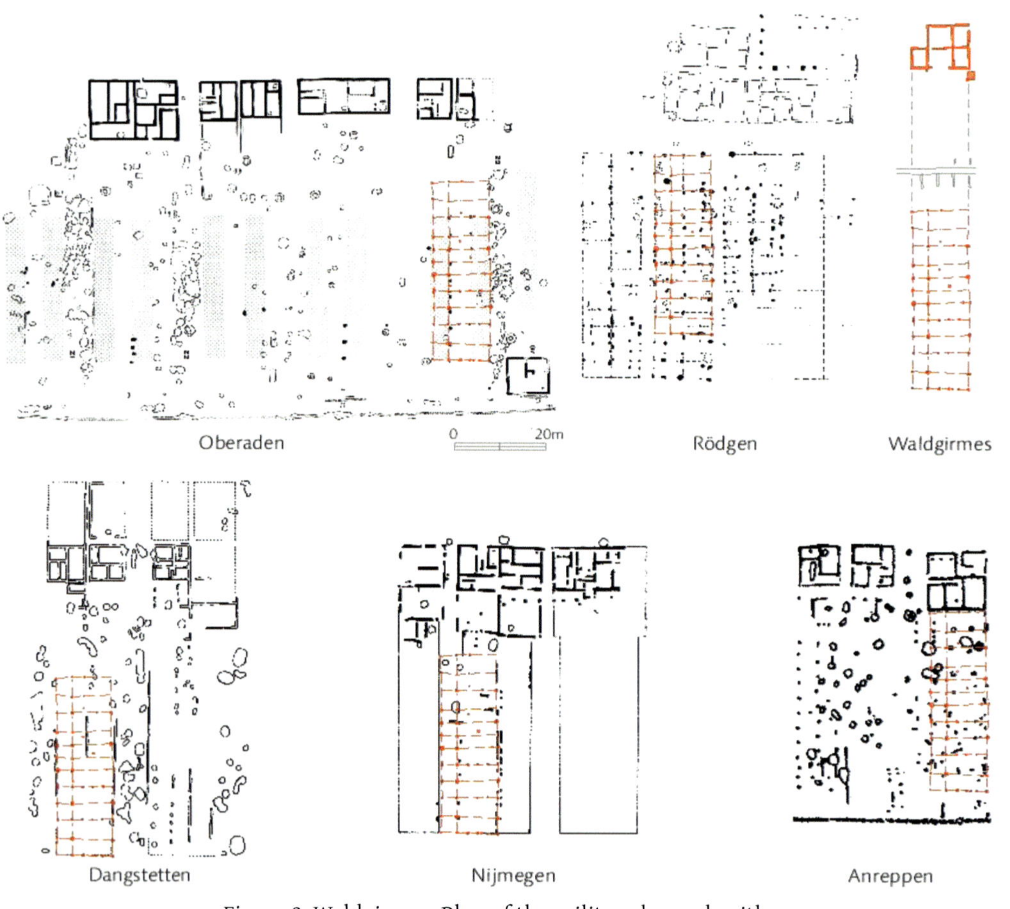

Figure 8. Waldgirmes. Plan of the military barrack with separate officer's quarters.

Figure 9. Waldgirmes. Plan of the Augustan civil site.

were constructed in a style similar to small Mediterranean atrium houses, and along the streets there were various workshops – a blacksmith's workshop and two pottery kilns. Two wells and several granaries completed the picture of a small Roman settlement in a newly conquered region. But there are various features and layers which overly each other, and apparently the function of the settlement changed. This process became distinctly visible when the forum was erected. One house (Figure 9, no. 5) was demolished, and the forum – this main building – was erected on a slightly different orientation to the south gate. This indicates that in the second phase the main gate was in the south; today it has been destroyed by modern buildings.

To consolidate Roman power after Tiberius' campaigns a new administrative centre was created at Waldgirmes. We cannot date this moment exactly but in the context of historical reports it may be possible to connect this development with appointment of Publius Quinctilius Varus as *legatus augusti pro praetore* in AD 7.

The forum was constructed on stone foundations in half-timber technique. It consists of three wings surrounding a courtyard closed with a basilica to the north. The forum covers 2200 m^2 and is – at the moment – the earliest building with stone foundations to be found in Germany. In contrast to this development and to the physical urbanisation of the settlement modelled in a Mediterranean style, the small finds and architectural elements show the presence of different cultural groups of inhabitants. In contrast to Roman wooden architecture, non-Roman buildings were constructed with single wooden uprights similar to Roman granaries. This type of house is typical for Germanic settlements of this time.

A clue to the town's inhabitants may be found in the comparison of Germanic hand-made pottery with Roman pottery thrown on a wheel. The ratio of wheel-made to hand-made pottery is 85% to 15%; counting only the base sherds the proportion of Germanic ware rises to one quarter (75% to 25%). In all other Roman sites east of the Rhine hand-made pottery is extremely rare. In comparison to other Roman sites wheel-made cooking wares are rather rare, and probably the handmade ware filled the gap. Most of the wheel-made pottery belongs to the so-called 'Belgic wares', and chemical analyses have identified potters in the Champagne region around Reims.

From the same region the Romans transported blocks of shell-bearing limestone to Waldgirmes for the bases of probably five statues (Figure 10). The foundations of the bases were found in the inner courtyard of the forum in front of the basilica. Stone was very rare as building material in the Augustan period in Germany and the few known examples are restricted to important sites such as Mainz (Frenz 1991) and Cologne (Eck 2004: 80f).

Along with the handmade ceramics, the brooches also came from other regions. Most of them are of Gaulish types, but two are of particular interest: one is a unique Roman disk fibula of gold-plated silver, perhaps a product of northern Italy, and the other a silver eye-fibula ('Frühe Augenfibel') with a weight of three Roman *denarii* (Figures 11-12).

Figure 10. Waldgirmes. Foundation pit in the inner courtyard of the forum with fragments of shell-bearing limestone from the Champagne region.

Figure 11. Waldgirmes. Silver, gold plated disk fibula with inlays of different coloured glass.

This type of eye-fibula was distributed mainly in the northeast of Germany, south of the Baltic sea and in the Bohemian Basin. The finds from Waldgirmes show the presence of inhabitants of different ethnicities but on an equal social level.

In the first season of the excavation a small fragment of cast gilded bronze came to light, which could only be part of a statue. In the course of the excavations more than 160 fragments, mostly very small, were discovered in various pits, a ditch and certain areas of the settlement. The discovery of two floral ornate bronze pectorales of a horse harnesses indicated that there must have been at least two life-size equestrian statues at Waldgirmes.

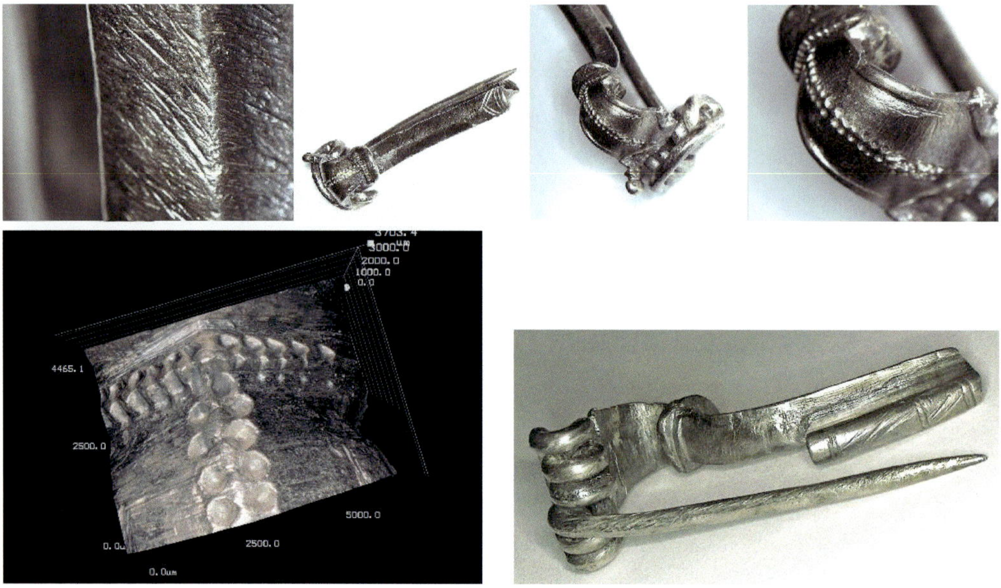

Figure 12. Waldgirmes. Early eye-fibula, silver.

The statues were originally located in the courtyard of the *forum*, where five robbed foundation pits were excavated. Numerous fragments of shattered stone plinths and very small fragments of gilded bronze were found around the foundations, which had been created for up to five statues. All these foundations are the appropriate size for equestrian statues.

These impressive statues emphasise the great importance of the forum as the centre of the Roman administration and jurisdiction. If there were indeed five statues (it is certain that we excavated fragments of at least three statues), they could have formed a group of the Imperial family (comprising Augustus, Drusus or Germanicus, Tiberius, Lucius and Gaius). Moreover the image of Augustus sent a powerful signal to the native population in the settlement and in the environment – impressive lifesize pictures in a cultural environment where human representations were extremely rare and very simple.

At a later stage in Waldgirmes' history the ditch of the E/W street was filled in and a new road surface was constructed. Surprisingly, a small fragment of a statue came to light beneath the new surface. This stratigraphic relationship clearly indicates that after the statues were damaged – which possibly is to be dated to AD 9, the year of the defeat of Varus in the Teutoburger Forest – the Roman settlement at Waldgirmes was still occupied and undertaking building projects.

The excavations in 2009 – the last year of the long-term Waldgirmes project financed by the German Research Foundation – concentrated on a well which had previously been detected by geophysical survey. The shaft was clearly distinguishable from the pit surrounding it, and from a depth of about 6m – the current groundwater level – the wooden box of the

Figure 13. Waldgirmes. The second well in photogrammetric reconstruction.

shaft was extremely well preserved (Figure 13). Interestingly, the well was completely filled with numerous wooden objects, apparently deposited there to put the well out of commission a short time after the statues were destroyed.

The dendrochonological analysis of the well casing produced the same date for all the timbers: the trees were felled in the winter of 4 to 3 BC. Most of the wooden objects from the well shaft, for example fragments of a shovel, parts of the well cover, the axle of a cart, wheel spokes and tool handles all provided no exact dendrochronological data. But on several parts of a ladder the tree bark was still preserved, and indicated that the struts had been felled in the autumn or winter of AD 9 to 10 (well after the battle in the Teutoburg forest in AD 9).

Below the well casing a large barrel was found that had acted as a settling tank. By the edge of the barrel a bronze *calcaeus* was found, the typical shoe of Roman patrician costume. Surprisingly, this statue fragment was not gilded, another indication of the presence of a second statue. The largest fragment of a statue, a life-size gilded bronze horse's head, was located at the bottom of the well between eight millstones (Figure 14). The richly decorated horse harness shows pictures of the goddess Victory and of the god Mars, resting on a rock. These two, Victory and Mars at rest, symbolically reflect the political situation perfectly in the newly conquered region (Figure 14).

The archaeological record surely has to be interpreted as the result of ritual deposition by the Gallo-Germanic, or even Roman inhabitants, of the settlement. But the episode that led to the destruction of the statues did not immediately result in

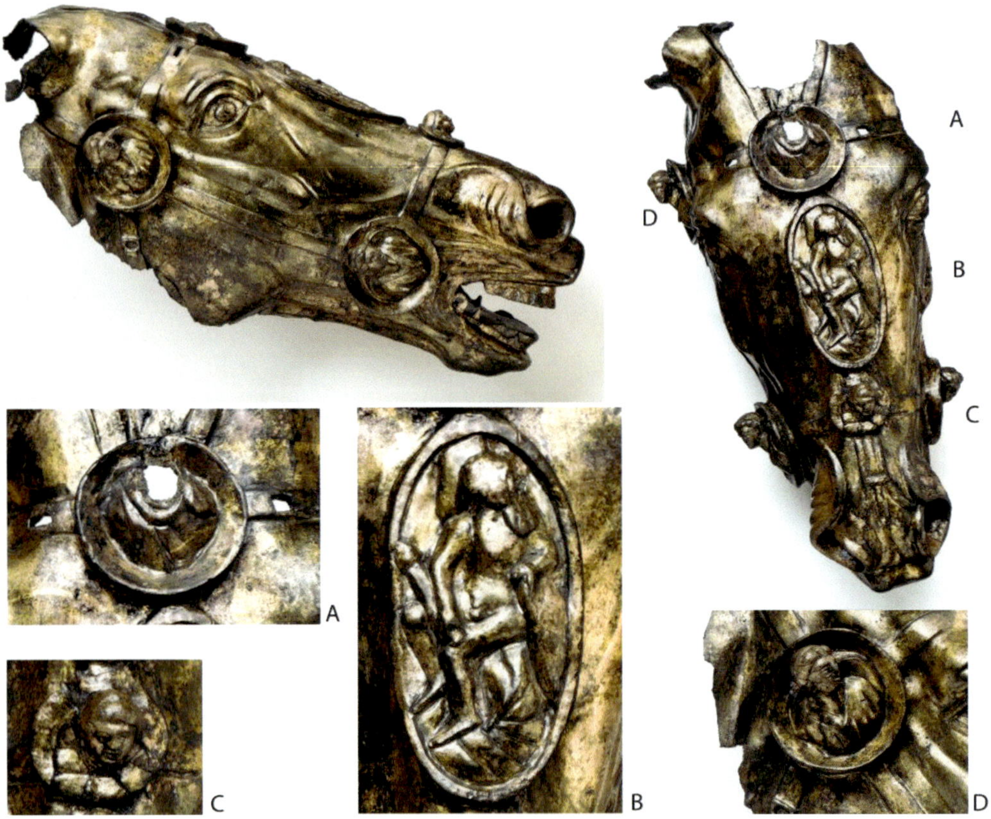

Figure 14. Waldgirmes. Life-size gilded bronze horse's head with images of Victory and Mars.

the demolition of the settlement or the abandonment of Roman Waldgirmes. However, the discovery of the horse's head was the extraordinary final event in the archaeological fieldwork in Waldgirmes.

Between the layer in which the horse's head and the millstones were found, and the various burnt wooden objets, was an horizon of sediments that contained no archaeological finds. In the entire filling of the well we found no fragments of burnt clay from demolished houses, but only on top of the well in the very last filling. In fact all of the wooden finds as well as the millstones had lost their metal elements. This indicates that some time elapsed between the three events: the destruction of the statues, the demolition of the well, and the burning down of the settlement. The filling of this well is the basis for our interpretation that Roman Waldgirmes was still populated until AD 16, when Tiberius had ordered the Roman withdrawal. We have no coins from Waldgirmes minted after AD 10, because after the battle in the Teutoburg Forest in AD 9 the settlement reverted to the status of an *emporion*, a small commercial settlement. Fresh coins were not necessary to collect tributes or to deal with the natives of the surrounding area, where coin-use was still not common. Trade could still take place in the form of bartering.

To build a new province the Romans needed central settlements as administrative centres, as well as native inhabitants who cooperated with them. In Germania the indigenous settlements mostly consisted of isolated self-sufficient farmsteads with longhouses, sunken houses or 'Grubenhäuser', and small agricultural buildings. There was no infrastructural basis such as that provided by the oppida in Gaul with an hierarchical social structure. It is clear that there was also no system of extensive cooperation between Germanic elites at this time. The Roman settlement of Waldgirmes was a melting pot of Gallo-Roman, Gallo-Germanic and Germanic inhabitants who were intended to create a new elite. This situation is described by Tacitus for Roman Britain at the very beginning of his Agricola (21). The Roman province in Germania Magna failed both as a result of the character and the structure of the splintered Germanic societies, and because of the lack of economic resources in the region, which would have been the main reason why Rome was interested in building a province in the first place.

References

Année Épigr. 1984, 137-145 Nr. 508. Le Roux, P. and Sánchez-Ostiz, A. (eds). 1999. *Tabula Siarensis.* Edición, traducción y comentario. Pamplona, Ediciones Universidad de Navarra.

Aßkamp, R. 2010. *Haltern, Haltern am See, Kreis Recklingshausen.* Römerlager in Westfalen 5. Münster.

Becker, A. and Rasbach, G. 2015. *Waldgirmes. Die Ausgrabungen in der spätaugusteischen Siedlung von Lahnau-Waldgirmes (1993-2009). 1. Befunde und Funde.* Römisch-Germanische Forschungen 71. Mainz, Philipp Von Zabern.

Eck, W. 2004. *Köln in römischer Zeit. Geschichte einer Stadt im Rahmen des Imperium Romanum. Geschichte der Stadt Köln 1.* Köln, Greven.

Frenz, H. G. 1991. Zum Beginn des repräsentativen Steinbaus in Mogontiacum. In R. Aßkamp and St. Berke (eds), *Die römische Okkupation nördlich der Alpen zur Zeit des Augustus. Kolloquium Bergkamen 1989. Vorträge, Bodenaltert*: 85-96. Westfalen 26. Münster, Aschendorff.

Grote, K. 2014. Römerlager Hedemünden: der augusteische Stützpunkt, seine Außenanlagen, seine Funde und Befunde. Veröff. Arch. Slg. Landesmus. Hannover 53 (Dresden 2012). – Dazu die Rezensionen: Baatz, D. 2014. Ein Römerlager auf dem Burgberg bei Hedemünden (Lkr. Göttingen)? *Archäologische Korrespondenzblatt* 44: 229-238. S. von Schurbein 2014. Hedemünden: Ein Römerlager? *Germania* 92: 163-170.

Grote, K. 2015. Die römischen Militäranlagen der augusteiscchen Germanienfeldzüge und Hinweise auf spätere Vorstöße im Werra-Leine-Bergland rings um Hedemünden. In G. A. Lehmann and R. Wiegels (eds), *'Über die Alpen und über den Rhein ...': Beiträge zu den Anfängen und zum Verlauf der römischen Expansion nach Mitteleuropa.* Abhandl. Akad. Wiss. Göttingen N. F. 37: 191-223. Berlin/Boston.

Hollstein, E. 1979. Dendrochronologische Daten von Funden aus Oberaden und Trier, Petrisberg. In *Festschrift 100 Jahre Rheinisches Landesmuseum Trier*: Beiträge zur Archäologie und Kunst des Trierer Landes. Trierer Grabungen und Forschungen 14: 315-318. Mainz, Philipp Von Zabern.

Ilkjær, J. 1989. The weapons sacrifices from Illerup Ådal, Denmark. In K. Randsborg (ed.), *The birth of Europe: archaeology and social development in the first millennium A.D.* International archaeological symposium, Rome 14th – 17th January 1987. Analecta Romana Inst. Danici Suppl. 16: 54-61. Roma, L'Erma di Bretschneider. Ilkjær, J. 2006. Illerup Ådal. *Jutland Archaeological Society Publications* 25.

Kühlborn, J. 2008. *Oberaden, Stadt Bergkamen, Kreis Unna, und Beckinghausen, Stadt Lünen, Kreis Unna*. Römerlager in Westfalen 3. Münster/Westf: Altertumskommission für Westfalen.

Löhr, H. 2003. Das frührömische Militärlager auf dem Petrisberg bei Trier. *Funde und Ausgrabungen im Bezirk Trier* 35: 21-35.

Löhr, H. 2005. Zum Stand der Untersuchungen im frühesträmischen Militärlager auf dem Petrisberg bei Trier. *Arch. Rheinland-Pfalz* 2004 (2005): 36-39.

Zum Ende von Haltern: S. v. Schnurbein. 2013. Zum Ende von Haltern. Arch. Korrbl. 43: 91-98. –Berke, St. 2013. Die römische Nekropole von Haltern. In St. Berke and T. Mattern (Hrsg.), *Römische Gräber augusteischer und tiberischer Zeit im Westen des Imperiums: Akten der Tagung vom 11. bis 14. November 2010 in Trier*: 58-92. Philippika 63. Wiesbaden, Harrassowitz.

Schönberger, H. and Simon, H.-G. 1976. *Das Römerlager Rödgen*. Limesforschungen 15. Berlin, Gebr. Mann.

Schulze-Forster, J. 2005. Der Dünsberg und die jüngsten keltischen Münzen in Hessen. In J. Metzler and David Wigg-Wolf (eds), *Die Kelten und Rom : neue numismatische Forschungen = Les Celtes et Rome: nouvelles études numismatiques*. Fond de Gras/Titelberg, Luxemburg, 30. 4. – 3. 5. 1998: 159-181. SFMA 19. Mainz.

Schulze-Forster, J. 2015. Die latènezeitlichen Funde vom Dünsberg. *Berichte der Kommission für archäologische Landesforschung in Hessen* 13, 2014/2015.

The Gallo-Roman temple 'Auf dem Spätzrech' (Schwarzenbach/Saarland) – From a Late La Tène cult place to a Gallo-Roman pilgrim shrine?

Daniel Burger-Völlmecke

Institut für Archäologische Wissenschaften, Goethe-Universität, Frankfurt am Main

Abstract

Post-excavation work and analysis of the Gallo-Roman 'Auf dem Spätzrech' temple in the civitas Treverorum of the province Gallia Belgica concluded in distinction of four building phases. They are preceded by a functionally unidentifiable horizon of the Late Iron Age, mainly from the periods La Tène D2a and D2b. Of particular interest are the questions of the meaning and function of the temple in the view of the nearby *oppidum* 'Hunnenring' that was abandoned in the Late Iron Age and the following finds horizon begun in the area of the temple. Also of interest is the strong domestic character of the later Roman finds.

Keywords: Gallo-Roman temple, Roman finds, Late La Tène

The area of land known as 'Auf dem Spätzrech', close to modern-day Schwarzenbach (county of St. Wendel/state of Saarland), is well documented by regularly collected surface finds since the 19th century. Some of the Roman structures were visible until the 1960s.[1] After the discovery of a bronze votive tablet, dedicated to the Gallo-Roman god Mars Cnabetius, archaeological excavations were conducted in 1984/85 (Miron 2000: 379-407; Kolling 2002: 77-93). Since 2006 the Institute of Pre- and Protohistory of the University of Mainz has been carrying out an archaeological landscape project to examine the surroundings of the 'Hunnenring' *oppidum* of the late La Tène period. During these investigations, because the straight-line distance from the Roman temple to the *oppidum* is only about 1.3km, the temple 'Auf dem Spätzrech' also attracted the interest of scientific research. The surveys and excavations brought to light a settlement area of 21ha, within which have been found a *vicus* and a sector for metal-producing crafts to the south of the Gallo-Roman temple.[2]

This new research[3] of the 'Auf dem Spätzrech' temple pursued the aim of a basis for further investigations in the area and to understand the transition of the Late La Tène

[1] Remains of the temple were visible in 1960 but were being dismantled by some villages in the vicinity: files of the cultural heritage of Saarbrücken/Saarland (9.3.1967); Miron 2000: 398.

[2] Previous results of research in summary: Hornung 2010; Hornung 2016. Results of the Roman settlement 'Auf dem Spätzrech': Jung 2010: 155-224; Burger 2010: 165-169. Analysis of the metallurgical testing of the slag: Kronz *et al.* 2010: 275-309.

[3] The following article based on the present author's Master's thesis *Der gallo-römische Umgangstempel 'Auf dem Spätzrech' bei Schwarzenbach (Saarland). Auswertung der Grabung 1984/85*, submitted in June 2010 at the Institute of

period to the Roman settlements. Furthermore, a particular interest lay in finding the earliest horizon of the temple in the second half of the 1st century BC, and the end of the 'Hunnenring' *oppidum* in the middle of the 1st century BC, to answer the question of whether the area was used continuously, or discontinuously occupied by local inhabitants.

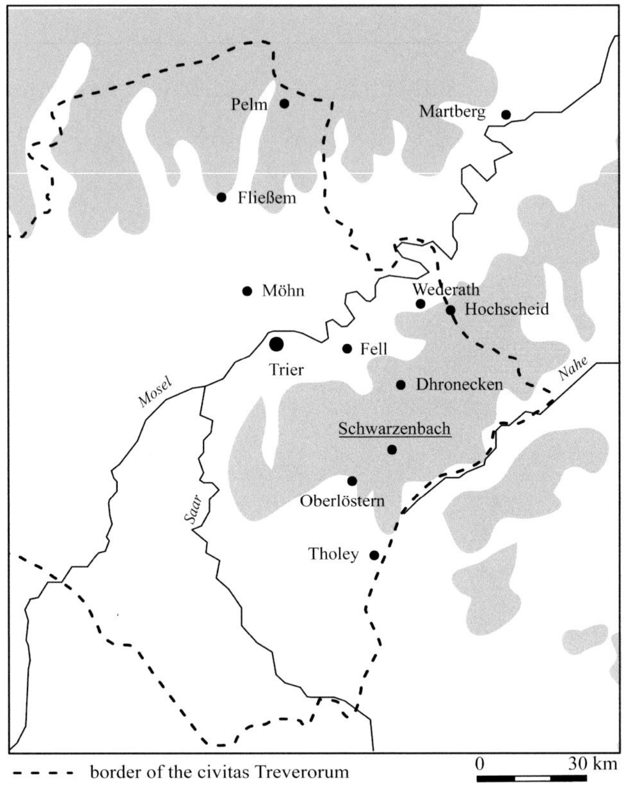

Figure 1. Eastern part of the civitas Treverorum with Schwarzenbach and the civitas-border. Map based on: Heinen 1985, supl. 1 (redrawing and processing: D. Burger-Völlmecke).

The 'Auf dem Spätzrech' temple

Modern Schwarzenbach was part of the Roman province of *Gallia Belgica* and part of the *civitas Treverorum*. The straight-line distance from *Augusta Treverorum*/Trier is 13km (Figure 1).

The temple is situated on an exposed hilltop about 500m above sea-level. Today the area is used for agriculture and a meadow plain bordered on three sides by woodland (Figure 2).

The outside dimensions of the temple are 22.8m x 21m and of the inner sanctuary 15.5m x 14.3m (Figure 3). The entrance may have been on the east side, as is known from many other temples (Fauduet 2010: 122). A specific characteristic is an outbuilding with dimensions of about 3.60m x 3.60m. This suggests that the gallery was closed, because from an architectural point of view an outbuilding on a *porticus* is rather unlikely.

A trench across the *cella* is the only section that gives an insight into the genesis of the temple. The *temenos* wall was located in two trenches and could be reconstructed with the help of LiDaR Scans (Figure 3). The *temenos*-site encompasses an area of 125m x 100m (*c.* 1.2ha). This temple is one of the largest Gallo-Roman sacred sites in the Treverian region. Similar in size is the Gallo-Roman temple of Dahlheim (Kt. Remich/L) at 25m x 18m (Ghetta 2008: 289f., with further literature). The temple of Dhronecken may have had a larger

Pre- and Protohistory, University of Mainz. A summarising article was published in 2012: Burger 2012: 225-243. The Master's thesis was published in 2016: Burger 2016: 137-292.

Figure 2. Situation of the temple (white) to the south-east of the Dollberg plateau.

gallery of 17m x 28.30m x 18.70m, but the *cella* is just 8.60m x 10.30m (Hettner 1901: 83-92. A summary and further literature can be found in Ghetta 2008: 302f.). Another example is temple II at Wederath-Belginum, of a similar size (gallery: 20m x 18m, *cella*: 11.50m x 9.50m) (Cordie-Hackenberg 2000: 412-418; Oldenstein 2000: 34-38.). In 2014 a temple similar to 'Auf dem Spätzrech' was discovered in the *vicus* of 'Wareswald' near Tholey, and also presented as an outbuilding. The distance from this sacred site to Schwarzenbach is about 20km (Henz 2014: 51; Henz 2014b: 33-36; Henz 2013: 62-63; Pers. com. 20.1.2015, K.-P. Henz). As with the temple building, there are only a few known comparable *temonos* areas, i.e. Neunhäuser Wald (118m x 88m), the temple-area I of Wederath-Belginum (120m x 70m), as well as Wallendorf (70m x 100m) (Neunhäuser Wald: Ghetta 2008: 332f.; Wederath-Belginum I: Binsfeld 1976: 39-44; Wallendorf: Krausse 2006: 211 Abb. 78. – For all three temples: Ghetta 2008: 339-342, with further literature). Only a very few temple areas have so far been discovered with complete *temenos* borders. This shows the unique relevance of Schwarzenbach and its importance within the architectural development of temple constructions in the province.

Criticism of sources: the excavations

Unfortunately the documentation of the 1984/85 excavation campaign is poorly archived and partly untraceable. It is known from the existing documentation that the area was divided into $5m^2$ quadrants with three stratigraphic levels, not always systematically documented. The finds were analysed for each quadrant but not in the context of each ground level. Therefore it is impossible to create a stratigraphic model. The earlier mentioned trial trench through the inside of the temple (Figure 3) was documented in two profiles, which are the only ones of the whole excavated area. The documentation of the archaeological contexts is thus incomplete. There are three layers within the individual quadrants, but not many finds can be assigned to any of them. The documentation connecting the finds and their contexts is also fragmentary.

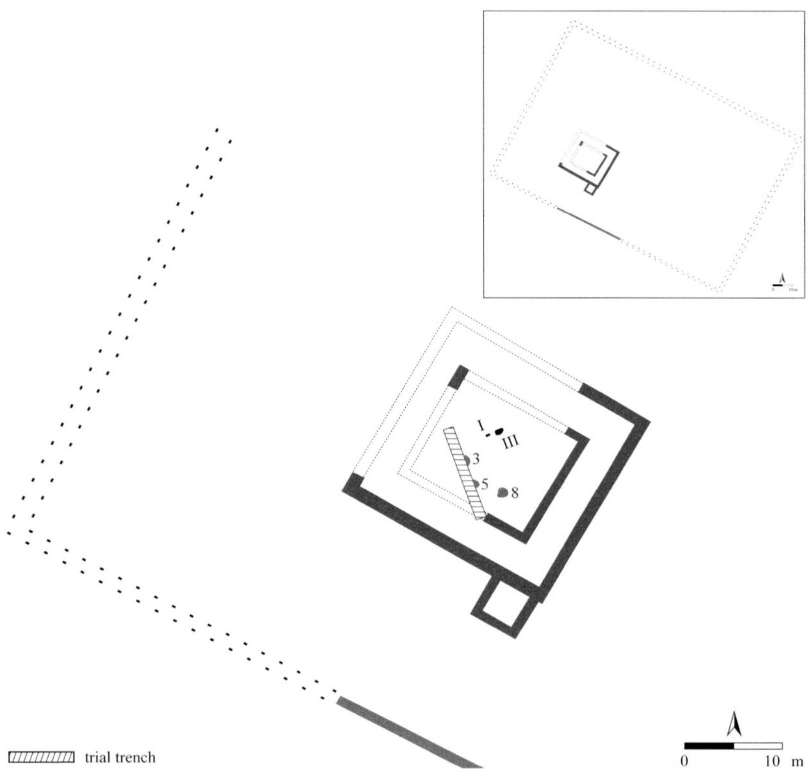

Figure 3. Section of the temenos area within the temple. The map shows post-pits 3, 5, 8 and offering pits I and III. The allocation of find numbers follow the orientation of the original publication. The dotted line is the reconstruction of the temenos wall following the interpretation of the LiDaR scans (graph: D. Burger-Völlmecke).

The small finds were documented in some outline drafts, and were to be professionally drawn at a later stage. Sadly these small finds of ceramic, bronze and iron are missing today; altogether 25% of the finds are lost. For further analysis it was at least possible to identify and draw the ceramic artifacts, using the sketches of the outline drafts.

A Late La Tène Period building and a possible Augustan predecessor?

Along with the Roman ceramic artefacts (43%) there is an even larger number of Late La Tène ceramics (47%). This ratio tends to give the impression that the settlement area 'Auf dem Spätzrech' was already in use in the pre-Roman period. The artifact spectrum includes cup-shaped vessels from Hoppstädten and Wederath which are a characteristic feature of La Tène D2a und D2b. Some fragments of dishes can be dated to La Tène D1a (Figure 4, 1-3) (Cup Hoppstädten (Figure 4, 2): Thoma 1993: 39; 41 Abb.19, 1 Var. A; Cup Wederath (Figure 4, 3): Miron 1991: 163 Abb. 5, 42; Thoma 1993, 48; bowl (Figure 4, 1): Miron 2000: 401; Wiegert 2002: 210-211 Anm. 1530).

These are accompanied by some Celtic coins, especially the 'small sitting man' and 'square nose' types, and can be dated to La Tène D1 and D2a (Wigg/Riederer 1998: 664-665, figure 2). Generally Late Celtic coins found in the context of Gallo-Roman temples are interpreted as leftovers from older circulations in combination with Roman coins at sacred sites. The earliest of these coins date to 30 BC (Loscheider 1998: 184ff.). As described above, the documentation did not permit the contextual association of the Late La Tène finds with any features. Therefore it is uncertain whether the find horizon represents cultic activities contemporary with an earlier temple or if they are remains from earlier layers representing

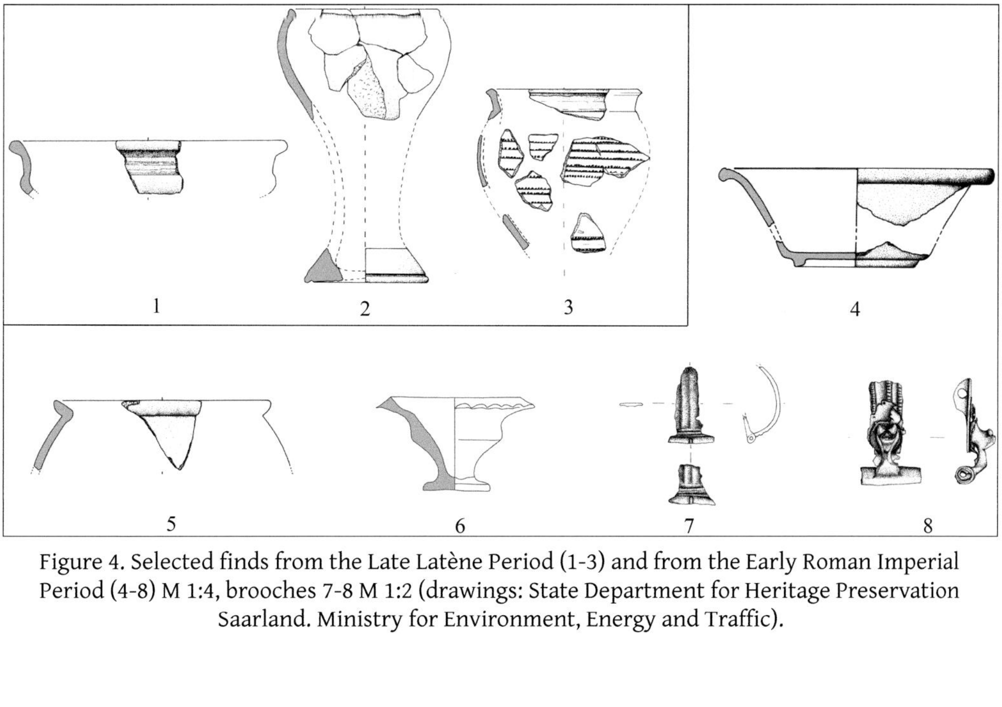

Figure 4. Selected finds from the Late Latène Period (1-3) and from the Early Roman Imperial Period (4-8) M 1:4, brooches 7-8 M 1:2 (drawings: State Department for Heritage Preservation Saarland. Ministry for Environment, Energy and Traffic).

a Celtic settlement. Other indications of Middle La Tène activity that might suggest an earlier site foundation have not been found.

The transition from Late La Tène to the Early Roman Imperial period is not characterised by a distinctive hiatus, and is represented by Gallo-Belgic ware, such as cups (Figure 4, 5), plates and bowls (Figure 4, 4) of the Augustan period. The artifact spectrum is completed by some *fibulae* of the Aucissa type (Riha 5.2.2c) (Riha 1979: 114; 118; Leifeld 2007: 202f.) and a thistle brooch with a lion-shaped pin (Riha 1979: 105; Leifeld 2007: 203 Abb. 36.), which also dates into the Augustan period (Figure 4, 7-8).

Indications of an earlier wooden building – Phase 1

During the excavations four post-pits were found. Whereas two of these were not especially clear, the other two were clearly formed by ancient posts. These features are also associated with feature 5 in the western profile (Figure 5). Two Roman coins, which are not described in detail, were found within feature 5. Another post-pit is documented in the second

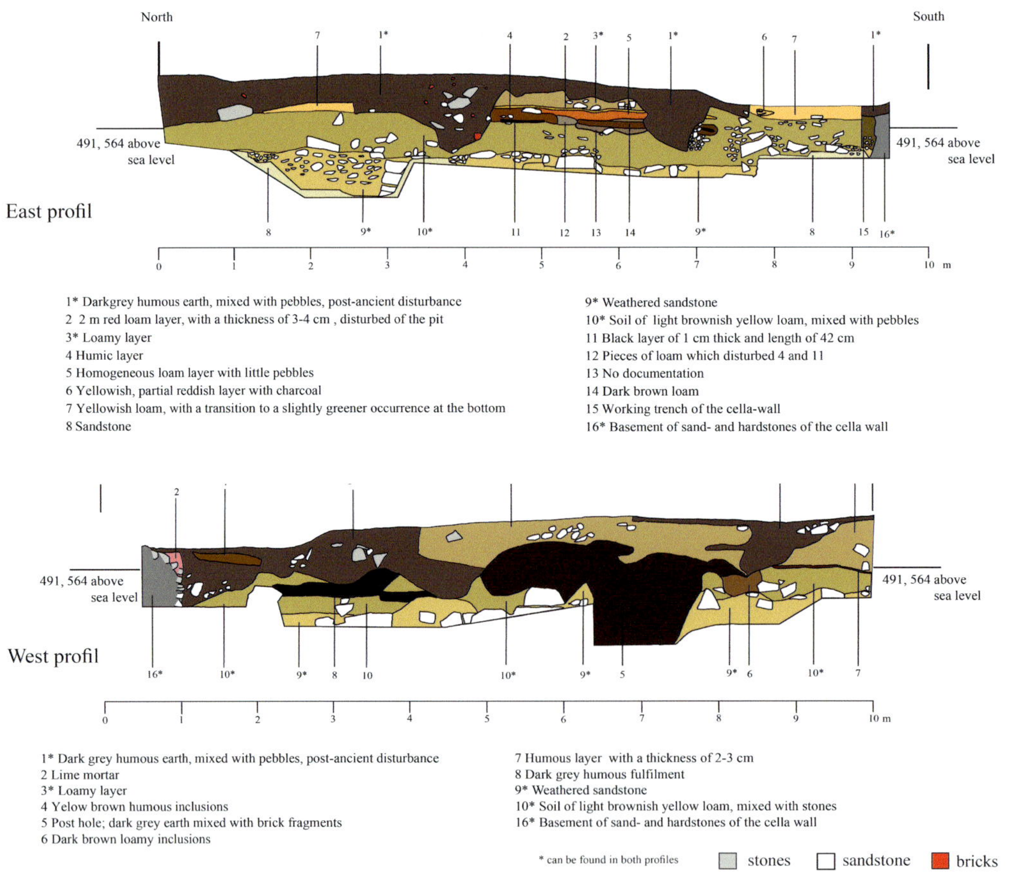

Figure 5. East and west profiles of the trial trench (redrawing and processing: D. Burger-Völlmecke).

layer, including wedges (Figure 3, 8). The eastern profile includes layers (features 2, 4-5, 11-14) which cannot be connected to the basement layers of the *cella* (Figure 5). They are interpreted as a minimum of two occupation layers. The earlier layer is a screed floor. In comparison with other temples, the use of screed floors is first documented in the Tiberian period (Fauduet 1993: 76).

In the western profile (Figure 5), at the same level as the screed floor of the eastern profile, a consistent layer of humus soil is documented (Figure 5, 7). This can be interpreted as the ground floor outside the earliest building. Two pits (Figure 3, I; III) are described which were found inside the *cella* and are considered also to belong to an earlier level.

The contents of the pits included metal and glass fragments, which have been lost and are only mentioned in the site notebook. In pit III an *as* of Domitian (RIC 371, dat. AD 88/89) was excavated. Pit I contained a cup of type Gose 443/444 (Figure 4, 6). Both artifacts are missing. The cup can be dated to the Tiberian/Claudian period. These pits are stratigraphically earlier than the stone wall of the temple and could be correlated with the early ground floors. This description is not compatible with an interpretation of the pits as *favissae* for deposits of cult objects that were no longer in use.

Although there is little evidence, the arguments suggest an earlier wooden building. The two ground levels described above could be indicators of a wooden construction of two phases.

On the basis of the described artifacts and features, the first construction phase is unlikely to have taken place later than the middle of the 1st century AD and is accompanied by a significant increase of the coins at the time of Emperor Vespasian (Figure 6, 2). An earlier date may be possible, as suggested by the Celtic coins as well as the Roman coinage. On the basis of the early finds, an Augustan dating is assumed for the temples of Möhn (Ghetta 2008: 322), Bastendorf (Reinert 2000), Gusterath (Gilles 1991: 105 Tab. 2) and Gillenfeld 'Hitzerath' (Henrich/Mischka 2006: 30f. However, there are no features at 'Auf dem Spätzrech' that support a dating into the beginning of the 1st century AD. Furthermore this hypothesis is in accordance with known construction phases of larger Gallo-Roman temples in the east of the province of Gallia Belgica (Fauduet 1993: 91).

The stone construction temple – Phases 2-4

The archaeological documentation only allows statements about relative chronological observations and architectural characteristics for classification of the construction periods of the stone building. These observations permit a classification into three construction phases. The outbuilding room shows a significant construction joint which implies a later construction, and furthermore separates phase 2 (temple without outbuilding) from phase 3 (temple with outbuilding). A simultaneous genesis of the temple and the *temenos* wall, which is oriented to the southwest of the temple, is conceivable. In a fourth period, the excavation documentation describes a flattening of brick powder that was created around the temple and over the foundation of the outbuilding. The brick powder marks the end of the earlier mentioned room, although at the same time the use of the temple continued.

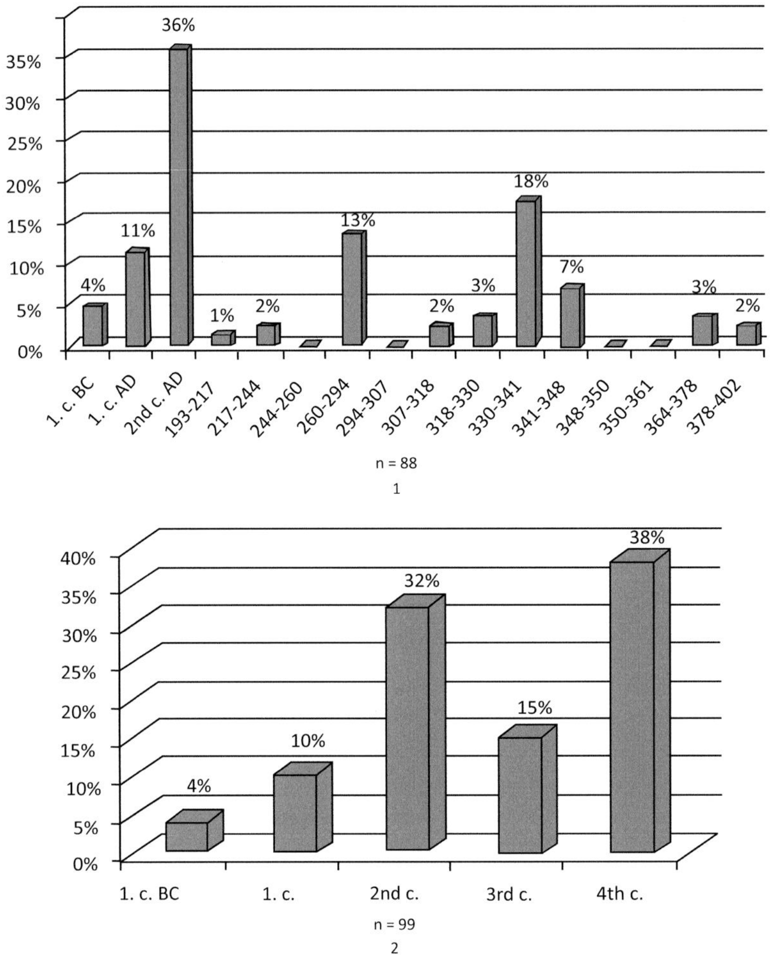

Figure 6. Diagram of the coins. 1: n=88 (phases by Peter 2001); 2: n=99.

Furthermore, as explained above, it must be assumed that the gallery was not a colonnade wall, but rather a closed wall. From an architectural point of view it is unlikely that a room would have been built next to a colonnade. The significance of the outbuilding is represented by the distribution pattern of small finds of terracotta. Therefore it is possible that the room was used as a *sacellum*, where dedications were presented.

The outbuilding is a special architectural feature in the Belgic and Germanic provinces. There are very few parallels in the Treverian region. The results of the geophysical prospection of the Gallo-Roman temple of Gillenfeld (Saarland/Germany) show a similar situation, where the northeast corner has a square anomaly (Henrich/Mischka 2006: 26-27, Abb. 1; 2). So far there has been no reliable argument for a classification as either an entrance or an outbuilding. A clear parallel has recently been excavated in the 'Wareswald' *vicus* at a distance of 20km from the 'Auf dem Spätzrech' temple (See also note 9). Next to the northern corner of the temple wall an outbuilding was added in a later construction phase during the 3rd century, with a comparable size of 3.40m x 3.60m. A third example is at temple 41 in Altbachtal (Augusta Treverorum/Trier), whose outbuilding was possibly used for cult activities (Gose 1972: 148, Abb. B. 269). This architectural peculiarity is perhaps a regional phenomenon of the civitas Treverorum.

Dated artifacts associated with the stone construction phase are very limited, and therefore only conditionally usable for any study based on absolute chronology. They cannot be assigned to one of the defined phases. Above the foundation of the *temenos* wall a burnt layer was documented and contained an *as* of Marcus Aurelius, dated AD 180. Inside the sanctuary a sacrificial victim, along with a Dragendorff-type 40 cup and a coin of Gallienus (undated), was deposited in the southern corner. Due to the unclear features, the interpretation of the deposit as a sacrificial victim must be considered with care.

Further results have been obtained by the analysis of a coin diagram. Overall there are 190 coins, of which 99 can be dated. The increase of the diagram curve is observable at the marker for the 2nd century and again at the marker of the first half of 4th century AD (Figure 6, 1). In consideration of an imprecisely dated *follis*, the concentration of the 4th-century coins within the sanctuary is more evident (Figure 6, 2).

The diagram shows that there was a higher accumulation of coins in the 1st century, slowly increasing during the Vespasianic period and reaching their highest number in the 2nd century. Although the results for the first two centuries seem extraordinary for Gallo-Roman temples, some similar examples can be seen from the neighbouring temples of Dhronecken and Zell (Cochem-Zell) (Gilles 1987: 197f., Tab. 1, with further coin diagrams for the surrounding sanctuaries). This is probably due to differing sacrificial practices, where coins played a more or less important role. Similar explanations could be given for the rise of coin numbers in the 4th century.

Considering the increasing numbers of coins, the low number of ceramic vessels seems unusual at first. Ceramic finds are present from the Early Roman Imperial period to the end of the 3rd century, although for the 4th century only a rim fragment of type Alzei 29 was found. The different amounts of coins and vessels are a phenomenon of Late Gallo-Roman sanctuaries in the Treverian region (Gilles 1987: 201, Anm. 22) and could have occurred for various reasons: the high production of the mints between AD 305 and the middle of the 4th century had an impact (Peter 2001: 154) on the high numbers of coins found in the archaeological evidence; and also the sacrificial practices changed at the end of the 3rd century. In this period the coins were thrown into the *cella* and were therefore better preserved and more visible to the site excavators (Henrich 2006: 54). For example, in the temple of Möhn the coins were found on the screed of the *cella* (Ghetta 2008: 322). The mapping of the coins at 'Auf dem Spätzrech' reflects a similar pattern (Figure 7).

This means that there are only a few absolute-chronological theories possible, as explained above. The gradient of the coin curve in the 2nd century AD runs parallel with a rise in the ceramics. This development can be explained by the increasing importance of cult activities that would have motivated the construction of the stone temple at this time. The steep decline of the coin curve by the end of the 2nd century until the time of the Gallic

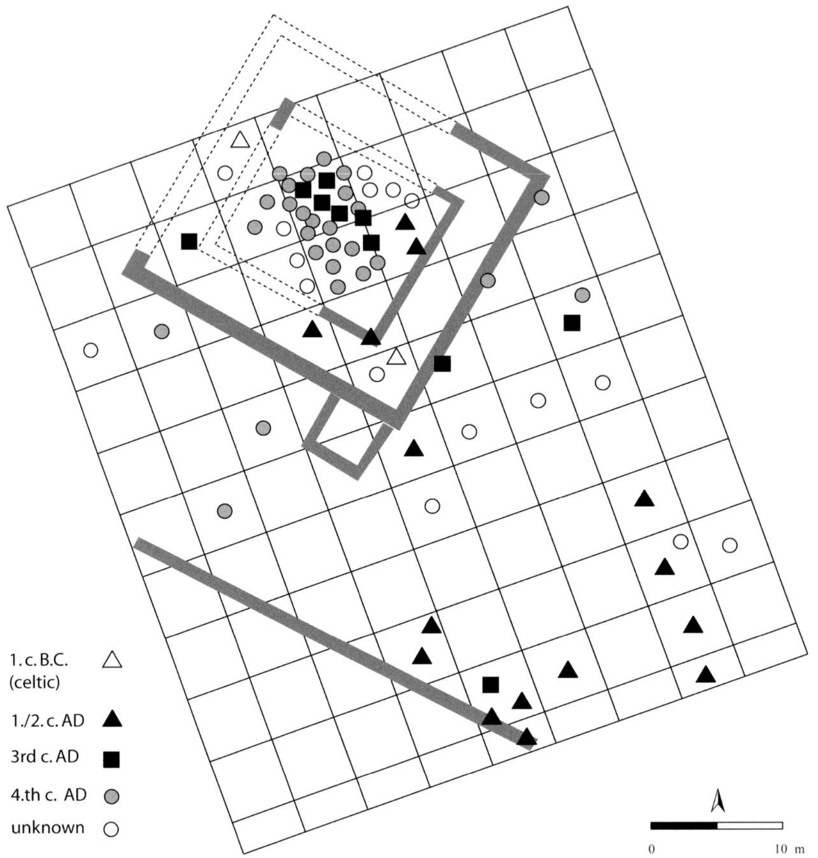

Figure 7. Distribution of the coins n=70.

Empire is probably related to the burnt levels in the area surrounding the *temenos* wall. The coin of Marcus Aurelius found in this burnt layer implies a *terminus post quem* of AD 180, and could reflect unsettled times. Another rise of the amount of coins at the end of the 3rd century AD coincides with the foundation deposit in the *cella* and suggests renovation or reconstruction works, although the uncertain documentation of the archaeological situation must be considered when stressing this hypothesis. However, the finds situation can be compared with similarities at the temple of Möhn.

The documentation of a coin in the *cella* wall is interpreted as a foundation deposit or a deposit after repair work at the end of the 3rd century AD,[4] but, once again, the unclear circumstances of the findings at the 'Auf dem Spätzrech' temple do not directly associate the construction of the outbuilding within the same chronological context. However, other structural modifications of sanctuaries in the Treverian region (i.e. Möhn, Wallendorf,

[4] Ghetta 2008: 322. Another example for a foundation deposit is the finding of a human skull with a ceramic vessel, dated in the first half of the 1st century AD, in the temple of Halatte, Oise/France. They were deposited under the screed in the *cella*: Durand 2000: 113-114, Fig. 20; 27.

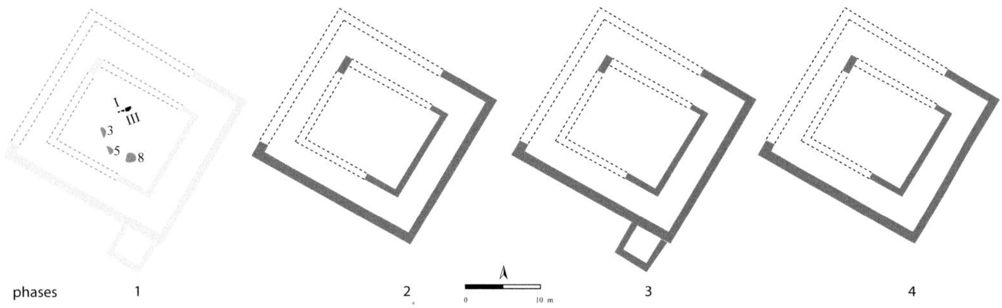

Figure 8. Phases 1-4 of the 'Auf dem Spätzrech' temple.

and the temple of Martberg: Ghetta 2008: 104f.) in the same period are known. This could suggest a similar construction development for the 'Auf dem Spätzrech' temple. Also the further development of the coin curve, representing a slight increase at the beginning of the 4th century AD, then climaxing in the 350s AD and a decline in the middle of the century, fits in with the overall view of other sanctuaries (Ghetta 2008: 105f., with a table of different types of coin curves for Treverian temples).

Here the temple at Möhn is also a good example of a possible parallel. The similar coin curve of these two sites could therefore be interpreted as a climax in cult activities in the 4th century (Ghetta 2008: 322). Because layers of the last occupation phases were disturbed, it is unclear whether the final decline was caused by devastating fires or the abandonment of the temples. This phenomenon is not unusual for the region and only a few Treverian sanctuaries show a burnt layer in the last-use- phase (Ghetta 2008: 111).

Selected finds

The most important find is a bronze *tabula ansata*, with a votive inscription which names the Gallo-Roman god Mars Cnabetius; the ordinand is Gaius Elvonius Caddimarus (Figure 09).

The inscription reads: MARTI CNAB/ETIO/CELVON CADDI/MARVS/[- -]DIVMIANO/II. (Translation: G(aius) Elvon(ius) Caddimarus has offered Mars Cnabetius an oblation.)

The last three lines are damaged and cannot be translated clearly (Burger 2012: 232-234). The *tabula ansata* cannot be dated precisely. This *tabula* is paleographically comparable to one found in the Gallo-Roman sanctuary near the *villa rustica* of Ottrang/Fliessem, which is dated on the basis of the formula INHDD between the second half of the 2nd century and the beginning of the 3rd century.[5]

The god Mars Cnabetius mentioned on the tabula is documented by six other inscriptions (Figure 10).[6] Two of these were found in the *civitas Treverorum* (Hüttigweiler, Tholey) and

[5] Merten 1985: 85. I. König is also convinced that the *tabula* of Mars Cnabetius dates to the time after the Severian period on the basis of palaeographical analysis (I. König, pers. com.).

[6] Tholey: CIL XIII, 04258; Wahlschied bei Saarbrücken: CIL XIII, 04507; Huttigweiler: CIL XIII, 04508; Osterburken: CIL XIII, 06572; Erbstetten: CIL XIII, 06455; Wiesloch: Wiegels 1992: 393f.

Figure 9. *Tabula ansata* (bronze) for Mars Cnabetius; 6cm x 4cm, scale not available (photo and drawing: State Department for Heritage Preservation Saarland, Ministry for Environment, Energy and Traffic).

one of them in Wahlschied, which is associated with the *civitas Mediomatricorum*, located directly across the border from the *civitas Treverorum* (Heinen 1985: Beil. 1). The other three inscriptions were found in the province of Germania superior, where two of them (at Osterburken and Erbstetten) are located along the earlier border of the Odenwald *limes*. With the four inscriptions found in the Treverian area, it can be assumed that Mars Cnabetius is of Treverian origin. The two inscriptions found at the *limes* could derive from Treverian soldiers, garrisoned at the border.

Altogether six bronze figurines were found near the 'Auf dem Spätzrech' temple. Four figurines display the Gallo-Roman god Mars, with the other two showing Apollo and Diana[7] (Figure 11, 1-4). The size of the figurines is between 4cm and 13 cm. These figurines reflect the typical types of a Gallo-Roman repertoire (Ibid. 235–237). Putting the four figurines of Mars in context with the votive inscription, it can be assumed that the temple was dedicated to Mars Cnabetius. The finds of 12 lance heads could also be connected with the cult of Mars. Sanctifications of weapons, especially lance heads, are typical of Treverian sanctuaries in the 1st century AD (Kyll 1966: 62f., with further examples).

[7] The find history of the Diana figurine is complicated and it is uncertain whether the figurine was from 'Auf dem Spätzrech': Wiegert 1997: 39; Miron 2000: 398; Burger 2012: 235.

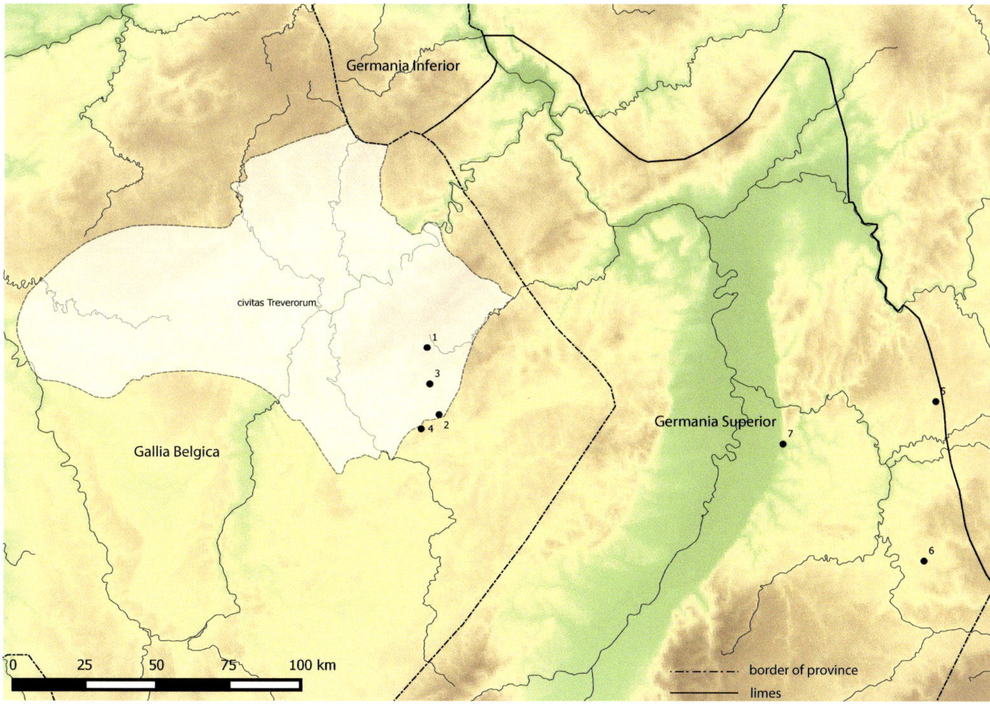

Figure 10. Inscriptions of Mars Cnabetius. 1) Schwarzenbach (St. Wendel); 2) Hüttigweiler (Neunkirchen) [CIL XIII, 04508]; 3) Tholey (St. Wendel) [CIL XIII, 04258]; 4) Wahlschied (Saarbrücken) [CIL XIII, 04507]; 5) Osterburken (Neckar-Odenwald) [CIL XIII, 06572]; 6) Erbstetten (Rems-Murr) [CIL XIII, 06455], 7) Wiesloch (Rhein-Neckar) [Wiegels 1992: 393f.].

Along with the bronze figures are some small bronze votive artefacts of genitals and snakes, suggesting a healing cult (Figure 11, 5-6). Votive artifacts of extremities are often considered to be associated with ancient healing cult activity, where the one who offers the votive object hopes for healing.[8] By contrast, snakes, especially adders, played a prominent role in Greco-Roman, as well as Gallo-Roman, healing cults. The snake was originally an animal accompanying the healing god Asklepios, but in the northern provinces it was adapted to local healing cults. It is not unusual for these snakes to be used in the same context as *genii loci* or images of accompanying animals.[9] The snakes of the 'Auf dem Spätzrech' sanctuaries could be seen in a similar context. However, the figurines that were found of Mars and Apollo are those of gods of healing, since, aside from his function as god of war, Mars was a god of healing and fertility.[10] The most important sanctuaries in the Treverian region were the temples of Martberg and

[8] Those votive of extremities are often wooden, but bronze examples are known; for a summary: Czysz 2010: 82-85; and for further examples: Fauduet 2010: 252-258.

[9] Matthäus 1987: 30-40. The snake is documented as an accompanying animal of Asklepios as well as of Hygieia/Salus and the Gallo-Roman goddess Sirona.

[10] Kuhnen 1996: 191f. For Caracalla thanking Apollo Grannus in Faimingen for his healing: Cass. Dio 77, 15, 5-7. Also Bender 2013: 110.

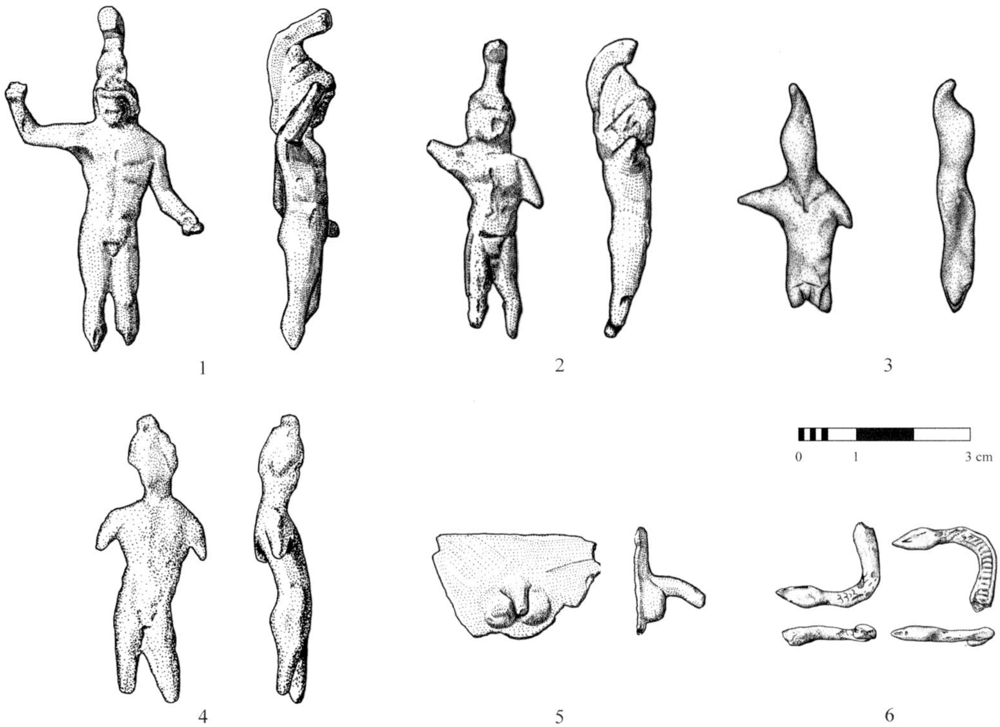

Figure 11. Selected small finds: 1-3) Figurines of Mars (bronze) M 1:1; 4) Figurine of Apollo (bronze) M 1:1; 5) Phallus (bronze) M 1:1; 6) Snake (bronze) M 1:2 (drawings: State Department for Heritage Preservation Saarland, Ministry for Environment, Energyand Traffic).

Irminwingert (Trier).[11] A similar importance can be assumed for the 'Auf dem Spätzrech' sanctuary. This theory is supported by the figurine of Apollo, who is equated in the northern provinces with the Celtic god Grannus.[12] Worship of the divine couple Mars/Apollo has also been documented for the temple at Möhn (Kuhnen 1996: 169; Ghetta 2008: 321). Ancient healing cults can be divided into the so-called mineral-water cure and the incubation cult. Whereas the mineral-water cure offers healing to the sick through the god acting with the help of the water, in the incubation cult the patient received divine healing through sleep in the temple or its surroundings (Merten 1985: 33ff.). At a distance of 70m from the 'Auf dem Spätzrech' temple there is a source, although a source protection has not been documented. For cult use, a source inside the sanctuary area is necessary (see, for example, the temples at Hochscheid and Wallenborn/Heckenmünster (Hochscheid: Weisgerber 1975: 79 f. Taf. 56 and 57,8; Wallenborn/Heckenmünster: Binsfeld 1969: 240-246)). For a sleeping cult it is usual to find lodging houses for patients in the sanctuary area within the archaeological context. So far, however, no structures of buildings inside the area have been found, although the dimensions of the area, as well as further developments in the surroundings, suggest a super-regional significance.

[11] Martberg in detail: Nickel/Thoma 2008; summarising: Ghetta 2008: 311. For the Irminwingert sanctuary: Ghetta 2008: 99-102, with further literature.

[12] Kuhnen 1996: 166-171. For a list of different sanctuaries of Apollo in the Treverian region: Schindler 1965: 80.

References

Bender, S. 2013. Der Feldzug gegen die Germanen 213 n. Chr. In *Caracalla. Kaiser, Tyrann, Feldherr*. Sonderb. Antike Welt: 104-109. Darmstadt/Mainz.

Binsfeld, W. 1969. Das Quellheiligtum Wallenborn bei Heckenmünster (Kreis Wittlich). *Trierer Zeitschrift* 32: 239-268.

Burger, D. 2010. Prospektionsbericht 2009. In P. Jung (ed.), *Neue Untersuchungen im Bereich der römischen Siedlung 'Auf dem Spätzrech' in Nonnweiler-Schwarzenbach (Lkr. St. Wendel) - Ergebnisse der Arbeiten 2006 bis 2009*: 165-169.

Burger, D. 2012. Der gallo-römische Umgangstempel 'Auf dem Spätzrech' bei Schwarzenbach (Lkr. St. Wendel) im Saarland. Ein Pilgerheiligtum für Mars Cnabetius in der civitas Treverorum? *Archäologisches Korrespondenzblatt* 42/2: 225-243.

Burger, D. 2016. Der gallo-römische Umgangstempel 'Auf dem Spätzrech' bei Schwarzenbach (Saarland). Auswertung der Grabung 1984/85. In S. Hornung, P. Brengel, M. König, D. Burger, A. and T. Lang, M. Smettan, A. Kronz (eds), *Mensch und Umwelt II. Vom Oppidum 'Hunnenring' bei Otzenhausen zum römischen Tempelbezirk und vicus 'Auf dem Spätzrech' bei Schwarzenbach, Gem. Nonnweiler, Lkr. St. Wendel*: 137-292. Bonn, Dr. Rudolf Habelt GmbH.

Cordie-Hackenberg, R. 2000. Der Tempelbezirk zu Belginum. In A. Haffner and S. Schnurbein (eds), *Kelten, Germanen, Römer im Mittelgebirgsraum zwischen Luxemburg und Thüringen. Akten des Internationalen Kolloquiums zum DFG-Schwerpunktprogramm 'Romanisierung' in Trier vom 28. bis 30. September 1998*: 409-420. Czysz, W. 2010. Neue Untersuchungen in den Karpfenteichen beim Kastell Dambach (Ausgrabung 2008). In P. Henrich (ed.), *Perspektiven der Limesforschung. 5. Kolloquium der Deutschen* Limeskommission: 73-88. Beitr. Welterbe Limes 5. Stuttgart, Theiss.

Durand, M. 2000. Le temple gallo-romain de la forêt d'Halatte (commune d'Ognon, Oise). Nouvelle interprétation du site à la suite des fouilles de 1996 à 1999. *Revue archéologique de Picardie*. Num. spécial 18: 93-142.

Fauduet, I. 1993. *Les temples de tradition celtique en Gaule romaine. Collection des hespérides.* Paris, Editions Errance.

Fauduet, I. 2010. *Les temples de tradition celtique en Gaule romaine*. Paris, Editions Errance.

Ghetta, M. 2008. *Spätantikes Heidentum. Trier und das Trevererland*. Geschichte u. Kultur des Trierer Landes 10. Trier, Kliomedia.

Gilles, K.-J. 1987. Römische Bergheiligtümer im Trierer Land. Zu den Auswirkungen der spätantiken Religionspolitik. *Trierer Zeitschrift* 50: 195-254.

Gilles, K.-J. 1991. Ein frühaugusteischer Münzschatz aus Gusterath, Kreis Trier-Saarburg. *Trierer Zeitschrift* 54: 95-106.

Gose, E. 1972. *Der gallo-römische Tempelbezirk im Altbachtal zu Trier*. Trierer Grabungen und Forschungen 7. Mainz am Rhein, Philipp v. Zabern.

Haffner, A. and Schnurbein, S. von (eds) 2000. *Kelten, Germanen, Römer im Mittelgebirgsraum zwischen Luxemburg und Thüringen. Akten des Internationalen Kolloquiums zum DFG-Schwerpunktprogramm 'Romanisierung' in Trier vom 28. bis 30. September 1998*. Koll. Vor- u. Frühgesch. 5. Bonn, Dr. Rudolf Habelt GmbH.

Hornung, S. (ed.) 2010. *Mensch und Umwelt I. Archäologische und naturwissenschaftliche Forschungen zum Wandel der Kulturlandschaft um den 'Hunnenring' bei Otzenhausen, Gem. Nonnweiler, Lkr. St. Wendel*. Universitätsforsch. Prähist. Arch. Bonn, Dr. Rudolf Habelt GmbH.

Hornung, S. 2016. *Siedlung und Bevölkerung in Ostgallien zwischen Gallischem Krieg und der Festigung der römischen Herrschaft. Eine Studie auf Basis landschaftsarchäologischer Forschungen im Umfeld des Oppidums 'Hunnenring' von Otzenhausen (Lkr. St. Wendel).* Röm.-Germ.-Forsch. 73. Darmstadt, Philipp von Zabern.

Heinen, H. 1985. *Trier und das Trevererland in römischer Zeit.* 2000 Jahre Trier 1. Trier, Spee.

Henrich, P. 2006. *Die römische Besiedlung in der westlichen Vulkaneifel.* Trier, Rheinisches Landesmuseum Trier.

Henrich, P. and Mischka, C. 2006. Der römische Tempelbezirk von Gillenfeld 'Etzerath', Kreis Daun. *Funde und Ausgrabungen im Bezirk* Trier 38: 25-33.

Henz, K.-P. 2013. Gallo-römischer VicusWareswald – Die Grabungskampagne 2012. Denkmalpflege im Saarland Jahresbericht 2012: 60-63. Saarbrücken, Ministerium für Bildung und Kultur/Landesdenkmalamt.

Henz, K.-P. 2014a. Gallo-römischer Umgangstempel mit unüblichem Anbau. *Archäologie in Deutschland* 4, 51.

Henz, K.-P. 2014b. Gallorömischer Umgangstempel mit Annex im Wareswald. *Denkmalpflege im Saarland Jahresbericht 2013*: 33-36.

Hettner, F. 1901. *Drei Tempelbezirke im Trevererlande: Festschrift zur Feier des hundertjährigen Bestehens der Gesellschaft für nützliche Forschungen in Trier.* Trier, Lintz.

Jung, P. 2010. Neue Untersuchungen im Bereich der römischen Siedlung 'Auf dem Spätzrech' in Nonnweiler-Schwarzenbach (Lkr. St. Wendel) – Ergebnisse der Arbeiten 2006 bis 2009. In Hornung (ed.), *Mensch und Umwelt I. Archäologische und naturwissenschaftliche Forschungen zum Wandel der Kulturlandschaft um den 'Hunnenring' bei Otzenhausen, Gem. Nonnweiler, Lkr. St. Wendel*: 155-224.

Kolling, A. 2002. *Ein gallorömisches Quellheiligtum. Kasbruch Neunkirchen Wellesweiler. Neunkirchen-Wellesweiler.* Wellesweiler Arbeitskreis für Geschichte, Landeskunde und Volkskultur.

Krausse, D. 2006. *Eisenzeitlicher Kulturwandel und Romanisierung im Mosel-Eifel-Raum. Die keltisch-römische Siedlung von Wallendorf und ihr archäologisches Umfeld.* Röm.-Germ. Forsch. 63. Mainz, Philipp v. Zabern.

Kronz, A., Smettan, M., Hornung, S. 2010. Zeugnisse spätlatènezeitlicher und römischer Metallurgie vom 'Hunnenring' bei Otzenhausen und aus dem vicusSpätzrech bei Schwarzenbach, Lkr. St. Wendel. In Hornung (ed.), *Mensch und Umwelt I. Archäologische und naturwissenschaftliche Forschungen zum Wandel der Kulturlandschaft um den 'Hunnenring' bei Otzenhausen, Gem. Nonnweiler, Lkr. St. Wendel*: 275-314.

Kuhnen, H.-P. (ed.) 1996. *Religio Romana. Wege zu den Göttern im antiken Trier. Ausstellungskatalog des Rheinischen Landesmuseums Trier. Schriftenreihe des Rheinischen Landesmuseums. Nr. 12.* Trier, Selbstverlag des Rheinischen Landesmuseums.

Kyll, N. 1966. Heidnische Weihe- und Votivgaben aus der Römerzeit des Trierer Landes. *Trierer Zeitschrift für Geschichte und Kunst des Trierer Landes und seiner Nachbargebiete* 29: 5-113.

Leifeld, H. 2007. *Endlatène- und älterkaiserzeitliche Fibeln aus Gräbern des Trierer Landes. Eine antiquarisch-chronologische Studie.* Universitätsforsch. Prähist. Arch. 146. Bonn, Dr. Rudolf Habelt GmbH.

Loscheider, R. 1998. Untersuchungen zum spätlatènezeitlichen Münzwesen des Trevererlandes. *Archaeologia Mosellana* 3: 63-225.

Matthäus, H. 1987. *Der Arzt in römischer Zeit*. Literarische Nachrichten – archäologische Denkmäler. I. Teil. Schr. Limesmus. Aalen 39. Stuttgart.

Merten, H. 1985. Der Kult des Mars im Trevererraum. *Trierer Zeitschrift* 48: 7-113.

Miron, A. 2000. Der Tempel von Schwarzenbach 'Spätzrech', Kr. St. Wendel. Zur Aufarbeitung eines Altfundkomplexes. In A. Haffner and S. Schnurbein (eds.), *Kelten, Germanen, Römer im Mittelgebirgsraum zwischen Luxemburg und Thüringen. Akten des Internationalen Kolloquiums zum DFG-Schwerpunktprogramm 'Romanisierung' in Trier vom 28. bis 30. September 1998*: 397-407.

Nickel, C. and Thoma, M. 2008. *Martberg. Heiligtum und Oppidum der Treverer 1. Der Kultbezirk. Die Grabungen 1994-2004*. Berichte zur Archaëologie an Mittelrhein und Mosel 14. Koblenz, Generaldirektion Kulturelles Erbe Rheinland-Pfalz.

Oldenstein, J. 2000. Oldenstein, HWederath/Belginum. Gräberfeld, Lager, Siedlung und Tempelbezirk. In Haffner/Schnurbein, 23-40.

Peter, M. 2001. *Untersuchungen zu den Fundmünzen aus Augst und Kaiseraugst*. Studien zu Fundmünzen der Antike 17. Berlin, Mann.

Reinert 2000. Bastendorf – ein frührömischer Kultplatz mit Münzopfer im nördlichen Treverergebiet. In A. Haffner and S. Schnurbein (eds), *Kelten, Germanen, Römer im Mittelgebirgsraum zwischen Luxemburg und Thüringen. Akten des Internationalen Kolloquiums zum DFG-Schwerpunktprogramm 'Romanisierung' in Trier vom 28. bis 30. September 1998*: 369-382.

Riha, E. 1979. *Die römischen Fibeln aus Augst und Kaiseraugst*. Forschungen in Augst 3 (Liestal).

Schindler, R. 1965. *Gallorömische Götter, Kulte und Heiligtümer im Saarland*. Bericht der Staatlichen Denkmalpflege im Saarland 12: 79-107. Saarbrücken.

Thoma, M. 1993. *Das reich ausgestattete Brandgrab 1726 der Spätlatènezeit aus Wederath. Eine antiquarische, soziologische und historische Analyse*. Ungedr. Diss Kiel. Erschienen in Mikrofiche-Druck.

Wiegels, R. 1992. Adnotationes Epigraphicae –Inschriftliches aus Baden-Württemberg. *Fundberichte aus Baden-Württemberg* 17/1: 379-404.

Weisgerber, G. (ed.) 1975. *Das Pilgerheiligtum des Apollo und der Sirona von Hochscheid im Hunsrück*. Bonn, Dr. Rudolf Habelt GmbH.

Wiegert, M. 2002. *Der 'Hunnenring' von Otzenhausen, Lkr. St. Wendel. Die Siedlungsfunde und Bebauungsstrukturen einer spätlatènezeitlichen Höhenbefestigung im Saarland*. Internationale Archäologie 65. Rahden/Westf, M. Leidorf

Wigg, D. G. and Riederer, J. 1998. Die Chronologie der keltischen Münzprägung am Mittelrhein. In U. Peter (ed.), *Stephanosnomismatikos. Edith Schönert-Geiss zum 65. Geb.*: 661-674, Berlin.

After the 'Great War' (AD 166-180) – A 'New Deal' in internal relations within the Central and Northern European Barbaricum?

Hans-Ulrich Voß

Römisch-Germanische Kommission des Deutschen Archäologischen Instituts, Frankfurt am Main

Abstract

Outside the boundaries of the Imperium Romanum, grave finds testify to the self-representation and 'internationality' of the elites of indigenous peoples. Research on the 'Royal Tomb' of Mušov in Moravia (CZ) and the 'Princely Grave' of Gommern on the middle Elbe near Magdeburg (D) provide valuable information on the period immediately before, during, and after the Marcomannic Wars (AD 166/168-180). A detailed analysis of personal equipment allows us to recognise a network between the elites of Germanic and other populations on a geographically large scale that had grown over generations. We can see the extent to which the Marcomannic Wars altered this network, and thus influenced the spread of Roman material goods in Central European Barbaricum. That there were changes is beyond doubt. The discovery of a battlefield on the Harzhorn near Kalefeld, north of Göttingen (D), dated to the year AD 235 or 236 highlights the immediate influence of Rome on intra-Germanic affairs. The change in the balance of power in the lower and middle Elbe region was not without effect on Romano-Germanic relations.

Keywords: Northern European Barbaricum, Central European Barbaricum, Romano-Germanic relations

The interaction of indigenous populations of the European Barbaricum with the Roman Empire, more precisely with the various provinces of the Empire, has always been the interest of both ancient history and archaeological research. In this paper an aspect is to be singled out which is of central importance for understanding the relationship between 'Barbarians' and 'Romans': the internal relationships of indigenous groups outside the Imperial borders. Distribution maps of Roman material goods (e.g. Eggers 1951; Kunow 1983; Lund Hansen 1987; Bemmann 2005; 2015; Rau 2012; Luik 2015) and the analysis of indigenous personal equipment are the background for the discussion of the influence of Rome on the realignment of intra-Germanic elite networks.

With the 'Royal Tomb' of Mušov in Moravia and the 'Princely Grave' of Gommern on the middle Elbe at Magdeburg, two assemblages are available for research that spotlight the self-image and the 'internationality' of Germanic elites immediately before and during the Marcomannic Wars (AD 166/168-180), as well as over subsequent generations (Peškar/ Tejral 2002; Becker 2010) (Figure 1).

These wars are useful as a chronological marker since, among other reasons, in the second half or the last third of the 2nd century AD a clear change in the form of material culture can be observed, accompanied in many Germanic settlement areas with changes in the population structure and differentiation of the settlement system. An example of this is the settlement of Erfurt-Frienstedt in Thuringia, which includes a richly furnished inhumation grave. The immense spectrum of Roman material recovered by the use of metal detectors (Figure 2), in conjunction with other finds, provide completely new insights into the extent of Roman influence in the various regions of Germania (Schmidt 2013).

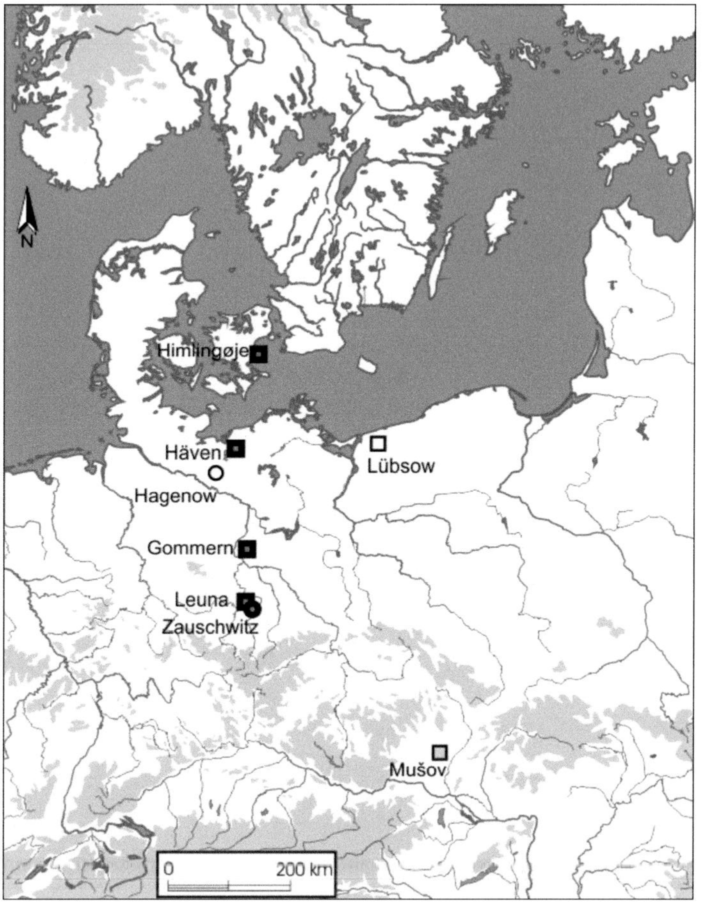

Figure 1. Overview of the geographical position of the cemeteries of Himlingøje on Zealand (DK), Hagenow and Häven in Mecklenburg (D), Lubieszewo/Lübsow in Pommerania (PL), Gommern and Leuna in Central Germany, Zauschwitz in Saxony (D) and Mušov in Moravia (CZ). Early Roman Iron Age: filled signature, Late Roman Iron Age: open signature; cremation graves: circle.

On the other hand, the spectacular discovery of a battlefield on the Harzhorn near Kalefeld in Lower Saxony, in the western Harz foothills, is a stark reminder that an archaeological discovery can confirm information provided by Roman historians, but which for a long time has been doubted (Berger *et al.* 2013; Pöppelmann *et al.* 2013). The reason is that the site of the battle between a Roman army, which included the Legio IIII Flavia, led by Maximinus I Thrax and Germanic warriors during a campaign in AD 235 (236?) is located deep inside Germania. Probably settlements on the Elbe north of the Harz mountains were the goal of this enterprise (Meyer and Moosbauer 2013), since this is where the Langobards, who were involved in the Marcomannic wars, are thought to have lived. This discovery is also dramatic because the advance of a Roman army so deep into foreign territory is

Figure 2. Erfurt-Frienstedt, Thuringia (D), settlement. Roman and Germanic metal finds.
After Schmidt 2013: fig. 8; 9.

inconceivable without secure supply routes and local allies. This means that a key role must have been played by Germanic settlement areas in what are now Thuringia and Saxony-Anhalt, with the well-known late Roman Iron Age 'Princely Graves' of Gommern, Leuna, Haßleben and others (Schulz 1933; 1953; CRFB D 6, 2006).

But first the situation until the Marcomannic wars. Through the filter of burial customs – with the well-documented 'hole in the West' – an amazing continuity in burial practices in elite graves is visible, for example in the provision of buckets with facial handle attachments (see Gorecki 2011) and steep-sided bronze basins from the end of the Germanic wars of Augustus until the beginning of the Late Roman Iron Age (Figure 3). This is demonstrated by a grave at Valløby and finds from the initial phase of the Late Roman Iron Age cemetery at Himlingøje on Zealand (Lund Hansen 1995: 177 Taf. 9; 37; 62; 80).

In addition, identically furnished graves of elite warriors demonstrate that, over generations, lasting relationships existed between the Germanic power centre on the middle Danube opposite *Carnuntum*/Petronell-Bad Deutsch Altenburg in Lower Austria (Elschek 2006; Stuppner 2006), and the northern Elbe region, at least from the last third of the 1st century AD (the Flavian period) (Figure 4). The route to the Danube, and thus access to the Roman Empire, did not run along the Elbe, but, as is demonstrated by a number of indications, along the rivers Havel and Oder to the Moravian Gate. The allies were

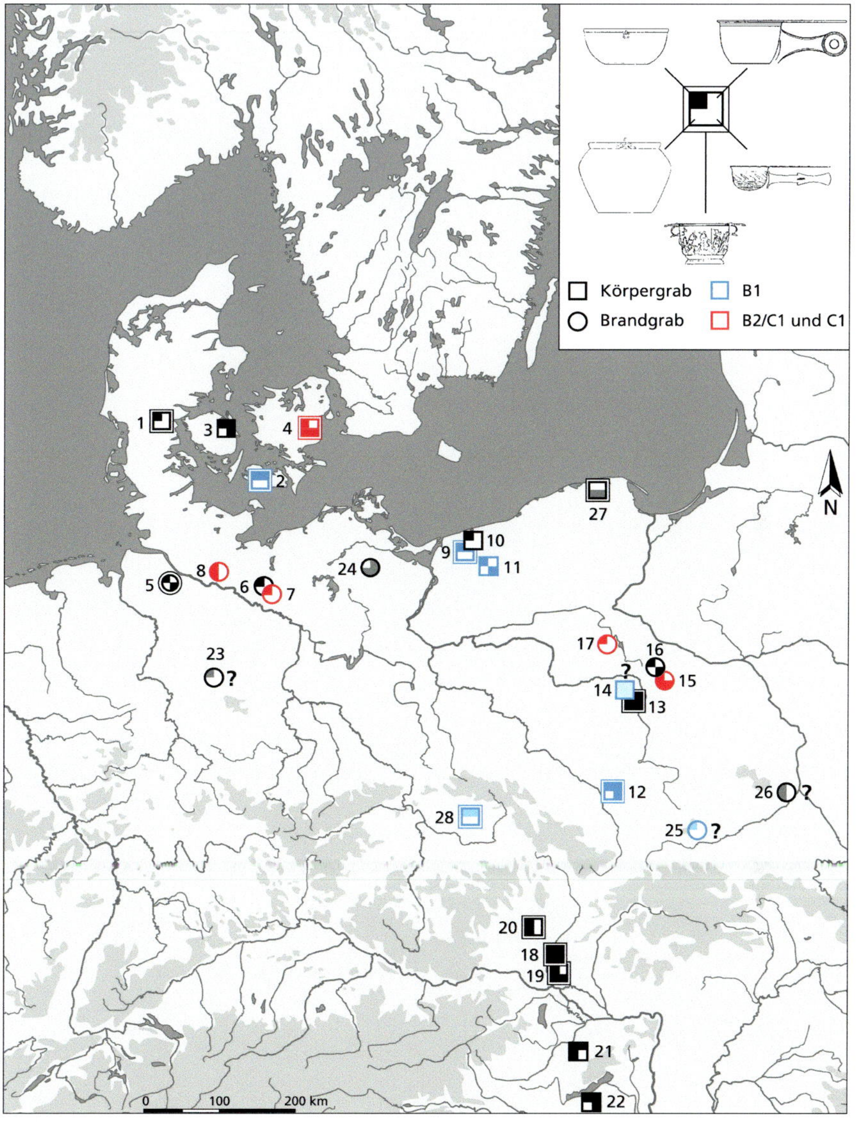

Figure 3. Combination of buckets with facial handle attachments and bronze basins in Early Roman Iron Age graves. Squares are inhumations, circles are cremations. B1: AD 1-70; B2: AD 70-215/220. After Voß 2005: Abb. 11.

located on this route and here, without involvement from central Germany, military elites established a communication network which was very probably also cemented by family ties (Voß 2005: 44-45 Abb. 14).

A pair of belt buckles decorated with gilded silver filigree from the 'royal tomb' of Mušov belong to the period immediately before or during the Marcomannic wars (see Carnap-Bornheim 2002: 195–198; 537–538 Taf. 56: C3.4 Farbtafel 4: 3.4). There is a very closely

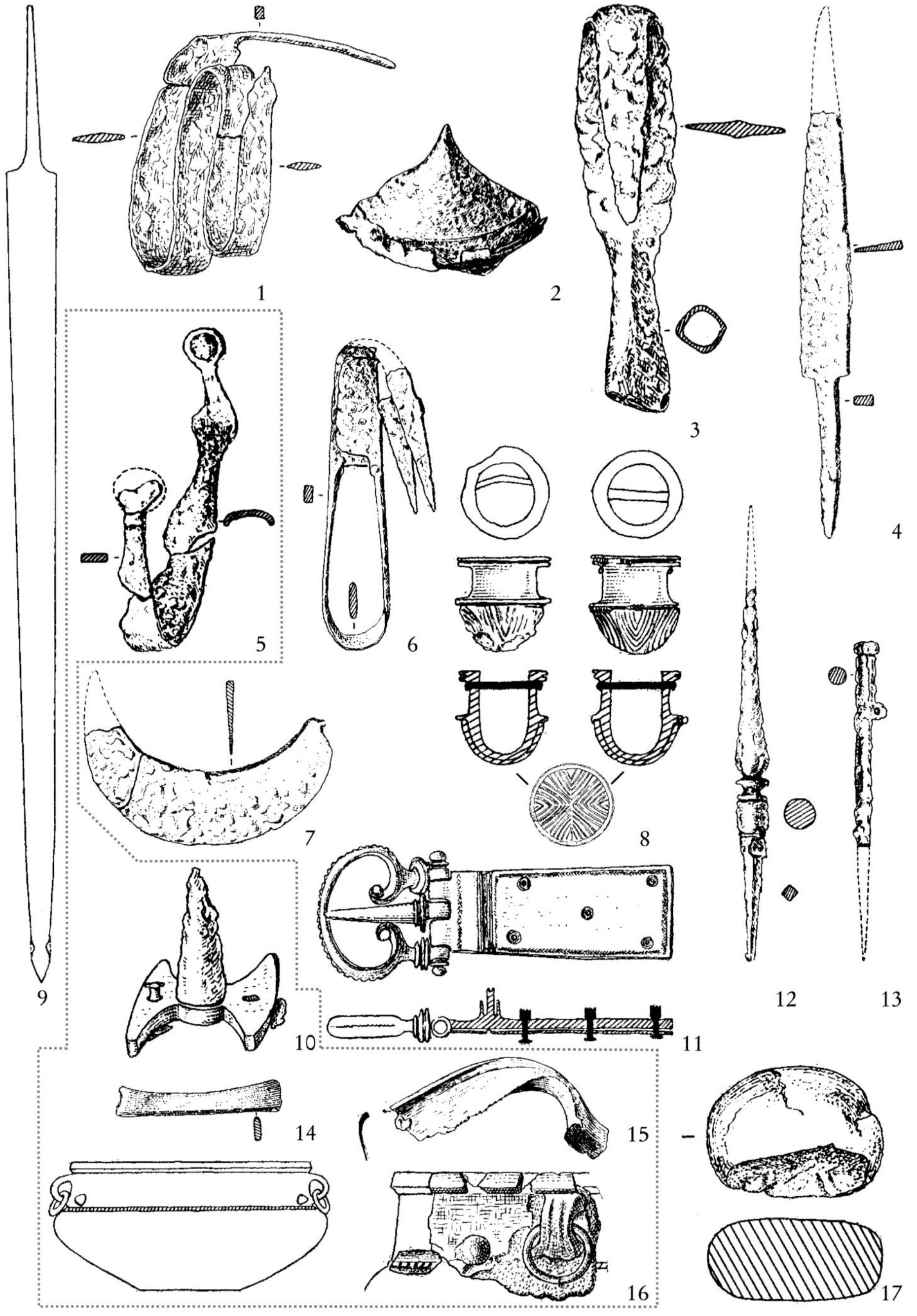

Figure 4. Furniture pattern of Early Roman Iron Age cremation graves: Kostolná pri Dunaji, western Slovakia, grave 37 (after Kolník 1980: 111 Taf. 9-93); 5.10.14-16 similar to Hagenow, Mecklenburg (D); grave 9/1995; all other except No. 7 identical with grave goods in Hagenow, grave 9/1995; 1.7.9.12.13 iron; 8.11 bronze with silver; 10 bronze with iron; 14-15 bronze; 16 ceramic and bronze; 17 stone. Not to scale (Voß 2005: Abb. 9).

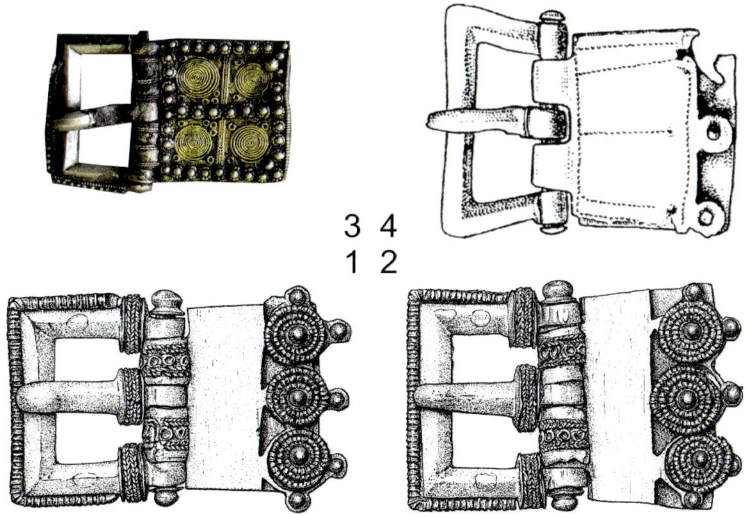

Figure 5. 1/2 Mušov, Moravia (CZ), 'Royal Tomb'. Pair of belt buckles, gilded silver, (object C 3, C 4); 3 Hagenow, Mecklenburg (D), grave1/1995, cremation. Belt buckle, silver, partly gilded; 4 Zauschwitz, Saxony (D), grave 14, cremation. Belt buckle, bronze; M. 1:1. After v. Carnap-Bornheim 2002: 538, Taf. 56: C3.4; Meyer 1969: Abb. 21.

related parallel from grave 1/1995 at Hagenow in Western Mecklenburg (Figure 5: 1–3), which was unfortunately not properly excavated (Voß 2005: 35–38 Abb. 11; 2008b: 46 Abb. 16; 219 Kat. 14). It also contained three golden finger rings, a bucket with facial handle attachment, form Eggers 27, used as an urn and a basin of form Neupotz NE 19 used as a lid (see Figure 3). Such basins were produced until the last third of the 2nd century on the evidence of the grave from Hagenow of similar date to the burial in Mušov. A similar, but much more simply-worked bronze belt set (Figure 5: 4) has been found in the urn grave (Grave 14) of a boy with weapons at Zauschwitz near Leipzig (Meyer 1969: 101 Abb. 21,1). This grave is dated to phase C1a (Kleemann 2007: 309–311; 319 Abb. 3) and is thus beyond dispute younger than those from Mušov and Hagenow, which date to the time just before or during the Marcomannic wars. The analysis of the technological details of the two silver buckles suggests that both pieces were made in the same workshop after the middle of the 2nd century AD, perhaps by the same hand. It has been suggested that there was a highly specialized workshop in the vicinity of Mušov hillfort, in which possibly even Roman specialists or at least craftsmen with Roman training were active (Tejral 2002: 158); or alternatively, as suggested by identically crafted belt fittings from the grave at Lubieszewo / Lübsow Tunnehult in Pomerania, at a workshop in southern Scandinavia (Schuster 2010: 158 Abb. 66). Undoubtedly, these gilded silver buckles are one of the leading objects marking status among the prestige goods of the time. Chronologically they belong to the final stages of the internal Germanic contacts between the lower Elbe region and the middle Danube which, as we have seen, lasted for several generations (eg. Böhme 1996; Tejral 1999; Voß 2005).

It is all the more surprising that a different picture, one that is more closely related to central Germany, is painted by the comparatively few finds that can be linked with the Marcomannic wars, be it weapons or parts of weapons such as – at least a few – Ringpommel swords or chapes of Novaesium-type, but also the characteristic fittings with a trumpet-shaped perforation pattern (Figure 6) and other pieces of military equipment (Voss 2008c:

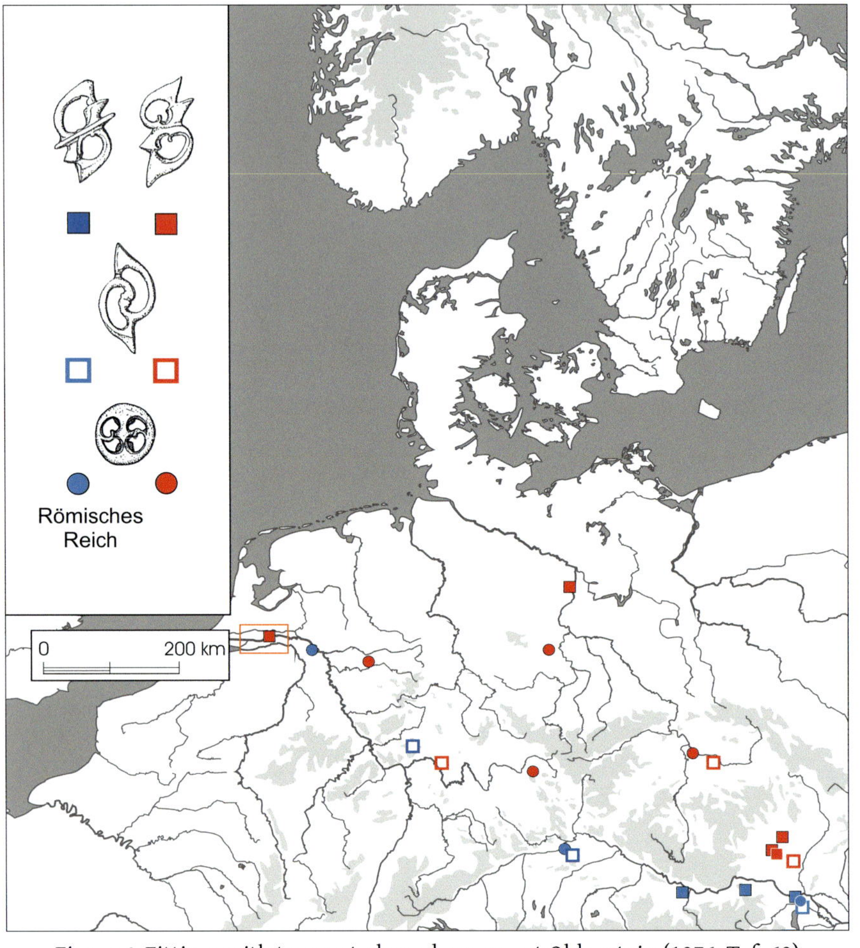

Figure 6. Fittings with trumpet-shaped ornament Oldenstein (1976: Taf. 69) type 897 und 905.

267 Abb. 10; 11; Pauli-Jensen 2008a: 121-127; 141-142; 2008b: 62-70 Abb. 34; 38). Certainly, the dominant burial rites, or those that now came into use in some parts of Barbaricum, play a important part in the picture we have, as does the state of research, in particular metal detector surveys. But a steadily increasing number of settlement finds may also serve to warn against jumping to conclusions.

After the Marcomannic wars contacts between Germanic groups from the lower Elbe region and the regions in present-day Moravia and western Slovakia were not broken off (Figure 7), as is indicated by finds of the earliest occupation phase from the urn-cemetery at Pritzier in west Mecklenburg, not far from the Early Roman Iron Age princely tombs at Hagenow (Schuldt 1955; Tejral 1975: 17-42; 1999: 200-204 Abb. 45-47; Voß 2008a: 62-67 Abb. 13). But studies involving the ceramics of the Elbian circle show that these groups now used a different route, down the Elbe (Hegewisch 2007: 220-290 Abb. 158; 159; 206-208).

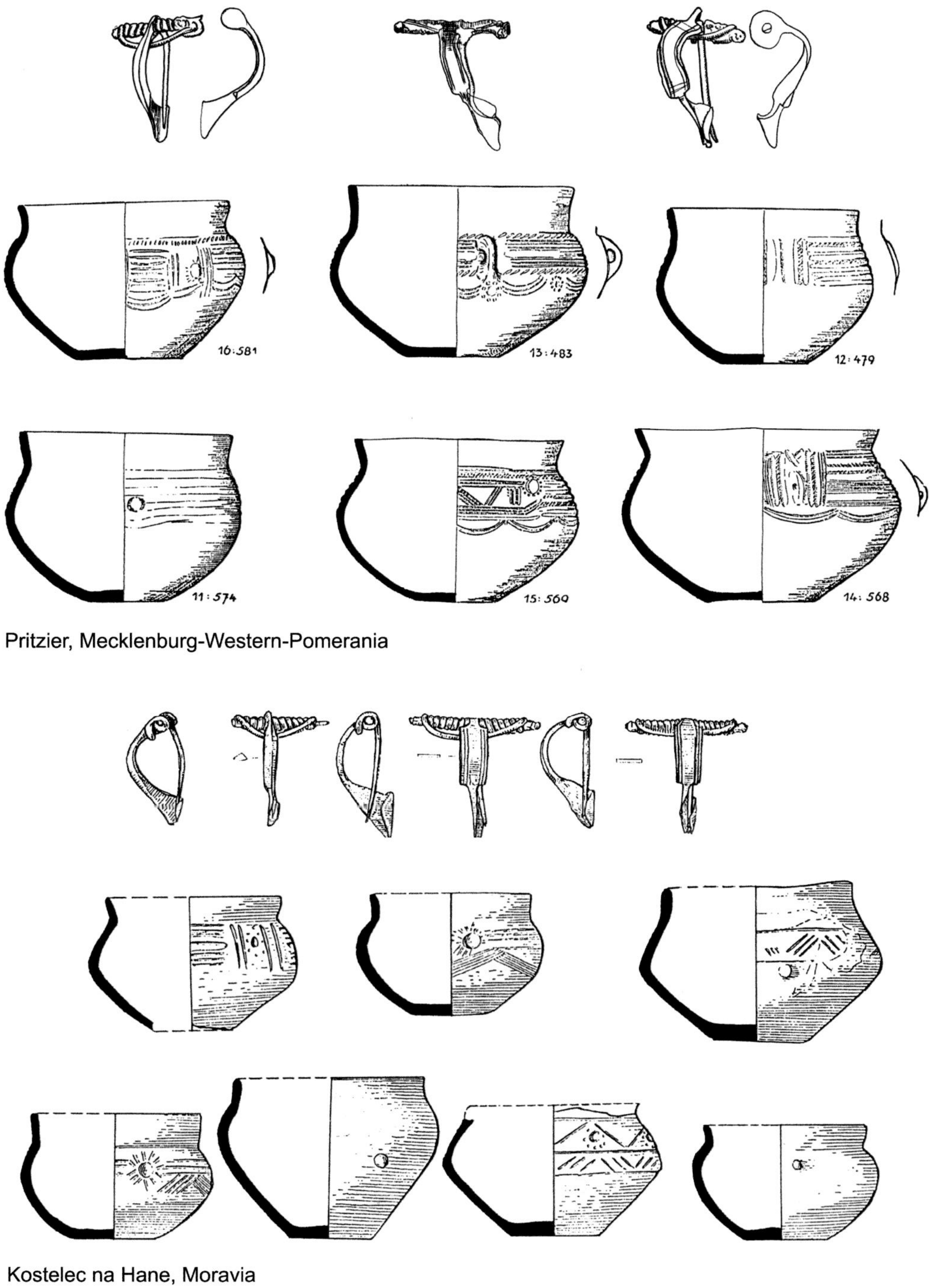

Figure 7. 'Schalenurnen' (bowl urn) and brooches with high catch-plate Almgren VII, from the Late Roman Iron Age cremation cemeteries of Pritzier, Mecklenburg (D) and Kostelec na Hané, Moravia (CZ) (after Voß 2008: Abb. 13).

The significant changes in the networks of Germanic elites after the Marcomannic wars are reflected in the necropolis of Häven, northeast of Lake Schwerin in west Mecklenburg (Voß 2014). In the 1860s/70s and 1960s/70s during earth-moving work several male and female burials richly furnished with Roman metal and glass vessels, as well as high-quality local products, were discovered (e.g. Lisch 1870; 1878; Schuldt 1969; 1972) (Figure 8). The cemetery was in use approximately between AD 230/250

Figure 8. 1 Häven, Mecklenburg (D), inhumation graves VII/1872 (1) and 2/1967 (2). Overview of the burial equipment.

and AD 300 (phases C1b/ C2a–C2b) and was located away from the major population concentrations; it seems to have been a deliberately chosen position at some distance from the coast (Schach-Dörges 1970). A survey of the tombs and the inventories of the graves shows three spatially separated groups: the first consisted of graves with and without stone packs in pits some 1.5m deep, without internal structures and with grave goods placed directly next to the skeleton. Some 100 years later in a separate zone, graves were laid out some 2m deep, with traces of wooden fittings and grave goods placed separately from the skeleton. The third group, discovered at a greater distance inland, differs in composition and furniture completely from the other two (Voß 2014: Abb. 21 Tab. 1).

The close ties between representatives of Germanic elites are also revealed by, among other things, a type of belt. In the burial of the Prince of Gommern at Magdeburg, east of the Elbe, dating probably before the middle of the 3rd century, a belt with silver fittings was found, interpreted as a body belt. The best parallel to its buckle is provided by Häven grave V found in 1869 (Lisch 1870: 127-128 Taf. 1: 7.8; Voß 2014: Abb. 26) (Figure 9). This remarkable, but probably incomplete grave ensemble of a 25-35 year-old man is dated to phase C2, which is somewhat later than the princely grave from Gommern (Becker 2010: 82; 415-417, Taf. 7: 1; 8: 1-4). Nevertheless, it is tempting to see the two persons as contemporaries, and to suggest the belts were also produced in the same workshop, or a group of related workshops.

How are the findings presented in this overview to be interpreted? The intermediary position of the Häven necropolis between Zealand and central Germany is obvious, as are some southern Scandinavian influences represented by 3rd-century material found in central Germany (e.g. Lund Hansen 1995; Bemmann 2005; Becker 2010; Rau 2012). Perhaps it was the cemetery of a staging post or 'station' settlement deliberately established to secure a part of the overland route between these two regions (Voß 2014: 84-88, Abb. 28) (Figure 10).

If the proposition of a deliberately maintained land connection with its own staging posts between southern Scandinavia and central Germany from the middle of the 3rd century onwards can be further substantiated, an intra-Germanic power constellation would be highlighted which coincides chronologically with references to the tribal associations as new actors in Romano-Germanic relations.

The interesting question is whether direct Roman interference in intra-Germanic affairs led to this constellation, and what role was played by the power struggles that are manifested in the southern Scandinavian offerings of military equipment. Evidence for the 'final stages of political power struggles' are the 'enormous complexes' of Illerup A (about AD 210) in central Jutland, and Vimose on Funen and Thorsberg in Schleswig from the first half of the 3rd century. These are of particular importance in this context, because some of the sacrificed objects dating to the second half of the 2nd century AD probably also came from central Germany (Blankenfeldt 2015: 278-291, Abb. 166-169; Ilkjær 1993: 374-386, Abb. 156, 157; Pauli-Jensen 2008a: 280-311; 2008b: Fig. 80-88; 2011: Fig. 6, 7; Rau 2010: 473-490, Abb. 198-204).

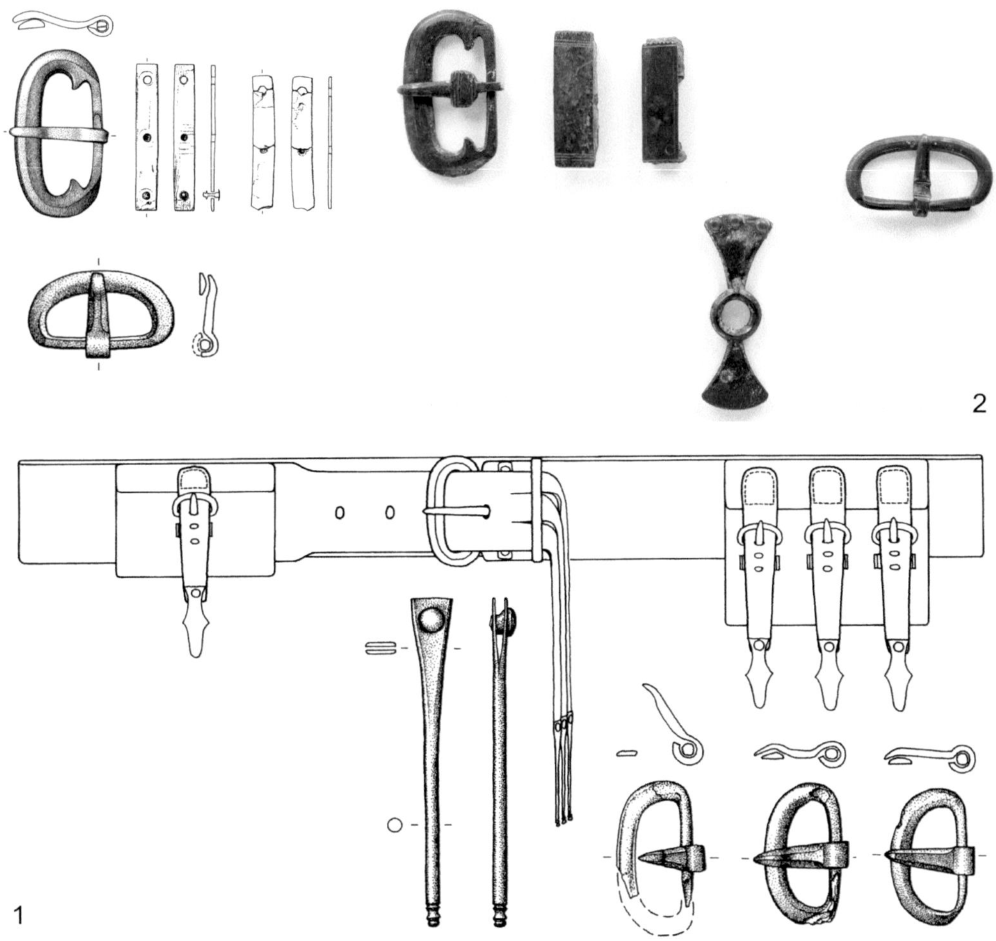

Figure 9. 1) Gommern, Saxony-Anhalt (D), 'Princely Grave', inhumation. Waist belt (belt 2), belt fittings, silver; 2) Häven, Mecklenburg (D), grave V/1869, inhumation. Waist belt, belt fittings, silver. M. 1: 1. 1 After Becker 2010: Taf. 7-9.

I also tend to believe that the military conflict in southern Scandinavia after the Marcomannic wars was part of a Roman game plan. Whether this was also accompanied by Roman influence on intra-Germanic alliances remains at present highly speculative.

In summary, it should be noted that despite the uncertainties due to difficulties with the sources, the so-called princely tombs provide an important indication of the changes in intra-Germanic relationships associated with the Marcomannic wars. Already a glance at the graves furnished with silver vessels shows a shift towards the Elbe area that is clearly visible in the distribution map of Late Roman Iron Age princely tombs with the inhumation groups on Zealand and in central Germany (Voß 2013: 305, ill. 19:1). The peripheral position of the 'Royal Tomb' of Mušov in Moravia and the grave at Czarnówko in Pomerania – both from the transitional phase between Early and Late Roman Iron Age

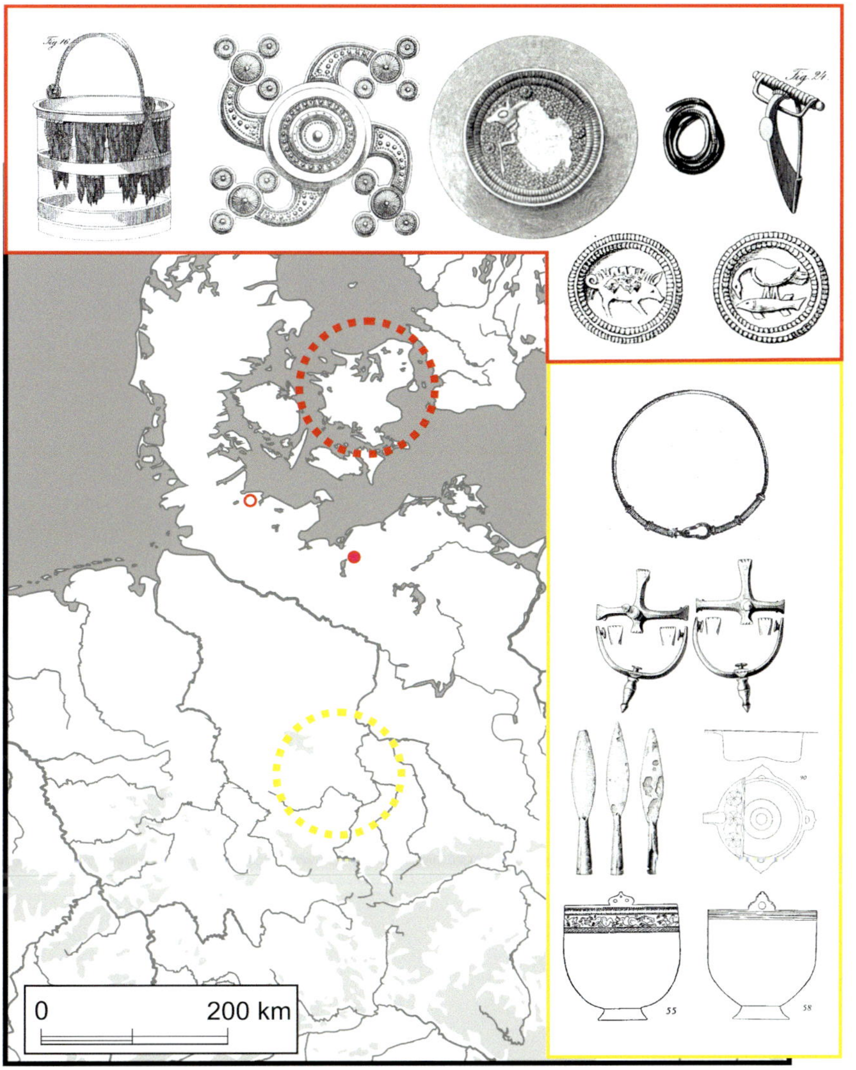

Figure 10. Häven, Mecklenburg (D), inhumation graves. Origin of grave goods (after Voß 2014: Abb. 28).

period, according to the conventional terminology for Barbaricum – is apparent (Figure 11).

One of the consequences of the transformation and reshaping of power relations inside Germania was that from the beginning of the 3rd century AD onwards Elbe-Germanic or Elbe-Germanic-dominated groups began to unsettle the Upper Germanic-Raetian *Limes*. With the invasions of the Alamanni in the north-western provinces on the one hand – represented by the Augsburg victory altar, dated to September AD 260 (Bakker 2006), and the so called 'Alemannic loot' from the Rhine near Neupotz, dated to the same year – and

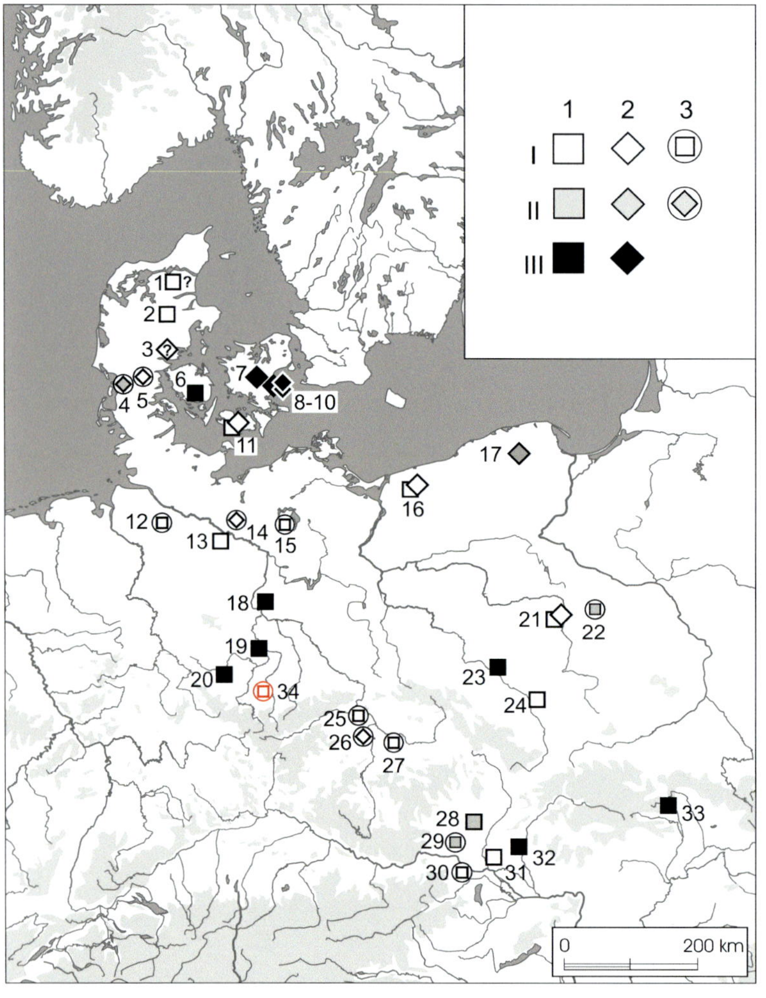

Figure 11. Silver vessels in 1st/3rd-century graves. I: AD 1-160/180; II: AD 150/160-200; III: AD 160/180-310/320. 1) Roman silver vessels; 2) Germanic imitations (or Dacian vessels). Encircled symbols are cremations, the remainder are inhumations (after Voß 2013: Ill. 19:1 (with addition).

the *ingentia auxilia germanorum* from central Germany as allies of the Gallic Empire (AD 260-274) on the other hand (Künzl 1993; Historisches Museum der Pfalz Speyer 2006; Bemmann 2015), all the ambivalence of Romano-Germanic relations is once more visible; but we can also see a lasting shift of power between the Roman Empire and the Barbarians visible in the distribution maps of Roman material goods, for example selected metal vessels.

Illustration credits

Base maps: K. Ruppel, Römisch-Germanische Kommission.

References

Bakker, L. 2006. Der Siegesaltar zur Augsburger Juthungenschlacht von 260 n. Chr. In Historisches Museum der Pfalz Speyer (ed.), *Der Barbarenschatz. Geraubt und im Rhein versunken*: 30-33. Stuttgart, Theiss.

Becker, M. 2010. *Das Fürstengrab von Gommern.* Veröffentlichungen des Landesamtes für Denkmalpflege und Archäologie Sachsen-Anhalt – Landesmuseum für Vorgeschichte 63. Halle/Saale, Landesamt für Denkmalpflege und Archäologie Sachsen-Anhalt, Landesmuseum für Vorgeschichte.

Bemmann, J. 2005. Zur Münz- und Münzersatzbeigabe in Gräbern der Römischen Kaiserzeit und Völkerwanderungszeit des mittel- und nordeuropäischen Barbaricums. In H.-J. Häßler (Hrsg.), *Neue Forschungsergebnisse zur nordwestdeutschen Frühgeschichte unter besonderer Berücksichtigung der altsächsischen Kultur im heutigen Niedersachsen.* Studien zur Sachsenforschung 15: 1-62.

Bemmann, J. 2014. Mitteldeutschland und das Gallische Sonderreich 260–274. Eine liebgewonnene These auf dem Prüfstand. *Kölner Jahrbuch* 47: 179-213.

Berger, F. *et al.* 2015. Die römisch-germanische Auseinandersetzung am Harzhorn, Lkr. Northeim, Niedersachsen. *Germania* 88, 2013: 313-402.

Blankenfeld, R. 2015. *Das Thorsberger Moor. 2. Die persönlichen Ausrüstungen.* Schleswig, Verein zur Förderung des Archäologischen Landesmuseums e.V. Schloss Gottorf.

Böhme, H.-W. 1996. Kontinuität und Traditionen bei Wanderungsbewegungen im frühmittelalterlichen Europa vom 1.-6. Jahrhundert. *Archäologische Informationen* 19: 89-103.

v. Carnap-Bornheim, C. 2002. Der Trachtschmuck, die Gürtel und das Gürtelzubehör. In J. Peškar and J. Tejral (Hrsg.), *Das germanische Königsgrab von Mušov in Mähren Teil 2.* Römisch-Germanisches Zentralmuseum, Monographien 55,2, Mainz, Verlag des Römisch-Germanischen Zentralmuseums.

CRFB D 6, 2006. Becker, M., Bemmann, J., Laser, R., Leineweber, R., Schmidt, B., Schmidt-Thielbeer, E. and Wetzel, I., *Corpus der römischen Funde im europäischen Barbaricum. Deutschland 6: Land Sachsen-Anhalt.* Bonn, Habelt.

Eggers, H. J. 1951. *Der römische Import im freien Germanien.* Atlas der Urgeschichte 1. Hamburg, Hamburgisches Museum für Völkerkunde und Vorgeschichte.

Elschek, K. 2006. Die spätlatènezeitliche und römerzeitliche Besiedlung des linken Marchufers und das germanische Herrschaftszentrum von Zohor (Westslowakei). In F. Humer (Hrsg.), *Legionsadler und Druidenstab. Vom Legionslager zur Donaumetropole. Textband.* Katalog des Niederösterreichischen Landesmuseums, N. F. 462: 190-197. [Bad Deutsch-Altenburg], Amt der NÖ Landesregierung, Abt. Kultur und Wissenschaft.

Gorecki, J. 2011. Die römischen Metallgefäße. In M. Mączyńska, Der frühvölkerwanderungszeitliche Hortfund von Łubiana, Kreis Kościerzyna (Pommern). *Bericht der RGK 90, 2009*: 154-194.

Grane, Th. 2007. *The Roman Empire and Southern Scandinavia - A Northern Connection.* Unpublished PhD-Thesis, University of København.

Hegewisch, M. 2007. *Plänitz. Ein kaiser- und völkerwanderungszeitliches Gräberfeld im Kreis Ostprignitz-Ruppin.* Bonner Beiträge zur Vor- und Frühgeschichtlichen Archäologie 7. Bonn, Vor- und Frühgeschichtliche Archäologie, Rheinische Friedrich-Wilhelms-Universität.

Historisches Museum der Pfalz Speyer (ed.) 2006. *Der Barbarenschatz. Geraubt und im Rhein versunken.* Stuttgart, Theiss.

Ilkjær, J. 1993. *llerup Ådal. 3–4. Die Gürtel. Bestandteile und Zubehör.* Jysk Arkaeologisk Selskabs Skrifter 25: 3–4. Aarhus, Aarhus University Press.

Kleemann, J. 2007. Das Gräberfeld von Zauschwitz. In M. Mączyńska and A. Urbaniak (Red.), *Okres rzymski i wędrówek ludów w północnej polsce.* Acta Universitatis Lodziensis, Folia Archaeologica 25: 307-328. Łódź, Wydawnictwo Uniwersytetu Łódzkiego.

Kolník, T. 1980. *Römerzeitliche Gräberfelder in der Slowakei. 1.* Archaeologica Slovaca monographiae. Fontes 14. Bratislava, Veda.

Künzl, E. 1993. *Die Alamannenbeute aus dem Rhein bei Neupotz. Plünderungsgut aus dem römischen Gallien.* Römisch-Germanisches Zentralmuseum, Monographien 34. Mainz, Verlag des Römisch-Germanischen Zentralmuseums.

Kunow, J. 1983. *Der römische Import in der Germania libera bis zu den Markomannenkriegen. Studien zu Bronze- und Glasgefässen.* Göttinger Schriften zur Vor- und Frühgeschichte 21. Neumünster, Wachholtz.

Lisch, G. C. F. 1870. Römergräber in Meklenburg. II Römische Alterthümer von Häven. *Jahrbücher des Vereins für Mecklenburgische Geschichte 35 B:* 106-163.

Lisch, G. C. F. 1878. Römische Alterthümer von Häven. Nachtrag zur vierten Aufgrabung, Grab 9. *Mecklenburger Jahrbücher* 43: 205-206.

Luik, M. 2015. Ein Hemmoorer Eimer von Rainau-Dalkingen, Ostalbkreis, Baden-Württemberg. *Germania* 91: 115-154.

Lund Hansen, U. 1987. *Römischer Import im Norden. Warenaustausch zwischen dem Römischen Reich und dem freien Germanien.* Nordiske Fortidsminder Ser. B 10. København Det Kongelige Nordiske Oldskriftselskab.

Lund Hansen, U. 1995. *Himlingøje - Seeland - Europa. Ein Gräberfeld der jüngeren Römischen Kaiserzeit auf Seeland, seine Bedeutung und internationalen Beziehungen.* Nordiske Fortidsminder Ser. B 13. København, Det Kongelige Nordiske Oldskriftselskab.

Mączyńska, M. and Rudnicka, D. 2004. Ein Grab mit römischen Importen aus Czarnówko, Kreis Lębork, Pommern. *Germania* 82, 2: 397-429.

Meyer, E. 1969. *Das germanische Gräberfeld von Zauschwitz, Kr. Borna. Ein Beitrag zur spätrömischen Kaiserzeit in Sachsen.* Arbeits- und Forschungsberichte zur sächsischen Bodendenkmalpflege 6. Berlin, Deutscher Verlag der Wissenschaften.

Meyer, M. and Moosbauer, G. 2013. Der Weg zum Harzhorn. In H. Pöppelmann, K. Deppmeyer, and W.-D. Steinmetz (eds), *Roms vergessener Feldzug. Die Schlacht am Harzhorn.* Veröffentlichungen des Braunschweigischen Landesmuseums 115: 265-268. Stuttgart, Theiss.

Oldenstein, J. 1976. Zur Ausrüstung römischer Auxiliareinheiten. Studien zu Beschlägen und Zierat an der Ausrüstung der römischen Auxiliareinheiten des obergermanisch-raetischen Limesgebietes aus dem zweiten und dritten Jahrhundert n. Chr. *Bericht der RGK* 57: 49-284.

Pauli Jensen, X. 2008a. *Våben fra Vimose - bearbejdning og tolkning af et gammelkendt fund. Text.* Unpublished PhD. Thesis, University of København.

Pauli Jensen, X. 2008b. *Våben fra Vimose - bearbejdning og tolkning af et gammelkendt fund. Katalog.* Unpublished PhD. Thesis, University of København.

Pauli-Jensen, X. 2011. Friend or Foe. Alliances and Power Structures in Southern Scandinavia during the Roman Iron Age. *Lund Archaeological Review*: 35-47.

Pöppelmann, H., Deppmeyer, K. and Steinmetz, W.-D. 2013. *Roms vergessener Feldzug. Die Schlacht am Harzhorn.* Veröffentlichungen des Braunschweigischen Landesmuseums 115. Stuttgart, Theiss.

Rau, A. 2010. *Nydam Mose 1. Die personengebundenen Gegenstände. Grabungen 1989–1999. Text.* Jysk Arkaeologisk Selskabs Skrifter 72. Højbjerg, Carlsbergfondet.

Rau, A. 2012. Das nördliche Barbaricum zur Zeit der Krise des 3. Jahrhunderts n. Chr. Einige kritische Anmerkungen zur Diskussion über provinzialrömisch-nordeuropäische Verbindungen. In Th. Fischer (Hrsg.), *Die Krise des 3. Jahrhunderts n. Chr. und das Gallische Sonderreich.* Schriften des Lehr- und Forschungszentrums der antiken Kulturen des Mittelmeerraumes – Centre Mediterranean Cultures: 343-430. Wiesbaden, Reichert.

Schach-Dörges, H. 1970. *Die Bodenfunde des 3. bis 6. Jahrhunderts nach Chr. zwischen unterer Elbe und Oder.* Offa-Bücher 23. Neumünster, Wachholtz.

Schmidt, Chr. 2013. Just recycled? New light on the Roman imports at the 'central farmstead' of Frienstedt (central Germany). *Journal of Roman Archaeology*: 57-70.

Schuldt, E. 1955. *Pritzier. Ein Urnenfriedhof der späten römischen Kaiserzeit in Mecklenburg.* Schriften der Sektion für Vor- und Frühgeschichte der Deutschen Akademie der Wissenschaften Berlin 4. Berlin, Akademie-Verlag.

Schuldt, E. 1969. Ein weiteres Körpergrab der späten römischen Kaiserzeit von Häven, Kr. Sternberg. *Ausgrabungen und Funde* 14: 186-191.

Schuldt, E. 1972. Sondierungen auf dem Friedhof der spätrömischen Kaiserzeit von Häven, Kreis Sternberg. *Jahrbuch für Bodendenkmalpflege in Mecklenburg*: 213-222.

Schulz, W. 1933. *Das Fürstengrab von Hassleben.* Römisch-Germanische Forschungen 7. Berlin, Leipzig, W. de Gruyter.

Schulz, W. 1953. *Leuna. Ein germanischer Bestattungsplatz der spätrömischen Kaiserzeit.* Schriften der Sektion für Vor- und Frühgeschichte der Deutschen Akademie der Wissenschaften zu Berlin 1. Berlin, Akademie-Verlag.

Schuster, J. 2010. *Lübsow. Älterkaiserzeitliche Fürstengräber im nördlichen Mitteleuropa.* Bonner Beiträge zur Vor- und Frühgeschichtlichen Archäologie 12. Bonn, Vor- und Frühgeschichtliche Archäologie, Rheinische Friedrich-Wilhelms-Universität.

Stuppner, A. 2006. Die germanische Besiedlung im nördlichen Niederösterreich bis zu den Markomannenkriegen. In F. Humer (Hrsg.), *Legionsadler und Druidenstab. Vom Legionslager zur Donaumetropole. Textband.* Katalog des Niederösterreichischen Landesmuseums, N. F. 462: 208-217. [Bad Deutsch-Altenburg], Amt der NÖ Landesregierung, Abt. Kultur und Wissenschaft.

Tejral, J. 1975. *Die Probleme der späten römischen Kaiserzeit in Mähren.* Studie Archeologického Ustavu 3,2. Praha, Academia.

Tejral, J. 1999. Die Völkerwanderungen des 2. und 3. Jh.s und ihr Niederschlag im archäologischen Befund des Mitteldonauraumes. In J. Tejral (Hrsg.), *Das mitteleuropäische Barbaricum und die Krise des römischen Weltreiches im 3. Jahrhundert.* Spisy Archeologického Ustavu AV ČR Brno 12: 137-213. Brno, Archäologisches Institut der Akademie der Wissenschaften der Tschechischen Republik.

Tejral, J. 2004. Mušov und Czarnówko. Bemerkungen zu weiträumigen Verbindungen zwischen germanischen Herrschaftszentren. In H. Friesinger and A. Stuppner (Hrsg.), *Zentrum und Peripherie. Gesellschaftliche Phänomene in der Frühgeschichte. Materialien des 13. Internationalen Symposiums 'Grundprobleme der frühgeschichtlichen Entwicklung im mittleren Donauraum' Zwettl, 4.-8. Dezember 2000.* Mitteilungen der Prähistorischen Kommission der Österreichischen Akademie der Wissenschaften 57: 327-385. Wien, Verlag der Österreichischen Akademie der Wissenschaften.

Voß, H.-U. 2005. Vortrag zur Jahressitzung 2005 der Römisch-Germanischen Kommission. Hagenow in Mecklenburg, ein frühkaiserzeitlicher Bestattungsplatz und Aspekte der römisch-germanischen Beziehungen. *Bericht der RGK* 86: 19-59.

Voß, H.-U. 2008a. Parum, Putensen, Pavia? Anmerkungen zur Archäologie der Langobarden an der Niederelbe. In J. Bemmann and M. Schmauder (Hrsg.), *Kulturwandel in Mitteleuropa. Langobarden - Awaren - Slawen.* Kolloquien zur Vor- und Frühgeschichte 11: 51-78. Bonn, Habelt.

Voß, H.-U. 2008b. Von Parum nach Pavia? Zur Archäologie der Langobarden an der Niederelbe. In Landschaftsverband Rheinland, Rheinisches Landesmuseum Bonn (Hrsg.), *Die Langobarden. Das Ende der Völkerwanderung*: 34-51; 218-220. Darmstadt, Primus-Verlag.

Voß, H.-U. 2008c. Zwischen Vannius Reich und Vimose – Die elitären Krieger von Hagenow. In A. Abegg-Wigg and A. Rau (Hrsg.), *Aktuelle Forschungen zu Kriegsbeuteopfern und Fürstengräbern.* Schriften des Archäologischen Landesmuseums, Ergänzungsreihe 4: 253-277. Neumünster, Wacholtz.

Voß, H.-U. 2013. Roman silver in 'Free Germany'. Hacksilber in context. In F. Hunter and K. Painter (eds), *Late Roman silver. The Traprain Treasure in context*: 305-320. Edinburgh, Society of Antiquaries of Scotland.

Voß, H.-U. 2014. Die Gräber von Häven in Mecklenburg und ihre Beziehungen nach Skandinavien. In A. Abegg-Wigg and N. Lau (Hrsg.), *Kammergräber im Barbaricum. Zu Einflüssen und Übergangsphänomenen von der vorrömischen Eisenzeit bis in die Völkerwanderungszeit.* Schriften des Archäologischen Landesmuseums, Ergänzungsreihe 9: 55-103. Neumünster/Hamburg, Wacholtz.

Inter-cultural and linguistic relations north of the Danube

Iulia Dumitrache, Roxana-Gabriela Curcă

Alexandru Ioan Cuza University of Iași, Romania

Abstract

Our purpose in this paper is to draw attention to the cultural activity and interactions between the Roman new-comers and the existing ethnic realities in Moesia Inferior, focusing on the socio-economic circumstances of the province, from a linguistic perspective, as reflected in the epigraphic evidence.

Keywords: Inter-cultural relations, linguistic relations, Roman Lower Danube

The theoretical and methodological assumptions that underlie this paper are linked to the idea that explanations for ancient social phenomena must be sought not only globally, but also in their local context. Moesia Inferior was, in its own way, both unique and typical.

The Roman Lower Danube was a buffer zone where two patterns of civilisation converged, and a special set of cultural features was created. In Moesia Superior, the older organisational structures were transformed, over time, to create an increasingly refined administration, in harmony with the economic importance of the province, and the wealth of its resources. Roman soldiers, veterans, colonists and administrative staff arrived in Dacia carrying a 'manual' for how to create a province. Moesia Inferior is the province where this element could be best seen. On a background characterised by a high Hellenistic cultural tradition and built upon typical Thracian organisation, Romans created and developed, both in the old Greek cities and in the Thracian communities, an administrative system adapted to existing realities.

The linguistic features reflected in the inscriptions in Moesia Inferior emphasise the fundamental aspects of bilingualism in the Roman world: the essential distinction between *contact* and *interference* (Biville 2005: 189-201), the opposition between *equal bilingualism* and *dominant bilingualism* (Hamers and Blanc 1989: 8), the differentiation between *elite bilingualism* and *sub-elite bilingualism*, the presence of code-switching as an intentional action (tag-switching, intra-sentential switching at lexical, morphologic and graphic level, inter-sentential code-switching (Hoffmann 1991: 46, 116, 104), etc.

The epigraphic documents revealed in Moesia Inferior and Dacia provided a wealth of economic data, which has been quickly subjected to analysis. Much time has now passed since the last systematic treatment of the subject; meanwhile much has changed. New readings and additions have added further data and rendered some earlier work out-of-date. Systematic study of provincial society has greatly expanded our understanding of the world that created these documents. New excavations have brought to light further evidence. The exploration of the Moesian and Dacian countryside has revealed private estates in a landscape previously considered to be empty. These advances have created a new context in which to place the socio-economic data that the provinces have provided. The time has come for reconsideration (Mihailescu-Bîrliba 2009; 2015; Bounegru 2013). More importantly, the theoretical framework, within which the data were to be interpreted, has changed radically. Analyses of the Lower Danube populations made so far, using mostly epigraphic data, have followed aspects such as social status and structures (focusing on freedmen, slaves, provincial aristocracy, and religious preferences of the diverse social categories), family relations, ethnic origin and onomastics (Glodariu 1974; Barnea, Suceveanu 1991; Rusu 1994; 1995; Mihailescu-Bîrliba 1996; 2000; 2006; 2009; Benea 2002; Ştefănescu 2002; Dana 2004; Rubel 2013, etc.).

In studying economic health, scholars have mostly focused on elite-values, which are relatively well documented. In an article published in 2009 on the concept of local elites, Danielle Slootjes defined basic local *potentes* through their political power, economic influence, their influence by means of religious functions, and influence by means of intellectual skills. The author includes merchants in this category: even if economic influence did not necessarily lead to political power, influence by means of wealth represents an indication of power at a local level and should be taken into consideration (Slootjes 2009; Verboven 2007).

Associations constituted the prime social framework within which businessmen lived and operated. To a large extent they moulded the social geography within which social positions at sub-aristocratic level were assigned, acquired and changed. Thus, the institutional structures of the associations, and of their symbolic order, were where the *ethos-habitus* of merchants was formed (Verboven 2007).

After a short review of the data we possess on the population involved in hand-made crafts and commercial activities, we can report that the epigraphic material is extremely poor, given the number of workshops and the diversity of craft activities of Moesia Inferior. Those that belonged to the craftsmen category (i.e. ceramics, metalworking or stone-working), remain, for the most part, anonymous. Those that appear epigraphically are only mentioned by name, and even the name does not always appear in a complete form. This fact does not allow for more consistent ethnical or social analyses. This situation may have many explanations, one of them being the possibility that these craftsmen or merchants would be hidden under the name of *consistentes* (in Moesia Inferior), leaving us uncertain as to their trade. We shall present a short review of the professional associations with activities within (see Bounegru 1986; Van Andringa 2003; Avram 2007) the Moesian business milieu.

At the beginning of the 2nd century AD in Callatis, functioned *cives Romani consistentur Callatis*, whose *quinquennalis perpetuus* was C. Iulius Produs (Rădulescu 1962: 275). The reference to this position confirms the organisational system of foreign merchants settled far away from their homes. This is also an important argument that supports the cohabitation of commercial structures of Hellenistic origin with those of Roman background (Bounegru 2007).

A Latin inscription has been discovered in Tomis (ISM II, 129) that contains a list of 11 names, all Roman, of some individuals of various origins, involved in the same cult association: Lucius Antonius Capito from Nicomedia; Caius Licinius Clemens, *natus Abonutichu*; Caius Aurelius Alexander, *natus Heraclia*; Claudius Secundus, *natus Abonuthicus*; Caius Gabinius Modestus *natus Perintho*; Titus Ailius Barbarius, *natus Nicomedia*; Aurelius, *natus Caesaria*; Vettius Ponticus, *natus Tio*; Fabius Paulinus *natus Mazaca*; Titus Ailius Pompeius *natus Tio*; and Papirius Celer *natus*... All of these men originated in Asia Minor, coming from Bithynia, Galatia, Cappadocia or Perinth. Their coming together had a religious character, but we consider that its professional nature must also have been a very important motivation for their association. They must have been implicated in commercial activities, which explains their presence in an important economic city. They all bear Roman names, most of them Italian, even if they come from the Eastern Empire (See also Bounegru 2006: 51).

There were many ways to acquire a Roman name, but the evidence suggests that many Greek bearers of such names were associated with economic interests. When named in a Greek environment, and at a relatively early date, individuals may be identified as Roman citizens of Italian origin when Latin-style filiation is used, or a Roman voting tribe is mentioned. If a *nomen* is a relatively rare one, it is more likely that it belongs to an Italian or Roman émigré rather than to a 'Romanised' Greek. A number of onomastic formulae, however, might indicate that a Greek had Roman citizenship as the result of patronage, and was not merely responding to Roman influence by adopting a single name, *praenomen* or *cognomen*. Roman family names – even when they are single names borne by members of a modest stratum of the local society – might not indicate citizenship, and yet are useful. A *nomen* together with a specific *praenomen* further increases the likelihood that a Greek – and all his sons – acquired that name from a particular Roman family. The most common combination for new Greek possessors of Roman citizenship is that of a Roman family name and a Greek personal name, while the use of a cognomen instead might indicate that the bearer is either an Italian or a Romanised inhabitant of the Greek East.

The prosopographical and physical evidence, interwoven over time, as well as place, can further show us that Greeks with Roman names participated in internal exchanges as much as, or more than, international trade. There was some degree of economic Romanisation in Moesia Inferior, but a more accurate term might be 'economic acculturation'.

Starting from an article by Zah and Suceveanu (1971), asking the question: why were the Bessi in Roman Dobruja colonised?, Mihailescu-Bîrliba analyses 19 individuals of Thracian origin called *magistri vici* and *quaestores* from *vicus Quintionis* (Mihailescu-Bîrliba 2016). Most of these are *magistri vici*, such as Derzenus Auluporis (*ISM* I, 324), Bizienis (*ISM* I, 325), Durisses Bithi (*ISM* I, 326), Mucaporus Ditugenti (*ISM* I, 327), Genicius Brini (*ISM* I, 328), Lupus T...(*ISM* I, 329), Mucatralis Doli (*ISM* I, 330), Valerius Cutiunis (*ISM* I, 331), and Derzenus Biti (*ISM* I, 332). Two individuals are *quaestores*: Dotus Zinebti (*ISM* I, 330) and Fronto Burtsitsinis (*ISM* I, 332), and two other texts mention several Thracian families. Zah and Suceveanu (1971) advance two hypotheses concerning the Thracian presence in

Roman Dobruja: the first stipulates that the Bessi arrived through deportation, or their retreat ahead of the pressure exerted by the Romans upon their territories in the Balkan mountains. The second hypothesis concerns the reasons for the presence of the Bessi in the north Danube region into the 2nd century. The quoted authors think that the Bessi were colonised in Dobruja in order to organise surface mining exploitation. The second theory seems more probable, because it is based on literary sources and on field research. Of course, the role played by the Bessi is not exclusively economic, as their skills as warriors are indirectly proven by their presence, at numerically important levels, within the Roman army (see Mihailescu-Bîrliba 2016).

If, as we have seen, all the epigraphic documents concerning the communities of *consistentes* are written in Latin, from a total number of 17 inscriptions mentioning traders as individuals, 15 are in Greek. More than half of these attestations are from Tomis. Thus, we note the local *Émporoß* Stratokles (ISM II, 248); an anonymous son of Arthemidoros (ISM II, 403); and another anonymous individual, *Émporoß burséwn* (ISM II, 320). The term *burseúß*, the Greek equivalent of the Latin *coriarius*, implies an activity linked to leather processing, suggests a combination of both industry and trade. It is not unusual that a producer sells his own products. Bounegru (2008: 95) considers that *Émporoß* implied a larger activity; otherwise the individual in question would have been called simply *burseúß* or *téxnh burséwn*. In comparison with Latin cases of *negotiatores artis cretariae* or *lanariae* or *macellariae*, widespread within the Western provinces, or with very specialised activities mentioned epigraphically in Thracia, restricting his field of activity, is not completely sustainable. In Tomis there also lived Pontianos, *xrusoxóoß*, a goldsmith, who sold his products at the local market (ISM II, 253); and Metrodoros, son of Caius and Hypias from Prusias and Seppon, an *oœnémporoß*, representing the business interests of an important wine-trader from Alexandria, on the western shore of the Black Sea (ISM II, 463). Bounegru (2008: 93-94) remarks that the latter individual calls himself *oœnémporoß*, not *oœnopôlhß*, and therefore he is not simply a wine-seller: this implies that he was involved in a large import-export commercial activity. From other regions came Aurelius Sozomenos from Byzantium (ISM II, 257), and Perinthos and his wife, Caecilia Artemisia, from Perinth (ISM II, 365). They bear Roman names and Greek *cognomina*, a usual onomastic habit, as we have seen earlier. Another interesting case is that of Lucius Euaristos (ISM II, 337), whose name also occurs in inscriptions in Dalmatia (in Epetium and Salona: CIL III, 9064; 10830), in Macedonia (at Stobi: CIL III, 8520), in Italy (at Aquileia CIL V, 8110) and in Dacia (CIL III), 8077, and who was linked to the pottery industry. If the editors of ISM are correct about the membership of our Lucius Euaristos from Tomis in this family selling luxury pottery in Dacia Inferior and Moesia Inferior, then this is an interesting situation. All the other inscriptions are written in Latin. But Lucius orders an inscription in Greek. Was this 'good for business'? Was he aiming to impress the local business community, which was mainly hellenophone?

Obviously, as regards the ethnicity of a certain person, the anthroponomy could be misleading. For example, in a bilingual funerary inscription discovered at Tomis (ISM II, 195), dating from the 2nd century AD, the anthroponym *Kornhlía Fortounáta he kè Doutoûroß* has the Thracian *agnomen* mentioned only in the Greek version. In the Latin version, she appears only with the Latin names Cornelia Fortunata.

In the 2nd century AD a family of merchants is attested in Histria (ISM I, 356). Asklepiades, son of Menophilos, is 'citizen' of both Nikomedia and Aizanoi. The family business brought him, his brother, Menophilos Bassos, probably his partner, and his son to Histria. Asklepiades carries out his activities here until the end of his life. We do not know if his son followed his family tradition, as long as only Asklepiades and his brother were Émporoi. Also active as traders in Histria were Diomedes, son of Diomedes from Heraklea (ISM I, 310) and Sextus from Corinthus (ISM I, 271; see also Bounegru 2008: 121), the latter having a ship represented on his tomb as the symbol of his activities.

The same is the case with Evandros, son of Fronto, from Callatis (ISM III, 177); with Dionysos, son of Demosthenes (IGB I, 139), and Adys, son of Herakleon, who came from Heraklea and settled in Odessos, very probably in pursuit of some economic interests (IGB I, 122).

The only *negotiator* from Moesia Inferior, a certain Iulius ...ero died aged 60 in Novae (ILB, 320).

Lucius Treius Faustus, freedman of Lucius, died in Oescus at 50 (Ivanov 1990: 131-135). He was *lixa legionis V Macedonicae*. *Lixae* accompanied the military units (both legions and auxiliary troupes). Their task was to assure the sale of different merchandise, mainly alimentary, within the civil settlements situated near the important military camps (for the discussion on *lixa*, see: Kleberg 1957: 14-16; Roth 1999: 95-97). The case of Lucius Treius Faustus is currently unique for the area we are studying.

It is impossible to say to what extent any of the conclusions or explanations suggested here are specific to a given area or could be generally applicable to all situations of Imperial or colonial interaction with native groups. Few of the changes mentioned in this paper reflect substantial modifications of the social system, but are instead relatively superficial modifications to it. There seems to be a difference in the extent of Roman activities in the Pontic cities, on the one hand, and at all the other contemporary sites on the other. This difference might be the result of the respective wealth of the inhabitants of a city, which would, to some extent, reflect the activities carried out there at each level. Administrative and religious facilities, markets and public activities tend to occur at the larger settlements. Consequently, the inhabitants of such towns would have had the opportunity to partake in activities exposing them to Roman practices and values and resulting in the accumulation of wealth through the control of trade and taxes. Immigrants settled the west-Pontic cities and the military camps. Together with the local elite, who had adopted Roman characteristics and habits, these people developed a new culture. The general picture that emerges is that the local inhabitants of Moesia Inferior abandoned *some* of their local habits and practices. But they did not replace these customs with Roman ones. Instead, aspects of Roman culture were adopted and new patterns of behaviour created that incorporated both local traditional and intrusive Roman traits. The major impact of the Roman occupation on the area was not the imposition of Roman culture and language, but the introduction of a larger framework, in which people needed to function, economically, politically and socially.

The bilingual phenomenon in Moesia Inferior is emphasised by a limited number of bilingual inscriptions (official and private). Their importance is, however, crucial for determining the relations between Greeks, Romans and natives at various levels, and also to understand the linguistic panorama in the area. To emphasise their relevance, it is fitting also to take into account the extra-linguistic context and the trigger factors that led to the bilingual occurrences in the epigraphic records: commerce; Roman administration and the army; feeling of inclusion within a certain ethnic group, underlying one's own identity; etc. The linguistic mosaic in this province makes various glottic interferences inevitable between Greek and Latin, and vice-versa, at the phono-morphological, syntactic and lexical levels, as attested in particular in the hellenophone area of the province (Curcă 2012: 184). Ascertained for this area is the double-dynamic of 'Graeco-Latin (explainable by the need of Greeks to learn the official language) and Latin-Greek (prompted by the need of the Latinophones to communicate with the majority population)' bilingualism (Alexianu 2004: 155-156).

In economic life, even if a *lingua franca* is necessary, it does not necessarily intrude decisively into the linguistic framework of the province. Using Latin is specific for integrating into the associative system. The quality of membership of a professional association implies adopting the administrative language (most of the epigraphic evidence mentioning associations come from the provincial interior; the examples are mainly rural and from sites situated near the military camps). On the other hand, individual businessmen are closer to their partners, producers, transporters and consumers. Using Greek or Latin is not particularly a matter of origin, or of self-representation or wealth and status. Rather it is linked, as Tacitus observed in the 1st century AD, to 'the thirst for gain and the oblivion of their homeland' – *cupido augendi pecuniam, postremum oblivio patriae* (Ann. II, 62).

Acknowledgement

This work was supported by a grant from the Romanian National Authority for Scientific Research, CNCS-UEFISCDI, project number PN-III-P4-ID-PCE-2016-0669, *Beyond the fringes of empire. Roman influence and power north of the Danube and east of the Rhine* — arheo.ro/romaninfluence.

References

Alexianu, M. 2004. La situation linguistique de la province romaine Scythie Mineure. Repères d'une recherche. In S. Santelia (ed.), *Italia e Romania: Storia, Cultura e Civiltà a confronto. Atti del IV Convegno di Studi italo-romeno* (Bari, 21-23 ottobre 2002), Quaderni di 'Invigilata Lucernis' 21: 145-156. Bari, Edipuglia.

Avram, A. 2007. Les ciues Romani consistentes de Scythie Mineure: État de la question. In: R. Compatangelo-Sossignan, G.-Chr. Schwentzel, (eds.), *Étrangers dans la cité romaine. Actes du colloque de Valenciennes (14-15 octobre 2004) 'Habiter une autre patrie: des incolae de la République aux peuples fédérés du Bas-Empire'*: 91-107. Rennes, Presses universitaires de Rennes),

Barnea Al., Suceveanu, Al. 1991. *La Dobroudja romaine*. Bucarest, Editura Enciclopedică.

Benea, D. 2002. Integrarea culturală a palmyrenilor în Dacia Romană. *Apulum* 39: 185-199.

Bounegru, O. 1986. Über die cives Romani consistentes von Scythia Minor. *MBAH*, 5.1: 59-73.

Biville, F. 2005. Contacts linguistiques. *StudClas* 37-39 (2001-2003) (Volum dedicat memoriei profesorului I. Fischer): 189-201.

Bounegru, O. 2007. Le Pont Gauche et Rome: traditions hellénistiques et modèles commerciaux romains. *Classica et Christiana* 2: 49-58.

Bounegru, O. 2008. *Comerț și navigatori la Pontul Stâng și Dunărea de Jos (sec. I III p. Chr.).* Iași, Demiurg.

Bounegru, O. 2013. *Mercator. Studien zur antiken Wirtschaft im Pontosgebiet und in der Ägäis.* Kaiserslautern und Mehlingen, Parthenon Verlag.

Bounegru, O. 2006. Trafiquants et armateurs de Nicomédie dans la Méditerranée à l'époque romaine. In A. Akerraz, P. Ruggieri, A. Siraj, C. Vismara (eds), *L'Africa Romana XVI. Mobilità delle persone e dei popoli, dinamiche migratorie, emigrazioni ed immigrazioni nelle province occidentali dell'Impero romano. Atti del XVI convegno di studio Rabat, 15-19 dicembre 2004*: 1557-1568. Roma, Carocci.

Curcă, R. 2012. *Elenism și romanitate în Moesia Inferior: interferențe etnice și lingvistice.* Iași, Editura Universității 'Alexandru Ioan Cuza' din Iași.

Dana, D. 2004. Onomastique est-balkanique en Dacie Romaine (noms thraces et daces). In L. Ruscu, C. Ciongradi, R. Ardevan, C. Roman, C. Găzdac (eds), *Orbis antiquus. Studia in honorem Ioannis Pisonis*: 430-448. Cluj-Napoca, Nereamia Napocae.

Glodariu, I. 1974. *Relațiile comerciale ale Daciei cu lumea elenistică și romană.* Cluj, Dacia.

Hamers, J. F., Blanc, M. H. A. 1989. *Bilinguality and Bilingualism.* Cambridge, Cambridge University Press.

Hoffmann, C. 1991. *An Introduction to Bilingualism.* London/New York, Longman.

Ivanov, R. 1990. Lixa Legionis V Macedonicae aus Oescus. *Zeitschrift für Papyrologie und Epigraphik* 80: 131-136.

Kleberg, T. 1957. *Hôtels, restaurants et cabarets dans l'antiquité romaine. Études historiques et philologiques.* Uppsala, Almqvist & Wiksell.

Mihailescu-Bîrliba L. (ed.) 2009. *Stucturi etno-demografice la Dunărea de Jos sec. I-VII p. Chr.* Iaşi, Editura Universității 'Alexandru Ioan Cuza' din Iași.

Mihailescu-Bîrliba, L. 1996. Le statut social des affranchis en Dacie par rapport à leur statut juridique; les affranchissements et les heritages. *Arheologia Moldovei* 21: 213-216.

Mihailescu-Bîrliba, L. 2000. Les esclaves et les affranchis impériaux sous le Haut Empire romain: apperçu général sur leur statut social. *Studia Antiqua et Archaeologica* 7: 393-398.

Mihailescu-Bîrliba L. 2006. Les origines de la population appartenant aux catégories sociales moyannes et humbles de la Dacie selon les sources épigraphiques. In L. Bîrliba, O. Bounegru (eds), *Studia historiae et religionis daco-romanae. In honorem Silvii Sanie*: 297-316. Bucureşti, Editura Academiei Române.

Mihailescu-Bîrliba, L. (ed.) 2015. *Colonisation and Romanisation in Moesia Inferior. Premises of a contrastive approach.* Kaiserslautern und Mehlingen Parthenon Verlag.

Mihailescu-Bîrliba, L. 2016. Les Bessi à Ibida (Mésie Inférieure). *Analele Științifice ale Universității 'Al. I. Cuza' din Iași. Istorie* 62: 13-16.

Rădulescu, A. 1962. Inscription inédite de Callatis. *Studii Clasice* 4: 275-279.

Roth, J. 1999. *The Logistics of the Roman Army at War: 264 B.C. - A.D. 235.* Leiden, Brill.

Rubel, A. (ed.) 2013. Romanizarea Impunere şi adeziune în Imperiul Roman. Iaşi, Editura Universității 'Alexandru Ioan Cuza' din Iași.

Rusu A. 1995. Les illyriens en Dacie. In *La colonisation de la Dacie Romaine. La politique édilitaire dans les provinces de l'Empire Romain II-IV siècles après J-C, Actes du II Colloque Roumano-Suisse, Berne 12-19.09.1993*: 19-37.
Rusu, A. 1994. Les illyriens en Dacie. *Sargetia* XXV: 137-153.
Slootjes, D. 2009. Local Potentes in the Roman Empire: a new approach to the concept of local elites. *Latomus* 68: 416-432.
Ştefănescu, A. 2002. Sociological aspects about the woman status in Roman Dacia. *Studii de Istoria Banatului* XXXV: 23-30.
Van Andringa, W. 2003. Cités et communautés d'expatries installées dans l'Empire romain: le cas des cives Romani consistentes. In N. Belayche, S.C. Mimouni (éds.), Les communautés religieuses dans le monde gréco-romain. Essais de définition: 49-60. Turnhout, Brepols.
Verboven, K. S. 2007. Good for business. The Roman army and the emergence of a 'business class' in the north-western provinces of the Roman Empire (1st century BCE – 3rd century CE). In De Blois Lukas and Lo Cascio Elio (eds), *The Impact of the Roman Army (200 BC – AD 476): Economic, Social, Political, Religious and Cultural Aspects (Proceedings of the 6th workshop of the network Impact of empire. Capri 2005)*: 295-313. Leiden, Brill.
Zah, E, Suceveanu, A. 1971. *Bessi consistentes, Studii şi cercetări de istorie veche* 22/4: 567-578.

Prosopographic notes on Flavius Reginus from Arrubium

Lucreţiu Mihailescu-Bîrliba
'Alexandru Ioan Cuza' University of Iaşi, Romania

Abstract

An inscription of Arrubium (Moesia Inferior) mentions a certain Flavius Reginus. The author tries to establish prosopographic connections between this magistrate (a *duumvir* probably at Troesmis) and the other Flavii from Troesmis.

Keywords: Flavius Reginus, Arrubium, Troesmis, Galatia, Bithynia

A fragmentary inscription on a statue base from Arrubium (Măcin, Tulcea county, RO) (Figure 1) mentions a certain Flavius Reginus, *duumvir*: *Iuliae Dom[nae] / Augustae [matri] castro[rum] Fl(avius) Reg[inus II]/vir* [(ISM V, 252).

The magistrate sets up a statue for the empress Julia Domna. The text dates between AD 195, when Julia Domna was awarded this title, and AD 217. Arrubium was the camp of *ala I Vespasiana Dardanorum*, as shown by the inscriptions found in the fortress.[1] The presence of Flavius Reginus and the erection of the statue was in connection with his status (*duumvir*) and the army relation. Moreover, it is presumed that he was magistrate in the nearest city (Troesmis), to which the status of municipium was granted at the end of Marcus Aurelius' reign (see latest Eck 2013: 199-213; Eck 2014: 75-88).

It is clear that this individual was a local magistrate in Troesmis at the beginning of the 3rd century AD. But to which family was he related?

In Troesmis the inscriptions do not attest the presence of many Flavii. There are eight Flavii mentioned by the monumental inscription of AD 134 (which is a list of released soldiers who took part in the Parthic wars of Trajan, AD 108-109) (ISM V, 137).

Other Flavii appear in family inscriptions, one votive and one funerary. In the first, Flavius Alexander, veteran of *legio V Macedonica* and *quinquennalis canabensium*, erected an altar, together with his wife and his children, to Jupiter, during the joint reign of Antoninus Pius and Marcus Aurelius.[2] Taking into account the governorship of Fuficius Cornutus, the

[1] ISM V, 218, 251. *Ala I Vespasiana Dardanorum* was one of the most active units in Moesia Inferior. Attested for the first time in AD 92 (Petolescu, Popescu 2004: 269-276), it was present in the provincial army during the whole of the 2nd c. AD (e.g. CIL XVI 45, 50, 78, 83; Mihailescu-Bîrliba 2008: 199-210; Weiß 2008: 293-296, 314-316; RMD I, 50; V, 399; Chiriac, Mihailescu-Bîrliba, Matei 2006: 383-389).

[2] ISM V, 155: *[I(ovi) O(ptimo) M(aximo) s(acrum)] / [pro sal(ute) Imp(eratoris) T(iti) Ael(i) Ha]/[driani Antonini Aug(usti) Pii et] / [Aur(eli) Veri Caes(aris)] / sub Fuficio Cornu/to leg(ato) Aug(usti) pr(o) pr(aetore) de/dicante Q(uinto) Caecilio / Reddito*

Figure 1. Map of Moesia Inferior.

inscription is dated between AD 151 and 154. The veteran also offers 250 *denarii* for being elected as *quinquennalis*. In fact, 250 *denarii* was the amount usually offered in the *canabae* of Troesmis for the *quinquennalitatis*, as indicated by another inscription (ISM V, 158). Flavius Alexander originated from Ancyra[3] and he was recruted in AD 129 or shortly before. This could have been a recruitment when units of the legion took part in the war against Bar-Kochba (see especially Mihailescu-Bîrliba, Dumitrache 2012, 43).

In the second text, another veteran, T. Flavius Valens and his brother, Flavius Alexander, set up a common epitaph for their wives, Valeria Fortunata and Marcia Basilissa.[4] It is unnecessary to detail the comment of the inscription, in connexion with another text, where a character also called Marcia Basilissa appears. The present author has written on

leg(ato) Aug(usti) T(itus) Fl(avius) Alexander vet(eranus) / leg(ionis) V Mac(edonicae) domu Fab(ia) / Ancyr(a) q(uin)q(ennalis) canaben(sium) / cum Iulia Florenti/na uxore et Flavio A/lexandro Valente / Pisone / Maximilla Res/pecta fili(i)s d(e) s(uo) p(osuit) item / (denarios) / CCL ob honor(em) q(uin)q(uennalitatis) cu/riae donavit ex quor(um) / incre[mentis sportulae] / [dividentur] om[nibus] / [. See also Matei-Popescu 2010: 71 ; Mihailescu-Bîrliba, Matei-Popescu 2019, 101-102.

[3] On the people originating in Ancyra in Moesia Inferior, see Curcă, Zugravu 2005: 313-329; Mihailescu-Bîrliba, Piftor 2005: 331-337.

[4] ISM V, 184: *D(is) M(anibus) / T(itus) Fl(avius) T(iti) f(ilius) Teretin(a) Valens A/mast(ri) vet(eranus) leg(ionis) V Mac(edonicae) an(norum) / LXV Valeria Fortunat(a) / uxor eiusdem an(norum) LX Fl(avius) Ale/xander frater an(norum) LXII / Marcia Basilissa uxor / eius an(norum) L in locum titu/lum posuerunt sibi.*

this before and thus only the conclusion is added here: T. Flavius Valens was enlisted in the legion probably at the beginning of the Bar-Kochba wars, and his brother came with him in Lower Moesia (Mihailescu-Bîrliba, Dumitrache 2012: 31-34. See also Mihailescu-Bîrliba 2008-2009: 17-23; Mihailescu-Bîrliba 2012: 125-132).

He was originally from Pontus and Bithynia (Amastris). Amastris was also the origin of another two families where soldiers were involved, that of Iulius Ponticus (ISM V, 186. See Mihailescu-Bîrliba, Dumitrache 2012: 34-35) and the other of P. Aelius F[---] (ISM V, 171. See Mihailescu-Bîrliba, Dumitrache 2012: 35-36).

Let us return to Flavius Reginus. His association with *gens Flavia* at Troesmis indicates he could belong to a branch of Flavii descendants of former soldiers. There are some examples at Troesmis of descendants from veterans' families who belonged to local elites. M. Antistius Domitius was an *aedil* and *quaestor*, and his brother M. Antistius Rufus was a *pontifex* (ISM V, 148. See Mihailescu-Bîrliba, Dumitrache 2012: 124). A first Antistius is attested in the monumental inscription of AD 134 (Antistius Vetus) (ISM V, 137). Other Antistii (C. Antistius Valens, veteran, and his son Antistius Zoticus) are mentioned in two funerary inscriptions (ISM V, 174-175. See Mihailescu-Bîrliba, Dumitrache 2012: 124). Valens originated in Ancyra; M. Antistius Domitius and M. Antistius Rufus were perhaps born in Troesmis, but they definitely belong to the Ancyrean *gens*. Another example is C. Egnatius Valens, himself a former soldier who became *decurio* of the *municipium* (ISM V, 183. See Mihailescu-Bîrliba, Dumitrache 2012: 125); he is supposed to be related to another *miles*, discharged in AD 134, named also Egnatius Valens (ISM V, 137). The *decurio* also came from Ancyra; he was probably recruited at the beginning of the Bar-Kochba war and was discharged around AD 150. He belongs most likely to the first generation of magistrates in the new *municipium*. Finally, another example is represented by L. Publicius Viator, who erected an epitaph for his wife, Tiberia Claudia (ISM V, 180. See Mihailescu-Bîrliba, Dumitrache 2012: 127-128). A certain L. Publicius Niger, soldier of the *legio V Macedonica*, is attested alongside his freedwoman and wife, and he came from Bithynia (ISM V, 193). L. Publicius Viator is certainly a descendant or relative of the Bithynian *miles*. The enlistments in Bithynia were mostly undertaken before the Bar-Kochba war (Mihailescu-Bîrliba, Dumitrache 2012: 31-41).

The aforementioned examples show that veterans originating in the Asia Minor provinces (especially Galatia, Pontus and Bithynia) settled in Moesia Inferior after their discharge and were even members of the local elite. Moreover, their descendants or relatives, although civilians, took part in official municipal events.

The Flavii of Troesmis are no exception. T. Flavius Alexander was from Ancyra and became after his military discharge *quinquennalis* in the *canabae* of Troesmis. T. Flavius Valens was from Amastris and he settled in Troesmis, together with his brother and their wives.

Flavius Reginus was a *duumvir* and, given his place in the local elite, he probably came from a rich family of Flavii settled in Troesmis. Who else among the Flavii could attain such fortune and position? As observed earlier, these could only be veterans' families and their descendants or relatives. That is why Flavius Reginus undoubtedly belonged to one of these families. His presence at Arrubium and the setting up of a monument to Julia Domna was perhaps due to a visit to the military camp of *ala II Aravacorum*, a camp which was ajacent to the municipium Troesmense.

Acknowledgement

This paper was achieved with the financial support of CNCS, Project PN-III-P4-ID-PCE-2016-0271.

References

Chiriac, C., Mihailescu-Bîrliba, L., Matei, I. 2006. Un nouveau diplôme militaire de Mésie Inférieure. In S. Conrad, R. Einicke, A. E. Furtwängler, H. Löhr, A. Slawisch (eds), *Pontos Euxeinos. Beiträge zur Archäologie und Geschichte des antiken Schwarzmeer und Balkanraumes*: 383-389. Langenweißbach, Beier & Beran.

Curcă, R.-G. and Zugravu, N. 2005. 'Orientaux' dans la Dobroudja romaine. Une approche onomastique. In V. Cojocaru (ed.), *Ethnic contacts and cultural exchanges North and West of the Black Sea coast from the Greek colonization to the Ottoman Empire*: 313-329. Iaşi, Trinitas.

Eck, W. 2013. La loi municipale de Troesmis: données juridique et politique d'une inscription récemment découverte. *Revue historique du droit français et étranger* 91, 2: 199-213.

Eck, W. 2014. Das Leben römisch gestalten. Ein Stadtgesetz für das municipium Troesmis aus den Jahren 177-180 n. Chr. In G. D. Kleijn, S. Benoist, (eds), *Integration in Rome and in the Roman world. Proceedings of the Tenth Workshop of the International Network Impact of Empire (Lille, June 23-25, 2011), Impact of Empire 17*: 75-88. Leiden-Boston, Brill.

Matei-Popescu, F. 2010. *The Roman Army in Moesia Inferior*. Bucharest, Conphys.

Mihailescu-Bîrliba, L. and Piftor, V. 2005. Les familles d'Ancyre à Troesmis. In V. Cojocaru (ed.), *Ethnic Contacts and Cultural Exchanges North and West of the Black Sea Area from the Greek Colonization to the Ottoman Conquest*: 331-337. Iaşi, Trinitas.

Mihailescu-Bîrliba, L. 2008-2009. Două familii de pontobithynieni la Troesmis, *Analele Ştiinţifice ale Universităţii 'Al. I. Cuza' Iaşi. Secţia Istorie* 54-55: 17-23.

Mihailescu-Bîrliba, L. 2008. Un nouveau diplôme militaire de Mésie Inférieure. *Dacia Nouvelle Série* 51: 199-210.

Mihailescu-Bîrliba, L. 2012. Les Pontobithyniens à Troesmis. In D. Boteva-Boyanova, L. Mihailescu-Bîrliba, O. Bounegru (eds), *Pax Romana. Kulturaustausch und wirtschaftliche Beziehungen in den Donauprovinzen des römischen Reichs*: 125-132. Kaiserslautern, Parthenon Verlag.

Mihailescu-Bîrliba, L. and Dumitrache, I. 2012. *La colonisation dans le milieu civil et le milieu militaire de Troesmis*. Iaşi, Editura Universităţii 'Al. I. Cuza'.

Petolescu, C. C. and Popescu, A.-T. 2004. Ein neues Militärdiplom für die Provinz Moesia Inferior. *Zeitschrift für Papyrologie und Epigraphik* 148: 269-276.

Weiß, P. 2008. Militärdiplome für Moesia (Moesia, Moesia superior, Moesia inferior). *Chiron* 38: 267-316.

Mihailescu-Bîrliba, L. and Matei-Popescu, F. 2019. A new album of the quinquennales and magistri canabensium at Troesmis. In L. Mihailescu-Bîrliba, Wolfgang Spickermann (eds.), *Roman Army and Local Society in the Limes Provinces of the Roman Empire*: 95-108. Rahden/Westf. , Verlag Marie Leidorf.

Some considerations on the coin finds in the sites of Roman *Dacia*

Lucian Munteanu

Institute of Archaeology of Iași, Romania

Abstract

This study presents our ambition to establish a pattern of the coin finds in the sites of the Roman province of *Dacia*. In order to accomplish this, we began by comparing the lists of the monetary finds in this region with those in other parts of the Roman Empire. The comparative analysis of numismatic data has revealed numerous similarities between the province north of the Lower Danube and neighbouring territories. The monetary circulation in the Dacian sites represents a part of a regional model that comprises the Empire's Rhenish and Danubian provinces. Within this overall pattern there is a monetary pattern in the Dacian sites, whose features can be highlighted both in the civilian and military centres of the province. The particular behaviour of *Dacian* sites occurs especially during the Severan dynasty, due to the unusually high percentage of copied denarii, and in the time of Philip the Arab, as a consequence of the local civilian coinage minting. Unlike other western Roman provinces, in the case of *Dacia* there are no outstanding differences between the coin finds within the civilian settlements and military camps, most likely due to the brief rule of the Romans north of the Danube.

Keywords: Coin finds, Roman *Dacia*, monetary circulation

The history and archaeology of the province have been exhaustively researched and the results are well known by specialists. *Dacia* was founded by the Emperor Trajan, at the beginning of the 2nd century AD. It had a short lifespan of only one century and a half. Several military events and important administrative changes took place during this period. At the beginning of Hadrian's reign, *Dacia* was divided into three separate provinces (*Dacia Superior*, *Dacia Porolissensis* and *Dacia Inferior*). During the Marcomannic wars, *legio V Macedonica* was brought from *Moesia Inferior* and settled at *Potaissa*. The three *Daciae*, renamed at that moment (*Dacia Apulensis*, *Porolissenis* and *Malvensis*), were kept under the authority of a single governor. Starting from the reign of Gallienus, the Empire seems to have lost authority over the province or some parts of it. However, Aurelianus was the one who would permanently abandon *Dacia*, withdrawing its army and administrative staff south of the Danube (Petolescu 2010: 161-307; Protase, Suceveanu 2001: 35-287; Zerbini, Ardevan 2007: 35-208).

The sites of the province have been classified into civilian settlements and military fortifications. In the territory of *Dacia* are twelve certified Roman cities (six *coloniae* and six *municipia*). There is no archaeological situation where there is an overlap between the old La Tène Dacian centres and the new Roman cities. Most of them were created around military camps. As for Roman urbanisation in *Dacia*, it may be considered to have reached its height during the reign of Septimius Severus (Ardevan 1998; Diaconescu 2004). Outside the area of the urban centres of the province, there were a great number of small rural and military settlements, such as *pagi*, *vici*, *castelli*, *stationes*, *villae rusticae* and *vici militares* (Benea 2003; Gudea 2009; Popa 2002). Given its strategic position within the Roman world, the province of *Dacia* had plenty of military units and fortifications (two *castra legionis* and at least one hundred auxiliary forts have been identified in the field) (Gudea 1997; Protase, Suceveanu 2001: 99-136).

The most challenging part of the work presented here was to find an appropriate method of research for site finds. The chosen method needed to satisfactorily answer the following questions: what does a site represent regarding numismatics? Should all sorts of coin finds associated with a site be taken into account, or should a preliminary selection be made? What is the minimum number of coins from a site for meaningful numismatic interpretation? How should we compare sites having distinct archaeological definition and different status? How should we compare sites of various sizes that provide different quantities of coin finds? The answers to most of these questions are to be found in the works of P. J. Casey (1974, 1986, 1999) and R. Reece (1987, 1991, 2002, 2003). Using this generous theoretical support and taking into account the particularities of the province, the research methodology was defined by dividing it into several steps:

1. the selection of sites: the coin finds were registered by categories of sites, taking into account their various archaeological definitions (their functionality – civilian/military) and status (for civilian sites – cities, rural and military settlements);
2. the selection of coins: in each case, we chose only coins that were certainly known to have come from a Roman site, as a result of archaeological research or stray finds. We did not include any discoveries that did not fit into a normal rhythm of unintentional loss (for example, coins found in hoards or in funerary contexts) or those of uncertain origin (i.e. coins from collections and without a discovery location);
3. the next stage was to find the best numismatic tools. The lists of coin finds for all sites were conceived using a chronological scheme, divided into seventeen periods. Due to the short lifespan of the province of *Dacia*, it was more appropriate to work with smaller time units, based primarily on the emperors' reigns (short reigns were grouped with their predecessors). For each period the annual average coin loss could be estimated using the well-known Ravetz formula (1964: 206). For practical reasons, the improved version by P. J. Casey was chosen, performing the calculations on a common numerical basis (*per millia*) (Casey 1974: 41; 1986: 89). The application of this formula allows for sites with varied coin totals to be uniformly presented and it eliminates the discrepancy created by the various lengths of the periods. In the case of the short-lived province of *Dacia*, major distortions may appear when the formula is used for sites with less than forty coins registered.
4. the last step was to define the method. Any methodological attempt must be based on a simple and clear principle: no list of coin finds from a site has any numismatic value *per se*; instead, it must be interpreted only by comparison with similar lists, and only against the general monetary background to which it belongs. Through

making these objective comparisons, the common features from the lists of site groups may be highlighted and they may define the monetary patterns of coin finds (Reece 1987: 80). The characteristics of these patterns are generated by various monetary, economic, military and political factors (i.e. debasements of coinage, devaluations, inflation, wars etc.), which unevenly affect the coin circulation from different parts of the Roman world. The influence of these factors may affect the coinage from specific geographical areas, generating regional monetary patterns, or it can be restricted to a single administrative unit, creating provincial monetary patterns. Sometimes particular internal variations, in the form of sub-patterns, may appear inside these general standards (Casey 1974: 41, 46-47; Casey 1986: 87; Kos 1997: 114; Reece 1996: 342).

The present research aims to identify and characterise the monetary patterns of Dacian sites. To this end, the lists of coin finds from this region were compared with those from other provinces of the Roman Empire: *Pannonia Inferior*, *Pannonia Superior*, *Noricum*, *Raetia*, *Germania Superior*, *Germania Inferior* and *Gallia Belgica* (but only the part related to the *Limes Germanicus*) (Appendix I-VIII). A separate list of sites from the *Agri Decumates* was drawn up (Appendix IX). We took into consideration the presence of important similarities between this ancient region referred to by Tacitus and the province of *Dacia*, because of its position within the Empire, its length of existence and certain political and military events (Dietz 1997: 354-356). It should be noted that similar methodological approaches to the analysis of monetary circulation in *Dacia*, the two *Pannoniae* and the two *Moesiae*, have recently been used by C. Găzdac (2002, 2003, 2010), who had consistent and viable results.

Four distinct periods of monetary circulation can be defined with regard to the sites of *Dacia*: a) the period of the Antonine emperors (AD 98-192) – representing the beginning and development of monetary circulation; b) the time of the Severan emperors (AD 193-238) – during which the strengthening of monetary circulation takes place; and c) the reigns of Gordianus III and Philip the Arab (AD 238-249) – are the 'peak' of monetary discoveries; and d) the last period (AD 249-275), including the withdrawal of the Romans from the province – when the progressive decrease and end of monetary circulation occurs. For each of these periods, both the evolution of the monetary index in different chronological sequences and the composition of coinage denominations and types of issues have been analysed.

Before analysing the features of each of the four periods, it should be noted that inside the Roman sites of *Dacia* coins have also been found that are dated before the reign of Trajan. There are Geto-Dacian, Greek, Roman Republican and early Imperial issues, which came up in most Roman settlements and fortifications, representing, on average, 10% of all coins found. Since most settlements founded by the Romans in *Dacia* were not built over those of the locals (Ardevan 1998: 106), it is likely that these earlier coins, prior to Trajan, either remained in the monetary pool of the province or arrived after the Roman conquest.

I. The first period (AD 98-192), which is that of the Antonine emperors, represents the beginning and development of monetary circulation in *Dacia*. It is generally thought that the high monetary indices that characterised the reigns of Trajan and Hadrian were associated with a 'much larger influx of money' or a 'massive injection of money' in the newly conquered region, which was about to be integrated into the Roman economy and subsequently monetised. This could have been achieved by paying numerous troops, financing public activities or by a massive influx of colonists, holding and carrying Roman money (Dudău 2006: 41-43; Găzdac 2008: 73).

But a more plausible image could be obtained if the comparison is extended to sites in the Rhine and Upper Danube areas. The values calculated for *Raetia* and both *Germaniae* are similar to the values calculated for *Dacia*. Those from *Agri Decumates* are even higher, although the annexation of this region began during the Flavian dynasty (Figures 6-7, 9). In these circumstances, the size of the monetary impact of the Roman conquest of *Dacia* should be reconsidered realistically. The money supply of the newly conquered territory is in the normal range, sometimes lower than the common parameters of the period (see also Katsari 2008: 246-247). The higher values of *castra* indicate without any doubt that a large amount of early currency entered the monetary circulation of the province through the military environment. It could also have been the main way of supply, at least in the beginning of the Roman rule north of the Lower Danube.

Starting from the reign of Marcus Aurelius, the number of monetary discoveries on the lists of all sites in Dacia decreases significantly. It is a general phenomenon that manifests itself on the level of the entire province, both in settlements and camps. In the other Rhineland and Danubian provinces the evolution of coin finds seems to be different. In almost all cases, the monetary indices during Marcus Aurelius' reign are superior (in *Pannonia Superior*, *Germania Inferior*, *Agri Decumates*, *Gallia Belgica*) or at least equal (in *Noricum*, *Pannonia Inferior*, *Germania Superior*) to those of the previous period. The explanations of these monetary changes are to be sought in the military events of the time. Rather exceptionally, and for a short period, the Marcomannic wars affected monetary circulation at certain sites (notably at Emona and Celeia) (Kos 1986: 86-91; 1997: 103, Figure 5; 113). It seems that the presence of the emperor and the troops merging in the conflict zones even prompted the increase of coin production and supply in these areas (Hobley 1998: 6, Table 1; 18, 24).

Still, the province of Dacia suffered only to a limited extent because of these wars. Probably only a few camps on the *limes* of *Dacia Porolissensis (Porolissum* – 'Citera' and Gherla) and *Dacia Superior* (*Tibiscum* – 'Iaz' and – 'Jupa' and *Micia*) were attacked directly (Ardeț 2004: 54-55, 64-65; Benea 2013: 71-72; Gudea 1994: 70, 72). Under these circumstances, the general shortage of coins, from all the Dacian sites, could be explained by an intentional decrease of the currency flow coming from the central mints. At least part of their production must have been directed towards the war zones of the Empire.

During the reign of Commodus, the monetary index collapsed in all provinces, reaching its minimum of this first period (Figures 1, 7, 9). In many sites of the Empire, the volume of coin finds diminishes critically. This general situation seems to reflect the central authority's decision to restrict significantly the minting of both silver and bronze issues (Duncan-Jones 1998: 168, Table 11.2; Hobley 1998: 19).

The composition of the coinage maintains a relatively constant level throughout the 2nd century, reflecting the economic stability and the consistency of the Antonine emperors' monetary policies. The bronze coins struck in the central mints are the best represented in the lists of sites, especially the military ones. Very possibly the army's payments in this period were made, at least in part, in base metal coins (Kemmers 2006: 193-194; Peter 1996: 316-318; Peter 2001: 91-92). The share of the main bronze denominations in the currency of the moment was significantly influenced by the monetary policy of Trajan, by which a serious reduction in the production of *asses* took place, while the number of *sestertii* increased (Hobley 1998: 13, 19, 38, 128). The effects of these changes are visible in the site finds from all provinces, including *Dacia*, starting with the reign of Antoninus Pius, during which the numbers of *sestertii* discovered are close to those of *asses*. But only in the next periods – of Marcus Aurelius and Commodus – will the bigger coins of *orichalcum* predominate the currency.

II. The second period (AD 193-238) broadly overlaps with the Severan dynasty. The issues dated at this time are very well represented on the lists of coin finds from the Dacian sites. The monetary indices calculated for each emperor have a fluctuating course throughout the entire period. Thus, the reign of Septimius Severus marks an overall recovery of the coinage that reached its lowest intensity under the last Antonine emperor. During the time of Caracalla, a reversal takes place, followed by the highest values in the entire second period, reached under Elagabalus` reign. This was followed again by a less important decline, under Severus Alexander. How to explain these obvious fluctuations of quantities of coin finds at the Dacian sites? Were they caused by particular events in this area, such as the intense urbanisation policy of the province under Septimius Severus or Caracalla's visit here (Zerbini, Ardevan 2007: 61, 63)? The most likely answer is no. If we look at the overall picture, we notice that the same variations of the monetary indices also appear on the lists of most sites from the Danubian and Rhenish provinces (both *Pannoniae*, *Noricum*, *Raetia* and both *Germaniae*) (Figures 6-7, 9). It is possible that they were mainly influenced by the volume of coin production during each reign. It is interesting to note that the presumed outputs of *denarii* for the Severan emperors, roughly estimated by R. Duncan-Jones based on the numbers of dies, seem to fluctuate similarly (1998: 167-171, Table 11.2). If this is true, this situation confirms the importance of monetary production in setting the framework of findings, including areas at considerable distances from the source (for the coin supply of the highly militarised northern Balkan provinces see Katsari 2011, 25, 43-47, 105, 121, 147, 161-163).

The same comparison shows unusually high monetary indices both in the civilian and military sites of *Dacia*, throughout the Severan dynasty (for similar results see Găzdac 2010: 189-190, Plate Q2). In the case of settlements, a significant difference between the Dacian values and those calculated for other provinces is constantly preserved, at two points, increasing by one unit in the time of Severus Alexander. This situation may be explained by the structure of coin finds. The composition of the currency is dominated by silver denominations. High quantities of debased *denarii*, both genuine and copied, appear on the lists of all sites in *Dacia*, starting with the reign of Septimius Severus. Mainly two types of counterfeited pieces occurred. The most numerous are *denarii subaerati*, made with a copper core, plated with a thin layer of silver, and often made by striking or, rarely, by another plating technique – 'the silver bath' or 'amalgam technique'. Very few copies were made by casting in moulds (Pîslaru 2009: 52, 66, 355-358, 363-365). The copied *denarii* (mostly plated) appear in an unusually high number and represent almost a quarter of the total number of *denarii* discovered in the sites of *Dacia* (Găzdac 2010: 190). They were found in most civilian settlements and especially in fortifications, all over the province, generating the high values of the monetary index for both types of site (Figures 1-6).

The plated coins come up constantly, during all periods, even before the Roman conquest, and their percentages always follow, proportionally, the fluctuations of the similar genuine denominations' percentages, up to the reign of Gordianus III (Găzdac 2010: 149, Plate Q 3). Of course, the majority bear the images of the Severan emperors. In many cases, both categories of *denarii* (good and copied) were found together in the same archaeological contexts, proving that they circulated side by side, and were accepted, used and lost in a similar manner (Găzdac, Gaiu, Marchiş 2011: 18, 72, no. 73 [for *Arcobadara*]; Găzdac, Pripon 2012: 19, 26-27, 44, no. 128; 52, no. 185 [Buciumi]; Gudea 1996: 41 [*Porolissum-statio*]).

The presumed workshops where these coins might have been counterfeited were located at *Porolissum* (Winkler, Ivănescu 1977: 88-93), *Arcobadara* (Ardevan 2002: 39-43), *Apulum* (Găzdac, Oargă, Alföldy-Găzdac 2015: 15) or *Potaissa* (Pîslaru 2009: 71-74). The attribution of these sites was mainly made by taking into account the great number of copied issues, of different quality, on their lists of coins. The most substantial clues are recent and come from the fortification at *Potaissa*. They consist in the identification of five possible scraps (of coins), three *pondera examinata* and possible traces of bronze melting activities (Pîslaru 2009: 71-74). Still, each of the three cases may be put under question and does not confirm the existence of a monetary workshop in this legionary fortress. As for the site of *Sarmizegetusa*, a lead mould with the reverse image of a *sestertius* of Lucius Verus was discovered, but it was used to cast seals (Găzdac 1997; Găzdac, Cociș 2004: 113, no. 1383, Plate XIX). Thus, in the present state of research, we are still missing strong proof of copying of Roman *denarii* in *Dacia*. In these circumstances, we have to seek different explanations for the impressive volume of imitations. It is possible that at least some of the plated copies came from official mints, alongside the good coins. Such a possibility would explain most of the similarities that characterise the behaviour of the two monetary species, at least in the Dacian sites. It is possible that the bad coins were mainly targeted in the provinces on the border of the Empire, with the aim of filling in the amount of silver coinage.

Outside our province, most representative samples of copied *denarii* come from the two *Pannoniae*, *Noricum*, *Germania Superior* and *Gallia Belgica* (Figure 1). There are important differences between these specimens and the similar finds from *Dacia*, both in quantities and characteristics. Thus, their total number is much smaller, and their share of all the amount of *denarii* is smaller. The distribution of these coins within the provinces seems to be unequal. They appear only on the lists of some of the sites, especially in the military milieu. In most cases, solid evidence has been found of their local production, such as dies, clay moulds or various pieces of scrap metal with the images of the Severan emperors. They prove the existence of monetary workshops that probably functioned for a short period, with the tacit consent of the authorities, even inside the site or nearby (Aubin 2003; Boon 1974; King 1996; Kunisz 1980; Peter 1990; Peter 2001). Also, one may notice that the lists not containing such copies are more numerous in these provinces.

Provincial coins seem to have had a minor role in the currency of *Dacia*. The present author has only registered about 650 such issues, recorded from all sites of the province. Most of them appear on the lists of the civilian settlements (urban and rural) (roughly 80%), and less on those of the fortifications. There is an obvious concentration of these in the southern sites, nearby the Danube, in the vicinity of the two *Moesiae*. In the rest of the province their presence is rather sporadic. The origin of this coinage is extremely varied; it comes from almost sixty different civic and provincial mints. The best represented is, by far, the city of *Nicaea Bythiniae*, from where more than half of the provincial coins come. A constant source of supply was provided by the neighbouring Greek mints located inside the Balkan area, in the provinces of *Moesia Inferior* (especially *Marcianopolis* and *Nicopolis*), *Thracia* (*Philippopolis*, *Hadrianopolis* and *Pautalia*) and *Macedonia* (*Stobi*). The issues of the workshops in Asia Minor (except for the one in *Nicaea*) appear in varying amounts. Most of them bear the names of cities located in *Bithynia*. Most of these issues are struck in base metal. The only silver denominations are *drachmas* (five examples) and a *cistophorus*.

The provincial coinage covers all the periods up to Philip the Arab. But starting with the reign of Septimius Severus, its abundance takes a slow upward course and reaches its highest point, suddenly, in the time of Severus Alexander. The values continue to remain significant during Gordianus III. These sudden changes are due to a massive infusion of coins originating from *Nicaea Bythiniae* and dated to these periods. Recent studies sustain the idea that this type of coinage was used as military payments for the Dacian army units involved in the eastern campaigns during the reigns of Severus Alexander and Gordianus III (Benea 2006; Petac 2011: 155, 157, 174; Poenaru Bordea, Nicolae 2002: 34). But such a hypothesis does not satisfactorily answer why the coin finds from *Nicaea* were only concentrated in the Danube area, in the southern part of the province, or why they appear in vast quantities (over 75%) on the lists of the civilian settlements. There is a need to consider the role of economic (Oberländer-Târnoveanu 2008: 255), and, perhaps, political factors, in conveying this category of Greek coins to regions far from their home mint. The provincial findings from the two *Pannoniae* and the two *Moesiae* have many common features with the situation discussed above in *Dacia*. There is mainly an intense influx of Nicaean issues that occurred exactly during the same two periods. Except that in the sites of *Moesia Inferior* they are outnumbered by local issues (Găzdac 2010: 41-42, 315-316, Tables Q 2-3; Oberländer-Târnoveanu, Oberländer-Târnoveanu 2000: 407, Table I; 411, 417).

III. The third period (AD 238-249) may be regarded as the 'peak' of coin finds in the sites of *Dacia*. The monetary indices calculated for the reign of Gordianus III generally maintain the high figures from the latter part of the Severan dynasty. Only the values of the two *Pannoniae* are closer to them, while those of the western provinces are very low (Figures 6-7, 9). The features of the coinage change in a significant manner, under the equal action of general factors and local events. On the scale of the Empire, the decision to strike massive amounts of *antoniniani* (Carson 1990: 234; Estiot 2004: 40, Figure 3; Harl 1996, 129) turns them into the only silver denominations found inside the sites during this period. In *Dacia*, they represent one-third of all coins discovered in the civilian settlements. This share doubles in the case of fortifications. The average percentages of plated *antoniniani* (over 20%) are the highest from all provinces studied by the present author. Most of the time they seem to behave in the same way as the good coins. As in the case of *denarii*, it is possible that at least some of the plated copies came from the official mints, alongside the genuine ones (Ardevan, Suciu, Ciugudean 2003: 37-40).

The main local event which influenced the base metal coinage was the opening of the mint of *Viminacium* in the year AD 239. It functioned for only sixteen years, striking bronze issues, according to the official denomination system: *sestertii, dupondii* and *asses* (Martin 1992: 9-83). The coins originating from *Viminacium*, with the effigy of Gordianus III (mostly *sestertii*), were discovered only in half of the sites of *Dacia*, located mainly in the southern part of the province, near the Danube. The proportions vary between 10% and 30% of all coin finds dated to this period. One may note their concentration within the civilian settlements, especially in the large settlements, while the volume of finds in fortifications is much lower. Moesian issues have been found in large quantities (over 800) in the sites of the two *Pannoniae*, where they have the same chronological distribution as in *Dacia* (Găzdac, Alföldy-Găzdac 2008). It seems that the mint at *Viminacium* consistently supplied, albeit in different amounts, the sites of neighbouring provinces.

The coin index for Philip the Arab's reign is very large and reaches the highest level in the duration of the province. The values estimated for Dacian sites in this period are double those from *Pannonia* and surpass by a few times those from the Rhineland *limes* region (Figures 2-7, 9). Again, the reasons that caused this situation might have been the particular monetary factors that affected the coinage of this region. In the year AD 246 a new mint opened and, for a brief period of eleven years, it struck bronze coins, similar in denominations, weights, size and design with those from *Viminacium*, but with a different legend on the reverse – 'PROVINCIA DACIA' (Cavagna 2012; Martin 1992: 9-21, 84-106). It is are not easy to identify precisely the mint that produced this monetary series.

According to the most likely hypotheses, it was located in *Moesia Superior*, at *Viminacium* (Martin 1992: 13) or in *Dacia*, at *Sarmizegetusa* (Ardevan 1996) or *Apulum* (Găzdac 2010: 157; Găzdac, Alföldy-Găzdac 2008: 146). It seems more plausible that the mint functioned at *Sarmizegetusa*, under the authority of *concilium provinciae*; this is the only site from the entire area whose list of finds contains a complete chronological series for all three types of denominations.

The coins from *Sarmizegetusa*, mostly dated to the first two years of local production, appear at the majority of Dacian sites, in different proportions, depending on their location within the province and their functionality. As a result, the sites situated in the central and northern regions (inside the Carpathians) have the highest amounts of this coinage (60-70% from all finds of this period). A gradual decrease of these percentages occurs as we move away from the intra-Carpathian area. The list of sites near the Danube contains only a small number of these bronzes. Also, the coins with the legend 'PROVINCIA DACIA' from the civilian settlements are twice as numerous as those from the fortifications.

This massive influx of local issues from *Sarmizegetusa* generated an unusual increase of the monetary index of Dacian sites, during the period of Philip the Arab (Găzdac

2010: 191, Plate Q 2). The opening of a new mint inside the province was meant to reduce the economic effects of the general crisis and the Carpic invasions. But these measures caused only an artificial increment of the monetary mass and, consequently, they do not depict the real situation of the economy (Ardevan 2006: 154-155; Zerbini, Ardevan 2007: 110). In his research on the fort at Richborough, R. Reece convincingly explains the abnormally high number of coins found in the penultimate phase of the site's existence. From the time of the end of Roman administration, when the coinage supply ceased, nearly all the coins available in the site were discovered (a so-called 'total loss') (Reece 1968: 215; Reece 1981: 53). It seems likely that a somewhat similar situation could have happened in *Dacia*, at least in most sites of the central and northern areas, where the issues dated in the time of Philip the Arab or immediately thereafter were the last coins registered on their lists. Probably many of them did not arise as a result of an accidental loss and gradual replacement of coinage by normal circulation. They represent the currency available on the market, used for a short period inside the settlements or camps, and left behind. One may take into account the fact that the state was not very interested in recovering, by fees or other obligations, such issues of common metal, with a limited circulation. Thus, the high amounts of 'PROVINCIA DACIA' coinage, from the central and northern parts of the province, do not reflect the real monetary circulation of the time and therefore the overall growth of the monetary index for the Dacian sites, in this period, is unnatural.

The coins belonging to this monetary series were also found in the sites of the *Pannoniae*, but in smaller quantities and having different chronological distributions. The major part of this coinage in *Dacia* was issued in the first two years, while most of the similar finds from the *Pannoniae* are dated only beginning with the third year of the local production (Găzdac, Alföldy-Găzdac 2008). According to a recent opinion, the main purpose of the two local mints, at *Sarmizegetusa* and *Viminacium*, was to supply the numerous troops in the middle and lower Danube region, during the monetary crisis of the mid 3rd century AD. Hence all their coin production was directed wherever military events required the presence of soldiers (Găzdac 2010: 156-157; Găzdac, Alföldy-Găzdac 2008: 145-146). Such an hypothesis is tempting, but it requires answers to questions such as: why were these bronze coins mostly found in the civilian settlements? Why did the Imperial authority use different coinages (silver and two bronze species) to pay the troops in the northern and southern part of the province? Why was the mint of *Sarmizegetusa* opened only after the war with the Carpi finished (see in this regard Petac 1998: 33-34; Petac 2011: 186-193)?

IV. The last period (AD 249-275) brings to the province a progressive decrease, followed by the end of coinage. The latest monetary discoveries in most of the auxiliary forts of *Dacia* (those situated in the north and eastern half of the province) date back to the time of Philip the Arab (Figure 5) (see also Dudău 2006: 87, 89-92; Petac 2011: 117-118, 123, 131, 133, 142, 149, 155). It is difficult to determine to what extent the numismatic sources could support the hypothesis of a possible early abandonment of these parts of the province (Ardevan 2006: 156).

To follow its monetary changes closely, this period was divided into two separate phases: AD 249-259 and 259-275. In the first chronological sequence (the years AD 249-259), the number of discoveries is remarkably modest; many sites are represented only by a few coins on their lists and other lists of coin finds are closed. There is a noticeable concentration of money in the two legionary fortresses and the large towns of the province, located along the Imperial road, connecting *Drobeta* with *Porolissum* (Figures 2-5). The distribution of coin finds within the sites north of the Lower Danube seems to reflect a certain immobility of currency in society, caused by the disruption of the internal economic circuits of the province. Imperial money was distributed only in major centres, without reaching the population living outside these centres (Ardevan, Suciu, Ciugudean 2003: 43-44). The geographical position of sites inside the province also seems to have affected the volume of finds. Those located near the Danube, in the vicinity of the *Moesiae*, such as *Dierna*, *Drobeta* and *Sucidava*, maintained a constantly large inflow, while the majority, situated near the Carpathians, received fewer coins. The coinage composition consists mainly of *antoniniani* and a small number of local bronzes.

The monetary index for Dacian sites is low in this period, along with the indices calculated for *Noricum*, *Raetia* and *Germaniae* (Figures 6, 8, 10). A possible explanation for the poor supply of these territories may rest on the reduced outputs of *antoniniani* from the central mints during this time (Ehling 2008: 845, Graph 2; Estiot 2004: 40, Figure 3). By comparison, the values of the *Pannoniae* seem to be only slightly higher, probably due to the constant arrival of local issues (from *Viminacium* and *Sarmizegetusa*) and, later, to the massive presence of troops in the region, during the riots of the usurpers Ingenuus and Regalianus (Găzdac 2010: 192; Găzdac, Alföldy-Găzdac 2008: 153, Graphs 11-12).

The second chronological sequence (the years AD 259-275) coincides with an episode that has generated much controversy in our historiography – the abandonment of *Dacia*. The level of coin finds in the reign of Gallienus (alone) is the lowest in the whole lifetime of the province (Figures 2-6). The collapse of monetary circulation after the year AD 260 can be explained by the decrease in the number of troops, who were moved to the conflict zones of the Empire. Some of the *vexillationes* belonging to the two Dacian legions have been attested in *Pannonia Superior* and in *Gallia*, and others were part of the Danubian intervention force or defended northern Italy (Hügel 2003: 167-168). The departure of soldiers caused a drastic reduction of the money entering the province and thus ruined the local economy. Most likely, in the latter period of Gallienus' reign, a major part of *Dacia* was outside Imperial control, at least from the financial point of view (Găzdac 2002a: 737-738; Găzdac 2010: 199; Petac 2011: 74-75, 86, 200-202). Coins disappear from most of the sites, and only some scattered finds were registered.

One particular evolution is known by two strategic Danubian centres – *Drobeta* and *Sucidava* (Figure 2). During this period they were reinforced to serve the Imperial defensive policy on the Danube (Bondoc 2009: 734, 736-738; Poenaru Bordea 1975: 96, 101). The numerous coin finds from these sites testify the existence of a prosperous monetary circulation. The monetary values of the Dacian sites estimated for the time of Claudius II and Aurelianus are misleading, as they are based only on these two lists of finds.

There are many monetary resemblances between the sites of *Dacia* and those from the *Agri Decumates* region, beginning with the reign of Gallienus (alone) (Figures 6, 8, 10). The quantity of coinage, both in the military and civilian areas of the two Roman territories, geographically apart, is very low, almost unnoticeable. In either case, the coin finds seem to reflect the same major event that occurred at almost simultaneous times: the cease of Imperial authority and the break in the regular money supply (Kos 1995; Okamura 1996: 12-14). The other parts of the Empire, characterised by a normal development of Roman life – such as the *Pannoniae*, *Noricum*, *Raetia* and the *Germaniae* – have high or very high monetary indices. They received large quantities of debased *antoniniani*, struck in the recently opened imperial mints (e.g. *Colonia*, *Augusta Treverorum*, and *Serdica*) (Ehling 2008: 853-860; Estiot 2004: 40, Figure 3; 55-128).

Conclusions

The coin finds in the sites of Roman Danubian and the Rhineland provinces show significant similarities, both in the evolution of the monetary indices and the coinage composition. They define a regional monetary pattern, specific to this wide area of the Empire, for a certain length of time (this study is limited only to the period from the beginning of the 2nd century AD until the reign of Aurelianus).

The Dacian monetary pattern of coin finds is a part of this general standard. Its characteristics were generated under the action of specific factors of limited, local impact. Several distinct features of the coinage in the Dacian sites appear in different periods, and thus they have been highlighted in our research. In particular two significant situations might draw attention: a large number of plated *denarii* spread all across the province and bronze coinage with the legend 'PROVINCIA DACIA' that caused an abnormal increase of the monetary index during Philip the Arab.

In the case of *Dacia*, the civilian and military sites do not seem to provide varied patterns of coin finds, as in the case of *Britannia* (Casey 1974: 48-50; Casey 1999: 49-51). There are some differences within their monetary lists, but they are not very obvious, most likely because of the short lifespan of the province.

The Dacian monetary pattern is composed of two sub-patterns of coin finds for sites with distinct geographical positions inside the province (Chițescu, Poenaru Bordea 1983: 188-191; Dudău 2006: 35; Găzdac 2002b: 80-82; Găzdac 2003: 190-194; Găzdac 2010: 169-173, Plate Q 1; Petac 2011: 70-174; Poenaru Bordea 1998: 58-67). The northern sites, located within the Carpathians (*Dacia Porolissensis* and most of *Dacia Apulensis*), have higher monetary indices during the 2nd century. A massive presence of the army is attested here and probably a significant amount of money entered the province through the military environment, in the first stage of Roman rule. In the southern sites, located outside the Carpathians (*Dacia Malvensis* and the rest of *Dacia Apulensis*), the rise of the monetary indices began with the reign of Elagabalus. These values will exceed those from the north until the Romans retreat. The general prosperity of the province during the Severan dynasty and the economic development of the Danubian centres, as a result of commercial activities, might explain these changes. In such circumstances, the influence of the army over civilian life in *Dacia* became limited.

APPENDIX. List of sites used in numismatic research

I. *Dacia*: 1. civilian settlements: a) cities: Alba Iulia (*Apulum-colonia* and *municipium*), Cluj-Napoca (*Napoca*), Corabia (*Sucidava*), Drobeta-Turnu Severin (*Drobeta*), Jupa-Iaz (*Tibiscum*), Moigrad (*Porolissum*), Orşova (*Dierna*), Reşca (*Romula*), Sarmizegetusa (*Ulpia Traiana Sarmizegetusa*), Turda (*Potaissa*); **b) rural settlements**: Cioroiu Nou (*Aquae* [?]), Cristeşti, Gârla Mare, Micăsasa, Orlea, Groups of rural sites from *Dacia Porolissensis* (19), *Dacia Apulensis* (45) and *Dacia Malvensis* (29); **c) military settlements**: Alba Iulia (*Apulum*), Bumbeşti-Jiu, Căşeiu (*Samum*), Gherla, Ilişua (*Arcobadara*), Moigrad 'Sub Ferice/Drumul Vacilor' (*Porolissum*), Romita (*Certiae*), Stolniceni (*Buridava*), Veţel (*Micia*); **2. military fortifications**: Alba Iulia (*Apulum*), Bologa (*Resculum*), Buciumi, Căşeiu (*Samum*), Gilău, Ilişua (*Arcobadara*), Jupa (*Tibiscum*), Moigrad (*Porolissum* – 'Pomet' and *statio portorii*), Răcarii de Jos, Slăveni, Turda (*Potaissa*).
Bibliography (selected): Ardevan 1991; Ardevan 1993; Ardevan 2005; Chirilă 1991; Chiţescu, Poenaru Bordea 1983; Dudău 2006; Găzdac 2002b; Găzdac 2003; Găzdac 2010; Găzdac, Cociş 2004; Găzdac, Gaiu, Marchiş 2011; Găzdac, Gudea 2006; Găzdac, Isac 2007; Găzdac, Pripon 2012; Găzdac, Suciu, Alföldy-Găzdac 2009; Găzdac, Voişian, Cociş 2003; Găzdac *et al.* 2015; Matei 2015; Mitrofan, Ardevan 1997; Oberländer-Târnoveanu 2008; Opreanu, Lăzărescu 2015; Pîslaru 2010; Petac 2011; Poenaru Bordea 1975; Poenaru Bordea 1998; Stîngă 1998; Winkler 1964; Winkler 1965; Winkler 1975; Winkler, Băloi 1971; Winkler, Băloi 1973; Winkler, Hopârtean 1973.

II. *Pannonia Inferior*: 1. civilian settlements: Budapest (*Aquincum-colonia* and *canabae*), Dunaújváros (*Intercisa*), Pécs (*Sopianae*), Százhalombatta (*Matrica*), Tác (*Gorsium-municipium* and *vicus*); **2. military fortifications**: Budapest (*Aquincum*), Dunaújváros (*Intercisa*), Százhalombatta (*Matrica*).
Bibliography: Biró-Sey, Lányi 1980; Biró-Sey, Lányi 1981; Biró-Sey, Lányi 1982; Biró-Sey, Lányi 1983; Biró-Sey, Lányi 1985; Biró-Sey, Lányi 1986; Biró-Sey, Lányi 1989; Biró-Sey, Lányi, Torbágy 1993; Fitz 1978; FMRU I; Fülep 1984; Găzdac 2002b; Găzdac 2003; Găzdac 2010; Pekáry 1953; Thúry 2000.

III. *Pannonia Superior*: 1. civilian settlements: Árpás (*Mursella*), Drnovo (*Neviodvnvm*), Eisenstadt, Epöl-Kőkút, Halbturn, Hegykő-Téglástó, Héreg, Illmitz, Marz, Müllendorf, Neckenmarkt, Neusiedl am See, Oslip, Petronell (*Carnuntum-colonia* and *canabae*), Pöttsching, Ptuj (*Poetovio*), Schützen am Gebirge, Sopron (*Scarbantia*), Strebersdorf, Szombathely (*Savaria*), Szőny (*Brigetio*), Tokod, Wien (*Vindobona-colonia* and *canabae*), Winden am See; **2. military fortifications**: Ács Bum-Bum Kút (*Ad Mures*), Esztergom (*Solva*), Győr (*Arrabona*), Petronell (*Carnuntum*), Wien (*Vindobona*).
Bibliography: Biró-Sey 1977; Fitz 1978; FMRSl I; II; III; IV; V; VI; FMRÖ I,2; III,1; III,2; IX; FMRU II; III; Găzdac 2002b; Găzdac 2003; Găzdac 2010.

IV. *Noricum*: 1. civilian settlements: Adriach, Celje (*Celeia*), Gleisdorf, Kalsdorf, Lorch-Enns (*Lauriacum*), Lupitsch, Rattenberg, St. Peter in Holz (*Teurnia*), Wagna (*Flavia Solva*), Wels (*Ovilavis*), Zollfeld (*Virunum*).
Bibliography: FMRÖ II,3; IV,1; VI; FMRSl II; III; IV; V; VI; Prokisch 1989.

V. *Raetia*: 1. civilian settlements: Augsburg (*Augusta Videlicum*), Eining (*Abusina*), Epfach (*Abodiacum*), Gauting (*Bratananium*), Heiden Heim (*Aquileia*), Hüfingen-Mühlöschle, Karlstein, Kempten (*Cambiodunum*), Nassenfels (*Vicus Scuttarensium*), Regensburg (*Castra Regina*), Riegel, Schierenhof, Steppberg; **2. military fortifications**: Aalen, Alkofen, Burghöfe (*Summuntorium*), Dambach, Eining (*Abusina*), Faimingen (*Phoebiana*), Gnotzheim (*Mediana*), Günzburg (*Guntia*), Kosching (*Germanicum*), Kumpfmühl, Künzing (*Quintana*), Pförring (*Celeusum*), Pfünz (*Vetoniana*), Regensburg (*Castra Regina*), Risstissen, Schierenhof, Seebruck (*Bedaium*), Straubing (*Sorviodurum*), Weissenburg (*Biriciana*).
Bibliography: FMRD I,1; I,2; I,3-4; I,5; I,7; II,2; II,2 N1; II,3; II,3 N1;II,4, II,4 N1.

VI. *Germania Superior*: 1. civilian settlements: Alzey (*Altiaia*), Augst (*Augusta Raurica*), Bad Dürkheim, Bad Wimpfen (*Alisinensium*), Baden-Baden (*Aquae*), Baden Weiler, Butzbach, Contwig, Dieburg (*Med*...), Eisenberg, Frankfurt am Main (*Nida*), Friedberg, Köngen (*Grinario*), Ladenburg (*Lopodunum*), Mainz (*Mogontiacum*), Mainz-Weisenav, Pforzheim (*Portus*), Rheinzabern (*Tabernae*), Rottenburg (*Sumelocenna*), Rottweil (*Arae Flaviae*), Saalburg, Speyer (*Noviomagus*), Stettfeld, Sulz, Wiesbaden (*Aquae Mattiacorum*), Worms (*Borbetomagus*), Zugmantel; **2. military fortifications**: Alteburg-Heftrich, Bad Ems, Bingen (*Bingium*), Butzbach, Echzell, Gernsheim, Gross-Gerau ('Auf Esch'), Heidelberg-Neuenheim, Heldenber gen, Holzhausen, Jag Sthausen, Kleiner Feldberg, Köngen (*Grinario*), Langenhain, Mainz (*Mogontiacum*), Mainz-Kastel (*Castellum Mattiacorum*), Miltenberg-Altstadt, Ober-Florstadt, Ober-Rosbach (Kapersburg), Obernburg am Main, Öhringen, Osterburken, Rückingen, Saalburg, Stockstadt am Main, Stuttgart - Bad Cannstatt , Walheim, Walldrün, Zugmantel.
Bibliography: IFS 3, 4; FMRD I,6; II,1; II,1 N1; II,2; II,2 N1; II,3; II,3 N1; II,4; II,4 N1; IV,1; IV,1 N1; IV,2; IV,5; V,1/1; V,1/2; V,2/1; V,2/2.

VII. *Germania Inferior*: 1. civilian settlements: Altdorf, Düren (Mariaweiler) (*Vicus Marcodurum* [?]), Jülich (*Vicus Iuliacum*), Kastell Alteburg, Kirchberg, Köln (*Colonia Claudia Ara Agrippinensium*), Neubourheim (Wackersmühle), Neuss (*Novaesium*), Növernich-(Alt-) Oberbolheim (*Vicus Narboniacum*[?]); **2. military fortifications**: Froitzheim, Kastell Alteburg, Neuss (*Novaesium castra* I and II), Reckberg.
Bibliography: FMRD VI,1/1; VI,2/1; VI,3/2.

VIII. *Gallia Belgica*: 1. civilian settlements: Trier (*Augusta Treverorum*), Ensheim, Pachten (*Vicus Contiomagus*), Saarbrücken (St. Johann), Schwarzenacker.
Bibliography: FMRD III; IV,3/1; IV,3/2; IV,3/4; IV,3/5.

IX. *Agri Decumates*: 1. civilian settlements: Baden Weiler, Dieburg (*Med*...), Frankfurt am Main (*Nida*), Heiden Heim (*Aquileia*), Ladenburg (*Lopodunum*), Rottenburg (*Sumelocenna*), Rottweil (*Arae Flaviae*), Köngen (*Grinario*), Nassenfels (*Vicus Scuttarensium*), Saalburg, Zugmantel; **2. military fortifications**: Aalen, Jag Sthausen, Kleiner Feldberg, Köngen (*Grinario*), Kosching (*Germanicum*), Langenhain, Obernburg am Main, Pfünz (*Vetoniana*), Rückingen, Saalburg, Stuttgart - Bad Cannstatt, Walheim, Weissenburg (*Biriciana*), Zugmantel.

Acknowledgement

This work was supported by a grant of the Romanian National Authority for Scientific Research, CNCS-UEFISCDI, project number PN-III-P4-ID-PCE-2016-0669, *Beyond the fringes of empire. Roman influence and power north of the Danube and east of the Rhine* — arheo.ro/romaninfluence.

References

Ardeţ, A. and Ardeţ, L. C. 2004. *Tibiscum. Aşezările romane*. Cluj-Napoca, Nereamia Napocae.

Ardevan, R. 1991. Monetary Circulation in the Ancient Settlement from Gherla (Cluj County). *Eos. Organ Polskiego Towarzystwa Filologicznego* 79: 223-235.

Ardevan, R. 1993. Aperçu sur la monnaie d'or dans la Dacie romaine. In T. Hackens and G. Moucharte (eds), *Actes du XIe Congrès International de Numismatique organisé à l'occasion du 150e anniversaire de la Société Royale de Numismatique de Belgique. Bruxelles, 8-13 septembre 1991, II*: 347-353. Louvain-la-Neuve, Association Professeur Marcel Hoc.

Ardevan, R. 1996. Monetăria provincială de la Sarmizegetusa. *Buletinul Societăţii Numismatice Române* 86-87/140-141: 117-122.

Ardevan, R. 1998. *Viaţa municipală în Dacia romană*. Timişoara, Mirton.

Ardevan, R. 2002. Officina falsaria din aşezarea romană de la Ilişua.*Buletinul Societăţii Numismatice Române* 90-91/144-145: 39-43.

Ardevan, R. 2005. Monetary circulation and provincial society in the Roman settlement of Ilişua (Dacia). In C. Alfaro, C. Marcosand P. Otero (eds), *XIII Congreso Internacional de Numismática (Madrid, 2003). Actas-Proceedings-Actes, I*: 663-671. Madrid, Ministerio de Cultura.

Ardevan, R. 2006. Circulaţie monetară şi societate provincială în aşezarea romană de la Ilişua. *Revista Bistriţei* 20: 153-163.

Ardevan, R., Suciu, V. and Ciugudean, D. 2003. *Tezaurul monetar roman 'Apulum VII'*. Alba Iulia, Altip.

Aubin, G. 2003. Les moules monétaires en terre cuite du IIIe siècle: chronologie et géographie. *Revue Numismatique* 6e, 159: 125-162.

Benea, D. 2003. *Istoria aşezărilor de tip vici militares din Dacia romană*. Timişoara, Excelsior Art.

Benea, D. 2006. *Dakien im Orientfeldzug des Severus Alexander*. Die in Nicäa geprägten Münzen. In C. Gaiu and C. Găzdac (eds), *Fontes Historiae. Studia in honorem Demetrii Protase*: 693-698. Bistriţa/Cluj-Napoca, Accent.

Benea, D. 2013. *Istoria Banatului în antichitate*. Timişoara, Excelsior Art.

Biró-Sey, K. 1977. *Coins from identified sites of Brigetio and the question of local currency*. Budapest, Magyar Nemzeti Muzeum.

Biró-Sey, K. and Lányi, V. 1980. Fundmünzenbericht 1977. *Acta Archaeologica Academiae Scientiarum Hungaricae* 32/1-4: 455-466.

Biró-Sey, K. and Lányi, V. 1981. Fundmünzenbericht 1978. *Acta Archaeologica Academiae Scientiarum Hungaricae* 33/1-4: 347-364.

Biró-Sey, K. and Lányi, V. 1982. Fundmünzenbericht 1979. *Acta Archaeologica Academiae Scientiarum Hungaricae* 34/1-4: 363-386.

Biró-Sey, K. and Lányi, V. 1983. Fundmünzenbericht 1980. *Acta Archaeologica Academiae Scientiarum Hungaricae* 35/1-4: 345-371.

Biró-Sey, K. and Lányi, V. 1985. Fundmünzenbericht 1981. *Acta Archaeologica Academiae Scientiarum Hungaricae* 37/1-2: 161-176.

Biró-Sey, K. and Lányi, V. 1986. Fundmünzenbericht 1982. *Acta Archaeologica Academiae Scientiarum Hungaricae* 38/3-4: 299-312.

Biró-Sey, K. and Lányi, V. 1987. Fundmünzenbericht 1983. *Acta Archaeologica Academiae Scientiarum Hungaricae* 39/1-2: 69-92.

Biró-Sey, K. and Lányi, V. 1989. Fundmünzenbericht 1984. *Acta Archaeologica Academiae Scientiarum Hungaricae* 41/3-4: 509-526.

Biró-Sey, K., Lányi, V. and Torbágy, M. 1993. Fundmünzenbericht 1987-1988. *Acta Archaeologica Academiae Scientiarum Hungaricae* 45/1-4: 75-89.

Bondoc, D. 2009. Fortified towns to the north of the Lower Danube in the late Roman period: Drobeta and Sucidava. In A. Morillo, N. Hanel and E. Martín (eds), *Limes XX. XX Congreso internacional de estudios sobre la frontera Romana/ XXth International Congress of Roman Frontier Studies, León (España), Septiembre 2006, III*: 731-740. Madrid, Polifemo.

Boon, G. 1974. Counterfeit coins in Roman Britain. In P. J. Casey and R. Reece (eds), *Coins and the Archaeologist*: 95-172. British Archaeological Reports 4. Oxford, British Archaeological Reports.

Carson, R. A. G. 1990. *Coins of the Roman Empire*. London/New York, Routledge.

Casey, P. J. 1974. The interpretation of the Roman-British site finds. In P. J. Casey and R. Reece (eds), *Coins and the Archaeologist*: 37-51. British Archaeological Reports 4. Oxford, British Archaeological Reports.

Casey, P. J. 1986. *Understanding ancient coins. An introduction for archaeologists and historians.* London, Batsford.

Casey, P. J. 1999, *Roman Coinage in Britain*[3]. Buckinghamshire, Shire.

Cavagna, A. 2012. *Provincia Dacia. I conî.* Società Numismatica Italiana, Milano.

Chirilă, E. 1991. Câteva date privind circulaţia monetară la Porolissum. *Acta Musei Porolissensis* 14-15: 153-174.

Chiţescu, M. and Poenaru Bordea, Gh. 1983. Contribuţii la istoria Diernei în lumina descoperirilor monetare din săpăturile arheologice din 1967. *Buletinul Societăţii Numismatice Române* 75-76/129-130: 169-208.

Diaconescu, Al. 2004. The towns of Roman Dacia: an overview of recent archaeological research. In W. S. Hanson and I. P. Haynes (eds), *Roman Dacia. The making of a provincial society. Journal of Roman Archaeology Supplementary Series* 56: 87-141. Portsmouth, Journal of Roman Archaeology.

Dietz, K. 1997. Decumates agri (s.v.). In H. Cancik and H. Schneider (eds), *Der Neue Pauly. Enzyklopädie der Antike. Altertum (Bd. 3, Cl-Epi)*: 34-356. Stuttgart/ Weimar, Metzler.

Dudău, O. 2006. *Circulaţia monetară în castrele de trupe auxilare din provincia Dacia.* Timişoara, Graphite.

Duncan-Jones, R. 1998. *Money and government in the Roman empire* (3rd ed.). Cambridge, Cambridge University Press.

Ehling, K. 2008. Das Münzwesen. In K.-P. Johne (ED.), *Die Zeit der Soldatenkaiser: Krise und Transformation des Römischen Reiches im 3. Jahrhundert n.Chr. (235-284), II*: 843-860. Berlin, Akademie Verlag.

Estiot, S. 2004. *Monnaies de l'Empire romain. XII.1. D'Aurélien à Florien (270-276 après J.-C.), I-II.* Paris/Strasbourg, Bibliothèque nationale de France/Poinsignon numismatique.

Fitz, J. 1978. *Der Geldumlauf der römischen Provinzen im Donaugebiet Mitte des 3. Jahrhunderts.* Bonn/Budapest, Dr. Rudolf Habelt GmbH/Akadémiai Kiadó.

Fülep, F. 1984. Sopinae. *The history of Pécs during the Roman era and the problem of the continuity of the late Roman population.* Budapest, Akadémiai Kiadó.

Găzdac, C. 1997. A Lead Mould from Ulpia Traiana Sarmizegetusa. *Pontica* 30: 351-353.

Găzdac, C. 2002a. Monetary Circulation and the Abandonment of Auxiliary Forts in Roman Dacia. In P. Freeman, J. Bennett, Z. T. Fiema and B. Hoffmann (eds), *Limes XVIII. Proceedings of the XVIIIth International Congress of Roman Frontier Studies held in Amman, Jordan (September 2000), II*: 737-756. British Archaeological Reports International Series 1084. Oxford, Archaeopress.

Găzdac, C. 2002b. *Circulaţia monetară în Dacia şi provinciile învecinate de la Traian la Constantin I.* Cluj-Napoca, Nereamia Napocae.

Găzdac, C. 2003. *Monetary Circulation in Dacia and the Provinces from the Middle and Lower Danube from Trajan to Constantine I (A.D. 106-337).* Cluj-Napoca, Nereamia Napocae.

Găzdac, C. 2008. The coinage and the Roman conquest of Dacia: a comparative study of the sites: Ulpia Traiana, Porolissum, Carnuntum, Ovilava, Poetovio. In V. Spinei and L. Munteanu (eds), *Miscellanea numismatica antiquitatis: in honorem septagenarii magistri Virgilii Mihailescu-Bîrliba oblate*: 69-80. Iaşi, Editura Academiei Române.

Găzdac, C. 2010. *Monetary Circulation in Dacia and the Provinces from the Lower Danube from Trajan to Constantine I (AD 106-337)* (2nd ed.). Cluj-Napoca, Mega.

Găzdac, C. and Alföldy-Găzdac, Á. 2008. The management of a monetary crisis?: the 'P M S Col Vim' and 'Provincia Dacia' coinages in the Roman monetary policy of the 3rd century AD. *Numismatische Zeitschrift* 116-117. In M. Alram and H. Winter (eds), *Festschrift für Günther Dembski zum 65. Geburtstag: 135-171. Wien,* Österreichische Numismatische Gesellschaft.

Găzdac, C., Alföldy-Găzdac, Á., Neagoe, M. and Neagoe, O. 2015. *Drobeta. The never abandoned city of Roman Dacia.* Cluj-Napoca, Mega.

Găzdac, C. and Cociş, S. 2004. *Ulpia Traiana Sarmizegetusa.* Cluj-Napoca, Mega.

Găzdac, C., Gaiu, C. and Marchiş, E. 2011. *Arcobadara (Ilişua).* Cluj-Napoca, Mega.

Găzdac, C. and Gudea, N. 2006. *Porolissum.* Cluj-Napoca, Mega.

Găzdac, C. and Isac, D. 2007. *The Auxiliary forts from Samum (Căşeiu) and Gilău.* Cluj-Napoca, Mega.

Găzdac, C., Oargă, O. and Alföldy-Găzdac, Á. 2015. *It was supposed to be Silver! The Scrap Coin 'Hoard' Apulum VI.* Cluj-Napoca, Mega.

Găzdac, C. and Pripon, E. 2012. *The Roman Auxiliary Fort at Buciumi (Roman Dacia, Romania). Coins in archaeological context.* British Archaeological Reports International Series 2381. Oxford, Archaeopress.

Găzdac, C., Suciu, V. and Alföldy-Găzdac, Á. 2009. *Apulum.* Cluj-Napoca, Mega.

Găzdac, C., Voişian, V. and Cociş, S. 2003. Coin finds from Napoca – The excavations on Deleu st. *Revista Bistriţei* 17: 77-96.

Gudea, N. 1994. Dacia Porolissensis în timpul războaielor marcomanice. *Acta Musei Napocensis* 18: 67-93.

Gudea, N. 1996. *Porolissum. Un complex daco-roman la marginea de nord a Imperiului Roman. II. Vama romană. Monografie arheologică.* Cluj-Napoca, Muzeul Naţional de Istorie a Transilvaniei.

Gudea, N. 1997. Der dakischer Limes. Materialien zu seiner Geschichte. *Jahrbuch des Römisch-Germanischen Zentralmuseums* 44/2: 497-610.

Gudea, N. 2009. Ländliche Siedlungen in den dakischen Provinzen (106-275 n.Chr.). Archäologische Beiträge zur Geschichte des Dorfes und der Landwirtschaft in der Römerzeit. *Jahrbuch des Römisch-Germanischen Zentralmuseums* 56: 187-319.

Harl, K. H. 1996. *Coinage in the Roman economy, 300 B.C. to A.D. 700*. Baltimore/London, Johns Hopkins University Press.

Hobley, A. S. 1998. *An Examination of Roman Bronze Coin Distribution in the Western Empire AD 81-192*. British Archaeological Reports International Series 688. Oxford, Archaeopress.

Hügel, P. 2003. *Ultimele decenii ale stapânirii romane în Dacia (Traianus Decius-Aurelian)*. Cluj-Napoca, Nereamia Napocae.

Katsari, C. 2008. The Monetization of Rome's Frontier Provinces. In W. V. Harris (ed.), *The Monetary Systems of the Greeks and Romans*: 242-266. Oxford/New York, Oxford University Press.

Katsari, C. 2011. *The Roman Monetary System: The Eastern Provinces from the First to the Third Century AD*. Cambridge/New York, Cambridge University Press.

Kemmers, F. 2006. *Coins for a legion: an analysis of the coin finds from Augustan legionary fortress and Flavian canabaelegionis at Nijmegen*. Mainz am Rhein, Philipp von Zabern.

King, C. E. 1996. Roman copies. In C. E. King and D. G. Wigg (eds), *Coin finds and coin use in the Roman world. The thirteenth Oxford Symposium on Coinage and Monetary History, 25-27.3.1993*: 237-263. Berlin, Gebr. Mann.

Kos, P. 1986. *The monetary circulation in the south-eastern alpine region: ca. 300 B.C.-A.D. 1000*. Ljubljana, Narodni Muzej.

Kos, P. 1995. *Sub principe* Gallieno ... amissa Raetia? Numismatische Quellen zum Datum 259/260 n. Chr. in Raetien. *Germania. Anzeigen der Römisch-Germanischen Kommision des Deutschen Archäologischen Instituts* 73: 131-144.

Kos, P. 1997. Interpretacija (antičnih) novčnih najdb. Metodologija – njene možnosti in pasti. *Arheološki vestnik. Acta Archaeologica* 48: 97-115.

Kunisz, A. 1980. *La monnaie de nécessité dans les provinces rhénanes et danubiennes de l'Empire Romain dans la première moitié du IIIe*. In G. Vallet (éd.), *Les 'dévaluations' à Rome: époque républicaine et impériale. 2 (Gdansk, 19-21 octobre 1980)*: 129-139. Rome, École Française de Rome.

Martin, F. 1992. *Kolonialprägungen aus Moesia Superior und Dacia*. Budapest/Bonn, Akadémiai Kiadó/Dr. Rudolf Habelt GmbH.

Matei, C. 2015. *Circulația monetară romană pe teritoriul anticului Tibiscum (sec. I-IV p.Chr), I*. Szeged, JATE Press Kiadó.

Mitrofan, I. and Ardevan, R. 1997. Découvertes monétaires dans l'établissement romain de Micăsasa. *Studii și Cercetări de Numismatică* 11: 119-133.

Oberländer-Târnoveanu, E. 2008. Monedele descoperite în complexul arheologic roman din secolele II-III de la Gârla Mare (com. Gârla Mare, jud. Mehedinți) – Un studiu de caz asupra economiei monetare în spațiul rural al provinciei Dacia. *Cercetări Numismatice* 14: 243-271.

Oberländer-Târnoveanu, E. and Oberländer-Târnoveanu, I. 2000. Quelques rémarques sur la circulation des monnaies en bronze dans la zone des Bouches du Danube à l'époque romaine (Ier-IIIe siècles après J.-C.). In M. Iacob, E. Oberländer-Târnoveanu and F.

Topoleanu (eds), *Istro-Pontica - Muzeul tulcean la a 50-a aniversare. 1950-2000. Omagiu lui Simion Gavrilă la 45 de ani de activitate*: 405-419. Tulcea, Consiliul Județean.

Okamura, L. 1996. Roman Withdrawals from Three Transfluvial Frontiers. In R. W. Mathisen and H. S. Sivan (eds), *Shifting Frontiers in Late Antiquity (Papers from the First Interdisciplinary Conference on Late Antiquity, The University of Kansas, March 1995)*: 11-19. Aldershot, Variorum.

Opreanu, C. H. and Lăzărescu, V.-A. 2015. *A Roman frontier marketplace at Porolissum in the light of numismatic evidence. Contribution to the knowledge of the Roman limes economy*. Cluj-Napoca, Mega.

Pekáry, T. 1953. Aquincum pénzforgalma. *Archaeologiai Értesítő* 80/1-2: 106-114.

Petac, E. 1998. Consideraţii cu privire la data finală a tezaurelor monetare îngropate la mijlocul sec. III p. Chr. în Dacia romană de la sud de Carpaţi. *Studii şi Cercetări de Numismatică* 12: 27-40.

Petac, E. 2011. *Aspecte ale circulației monetare în Dacia romană (105 - 275 p.Chr.)*. Wetteren, Moneta.

Peter, M. 1990. *Eine Werkstätte zur Herstellung von subaeraten Denaren in Augusta Raurica*. Berlin, Gebr. Mann.

Peter, M. 1996. Bemerkungenzur Kleingeldversorgung der westlichen Provinzen im 2. Jahrhundert. In C. E. King and D. G. Wigg (eds), *Coin finds and coin use in the Roman world. The thirteenth Oxford Symposium on Coinage and Monetary History, 25-27.3.1993*: 309-320. Berlin, Gebr. Mann.

Peter, M. 2001. *Untersuchungen zu den Fundmünzen aus Augst und Kaiseraugst*. Berlin, Gebr. Mann.

Petolescu, C. C. 2002. *Auxilia Daciae. Contribuţie la istoria militară a Daciei romane*. Bucureşti, Ars Docendi.

Petolescu, C. C. 2010. *Dacia. Un mileniu de istorie*. Bucureşti, Editura Academiei Române.

Pîslaru, M. 2009. *The Roman Coins from Potaissa. Legionary Fortress and Ancient Town*. Cluj-Napoca, Mega.

Poenaru Bordea, Gh. 1975. Descoperiri monetare din cetăţuia romano-bizantină de la Sucidava cu specială privire asupra perioadei 260-328. Campaniile 1966-1971. *Studii şi Cercetări de Numismatică* 6: 69-106.

Poenaru Bordea, Gh. 1998. Monede din vremea Imperiului roman din colecţia şcolii din cartierul Celeiu al oraşului Corabia, jud. Olt. *Studii şi Cercetări de Numismatică* 12: 41-81.

Poenaru Bordea, Gh. and Nicolae, E. 2002. Monede greceşti şi coloniale din colecția Emil Sachelarie. *Buletinul Societăţii Numismatice Române* 90-91/144-145: 27-37.

Popa, D. 2002. *Villae, vici, pagi. Aşezările rurale din Dacia intracarpatică*. Sibiu, Editura Economică.

Protase, D. and Suceveanu, Al. (coord.) 2001. *Istoria românilor. II. Daco-romani, romanici, alogeni*. Bucureşti, Editura Enciclopedică.

Ravetz, A. 1964. The Fourth-Century Inflation and Romano-British Coin Finds. *Numismatic Chronicle* 7th, 4: 201-231.

Reece, R. 1968. The Roman coins found in 1931-8, and Summary of the Roman coins. In B. W. Cunliffe (ed.), *Fifth Report of the Excavations of the Roman Fort at Richborough, Kent*: 188-217. Oxford, Oxford University Press.

Reece, R. 1981. The Roman coins from Richborough – a summary. *Bulletin of the Institute of Archaeology, University of London* 18: 49-71.

Reece, R. 1987. *Coinage in Roman Britain*. London, Seaby.

Reece R. 1991. *Roman coin from 140 sites in Britain.* Cirencester, Cotswold Studies.

Reece, R. 1996. The interpretation of site finds – a review. In C. E. King and D. G. Wigg (eds), *Coin finds and coin use in the Roman world. The Thirteenth Oxford Symposium on Coinage and Monetary History, 25-27.3.1993*: 341-355. Berlin, Gebr. Mann.

Reece, R. 2002. *The coinage of Roman Britain.* Gloucestershire, Tempus.

Reece, R. 2003. *Roman coins and archaeology. Collected Papers.* Wetteren, Moneta.

Stîngă, I. 1998. *Viaţa economică la Drobeta în secolele II-VI p. Ch.* Bucureşti, Vavila Edinf SRL.

Thúry, L. 2000. Money circulation. In P. Kovács, *Matrica – excavations in the Roman fort at Százhalombatta, 1993-1997*: 105-119. Budapest, Kirké.

Winkler, I. 1964. Despre circulaţia monetară la Porolissum. *Acta Musei Napocensis* 1: 215-225.

Winkler, I. 1965. Circulaţia monetară la Apulum. *Acta Musei Napocensis* 2: 215-256.

Winkler, I. 1975. Descoperiri monetare în Ulpia Traiana Sarmizegetusa. *Sargetia. Acta Musei Devensis* 11-12: 117-136.

Winkler, I. and Băloi, C. 1971. Circulaţia monetară în aşezările antice de pe teritoriul comunei Orlea (I). *Acta Musei Napocensis* 8: 161-172.

Winkler, I. and Băloi, C. 1973. Circulaţia monetară în aşezările antice de pe teritoriul comunei Orlea (II). *Acta Musei Napocensis* 10: 181-212.

Winkler, I. and Hopârtean, A. 1973. *Moneda antică la Potaissa.* Cluj, Muzeul de Istorie Turda.

Winkler, I. and Ivănescu, I. 1977. Imitaţiile de denari descoperite la Porolissum. *Acta Musei Porolissensis* 1: 83-96.

Zerbini, L. and Ardevan, R. 2007. La Dacia romana. Soveria Mannelli, Rubbettino.

Abbreviations

FMRD – *Die Fundmünzen der römischen Zeit in Deutschland.*

I. *Bayern.* 1. Kellner, H.-J. (bearb.) 1960. *Oberbayern.* Berlin, Gebr. Mann; 2. Kellner, H.-J. (bearb.) and Gorecki, J. (beitr.) 1970. *Niederbayern.* Berlin, Gebr. Mann; 3-4. Kellner, H.-J. and Overbeck, M. (bearb.) 1978. *3. Oberpfalz. 4. Oberfranken.* Berlin, Gebr. Mann; 5. Kellner, H.-J. (bearb.) 1965. *Mittelfranken.* Berlin, Gebr. Mann; 6. Kellner, H.-J., Overbeck, B. and Overbeck, M. (bearb.) 1975. *Unterfranken.* Berlin, Gebr. Mann; 7. Alföldi, M. R.-, Franke, P. R., Kellner, H.-J., Kraft, K. and Küthmann, H. (bearb.) 1962. *Schwaben.* Berlin, Gebr. Mann;

II. *Baden-Württemberg.* 1. Christ, K. (bearb.) 1963. *Nordbaden.* Berlin, Gebr. Mann; N 1. Kaiser-Raiss, M. R., Martin, P.-H. (bearb.) 1980. Berlin, Gebr. Mann; 2. Christ, K. (bearb.) 1964. *Südbaden.* Berlin, Gebr. Mann; N 1. Kaiser-Raiss, M. R., Martin, P.-H. (bearb.) 1980. Berlin, Gebr. Mann; 3. Christ, K. (bearb.) and Franke, P. R. (beitr.) 1964. *Südwürttemberg-Hohenzollern.* Berlin, Gebr. Mann; N 1. Stribrny, K. (bearb.) 1993. Berlin, Gebr. Mann; 4. Christ, K. (bearb.) 1964. *Nordwurttemberg.* Berlin, Gebr. Mann; N 1. Stribrny, K. (bearb.) 1993. Berlin, Gebr. Mann;

III. *Saarland.* Kienast, D. (bearb.) 1962. *Saarland.* Berlin, Gebr. Mann;

IV. *Rheinland-Pfalz.* 1. Franke, P. R. (bearb.) 1960. *Rheinhessen.* Berlin, Gebr. Mann; N 1. Gorecki, J. (bearb.) and Rupprecht, G. (einf.) 2006. *Stadt Mainz.* Berlin, Gebr. Mann; 2. Chantraine, H. (bearb.) 1965. *Pfalz.* Berlin, Gebr. Mann; 3/1. Alföldi, M. R.- (bearb.) 1970. *Stadt Trier (3001-3002).* Berlin, Gebr. Mann; 3/2. Alföldi, M. R.- (bearb.) and Wigg-Wolf, D. (beitr.) 2006. *Stadt und Reg.-Bez. Trier. Die sog. Römerbauten (3003-3020).* Mainz am Rhein, Philipp von Zabern; 3/4. Alföldi, M. R.- (bearb.) 2007. *Stadt und Reg.-Bez. Trier. Stadt Trier. Strassen rechts der Mosel A-K (3022-3110).* Mainz am Rhein, Philipp von Zabern; 3/5. Alföldi, M. R.- (bearb.) 2007. *Stadt und Reg.-Bez. Trier. Stadt Trier. Strassen rechts der Mosel L-Z (3111-*

3185). Mainz am Rhein, Philipp von Zabern; 5. Stribrny, K. (bearb.) 1985. *Montabaur*. Berlin, Gebr. Mann;

V. *Hessen*. 1/1. Gorecki, J. (bearb.) and Ritter, H. W. (beitr.) 1994. *Wiesbaden*. Berlin, Gebr. Mann; 1/2. Gorecki, J. (bearb.) and Ritter, H. W. (beitr.) 1994. *Wiesbaden*. Berlin, Gebr. Mann; 2/1. Schubert, H. (bearb.) 1989. *Darmstadt*. Berlin, Gebr. Mann; 2/2. Schubert, H. (bearb.) 1989. *Darmstadt: Frankfurt am Main*. Berlin, Gebr. Mann;

VI. *Nordrhein-Westfalen*. 1/1. Nuber, E. (bearb.) 1984. *Stadt Köln*. Berlin, Gebr. Mann; 2/1. Komnick, H., Heinrichs, J. and Päffgen, B. (bearb.) 2008. *Reg.-Bez. Aachen (Landkreise Düren, Erkelenz, Jülich)*. Mainz am Rhein, Philipp von Zabern; 3/2. Backendorf, D. (bearb.) 2006. *Stadt Neuss*. Mainz am Rhein, Philipp von Zabern.

FMRSl - Die Fundmünzen der römischen Zeit in Slowenien.

I. Kos, P. 1988. Berlin, Gebr. Mann;

II. Kos, P. 1988. Berlin, Gebr. Mann;

III. Kos, P. and Semrov, A. 1995. Berlin, Gebr. Mann;

IV. Semrov, A. 1998. Berlin, Gebr. Mann;

V. Semrov, A. 2004. Mainz am Rhein, Philipp von Zabern;

VI. Semrov, A. 2010. Wetteren, Moneta.

FMRÖ - Die Fundmünzen der römischen Zeit in Österreich.

I. *Burgenland*. 2. Dick, F. (bearb.) 1984. *Burgenland*. Wien, Österreichische Akademie der Wissenschaften;

II. *Kärnten*. 3.Schmidt-Dick, F. (bearb.) 1989. *Kärnten*. Wien, Österreichische Akademie der Wissenschaften;

III. *Niederösterreich*. 1. Hahn, W. (bearb.) 1976. *Carnuntum (Gemeinden Petronell, Bad Deutsch-Altenburg, Stadt Hainburg)*. Wien, Österreichische Akademie der Wissenschaften; 2. Alram, M., Schmidt-Dick, F. (Hgg.) and Dembski G., Humer, F., Pfisterer, M., Ruske, A., Schmidt-Dick, F., Vondrovec, K., Winter, H., Woytek, B. (beitr.) 2007. *Die AntikenFundmünzen in Museum Carnuntum. Numismata Carnuntina: Forschungen und Material*. Wien, Österreichische Akademie der Wissenschaften.

IV. *Oberösterreich*. 1. Vondrovec, K. and Miglbauer, R. (beitr.) 2003. *Die antiken Fundmünzen aus Ovilavis/Wels*. Wien, Österreichische Akademie der Wissenschaften;

VI. *Steiermark*. Schachinger, U. 2006. *Steiermark. Der antike Münzumlauf in der Steiermark*. Wien, Österreichische Akademie der Wissenschaften;

IX. *Wien*. Dick, F. (bearb.) 1978. *Wien*. Wien, Österreichische Akademie der Wissenschaften.

FMRU - Die Fundmünzen der römischen Zeit in Ungarn.

I. Lányi, V. (zsgest.) 1990. *Komitat Fejér*. Bonn/Budapest, Dr. Rudolf Habelt GmbH/Kultura International;

II. Bakos, M. and Lányi, V. (zsgest.) 1993, *Komitat Győr-Moson-Sopron*. Bonn/Budapest, Dr. Rudolf Habelt GmbH/Archaeolingua;

III. Lányi, V., Redő, F. and Torbágyi, M. (zsgest.) 1999, *Komitat Komárom-Esztergom*. Berlin/Budapest, Gebr. Mann/Archaeolingua.

IFS -Inventar der Fundmünzen der Schweiz.

3. Peter, M. 1996. *Augusta Raurica I. Augst 1949-1972*. Lausanne, Académie suisse des sciences humaines et sociales;

4. Peter, M. 1996, *Augusta Raurica II. Kaiseraugst 1949-1972*. Lausanne, Académie suisse des sciences humaines et sociales.

	Dacia				*Pan Inf*				*Pan Sup*				*Noricum*		*Raetia*				*Germ Sup*				*Germ Inf*				*Gal Bel*	
	Civ		Mil		Civ		Mil		Civ		Mil		Civ		Civ		Mil		Civ		Mil		Civ		Mil		Civ	
	D %	D* %	D %	D* %	D %	D* %	D %	D* %	D %	D* %	D %	D* %	D %	D* %	D %	D* %	D %	D* %	D %	D* %	D %	D* %	D %	D* %	D %	D* %	D %	D* %
Ante 98	84	16	88	12	100	0	95	5	94	6	100	0	94	6	100	0	100	0	91	9	98	2	100	0	100	0	85	15
98-117	83	17	72	28	100	0	100	0	95	5	95	5	95	5	100	0	100	0	93	7	98	2	100	0	100	0	81	19
117-138	84	16	83	17	92	8	100	0	97	3	80	20	96	4	100	0	100	0	85	15	97	3	100	0	100	0	100	0
138-161	87	13	76	24	100	0	86	14	97	3	98	2	93	7	100	0	100	0	89	11	91	9	100	0	100	0	83	17
161-180	85	15	74	26	95	5	50	50	96	4	57	43	85	15	100	0	100	0	74	26	95	5	100	0	100	0	100	0
180-193	92	8	81	19	100	0	100	0	97	3	100	0	92	8	100	0	100	0	82	18	90	10	100	0	100	0	33	67
193-211	66	34	41	59	83	17	98	22	92	8	80	20	85	15	100	0	100	0	88	12	88	12	100	0	100	0	86	14
211-218	70	30	47	53	100	0	100	0	86	14	80	20	88	12	100	0	100	0	86	14	89	11	100	0	100	0	71	29
218-222	85	15	76	24	98	2	100	0	95	5	85	15	94	6	100	0	100	0	97	3	97	3	100	0	100	0	93	7
222-238	81	19	72	28	71	29	90	10	91	9	84	16	94	6	100	0	100	0	90	10	88	12	100	0	100	0	86	14
238-244	91	9	79	21			100	0	89	11	100	0	93	7	100	0	100	0	96	4	100	0	100	0	100	0		
244-249																												
249-253																												
253-259																												
259-268																												
268-270																												
270-275																												

Figure 1. The chronological distribution of the share of *denarii subaerati* (D*) in the civilian settlements (Civ) and military fortifications (Mil) of *Dacia*, *Pannonia Inferior*, *Pannonia Superior*, *Noricum*, *Raetia*, *Germania Superior*, *Germania Inferior* and *Gallia Belgica* (years AD 98-275).

	Cities											Mean
	Alba Iulia *Col*	Alba Iulia *Mun*	Cluj-Napoca	Corabia	Drobeta	Jupa-Iaz	Moigrad	Orşova	Reşca	Sarmi-Zegetusa	Turda	
98-117	2,9	3,37	5,06	2,65	3,49	8,9	4,16	3,53	3,04	11,07	3,68	**4,71**
117-138	6,44	3,72	12,06	2,52	3,32	5,87	6,6	4,81	5	11,4	2,68	**5,85**
138-161	7,25	7,86	5,01	2,9	3,17	4,76	5,74	2,52	6,21	7,11	7,15	**5,42**
161-180	4,65	6,24	4,33	2,64	1,84	3,84	4,65	2,66	3,2	4,94	4	**3,91**
180-193	2,12	1,66	0,97	1,29	0,98	1,05	2,4	1,55	2,12	2,14	2,64	**1,72**
193-211	7,98	5,39	5,63	4,64	3,9	6,59	12,99	4,49	4,91	2,41	10,89	**6,35**
211-218	7,1	3,46	6,33	4,38	1,36	0,65	7,05	5,77	7,89	2,27	7,7	**4,91**
218-222	11,05	14,15	7,91	19,5	4,76	5,71	12,33	15,15	8,29	4,63	14,09	**10,69**
222-238	9,67	8,25	5,93	9,05	6,55	6,84	7,63	8,21	14,16	5,13	8,27	**8,15**
238-244	5,52	5,84	6,32	16,71	8,99	9,89	1,73	18,52	17,49	6,39	11,43	**9,89**
244-249	16,02	19,41	17,72	12,26	12,7	16,44	10,91	24,24	15,47	6,88	13,72	**15,07**
249-253	1,38	8,76	0	2,79	18,25	13,7	1,95	15,15	1,38	2,31	1,2	**6,08**
253-259	0,46	4,49	1,05	0,93	6,88	3,04	0,9	10,1	0	1,32	0,41	**2,69**
259-268	0,31	0,6	0,7	6,81	10,58	1,52	0	2,24	0	0	0,27	**2,09**
268-270	0	8,09	0	29,25	25,39	0	0	0	0	0	0	**5,7**
270-275	0	0	3,8	24,51	31,11	2,74	0	2,02	1,1	0	0,49	**5,97**

Figure 2. The monetary index (‰/year) of the cities of *Dacia*.

	Rural Settlements								Mean
	Cioroiu Nou	Cristeşti	Gârla Mare	Micăsasa	Orlea	Group I - *Dac Por*	Group II - *Dac Apul*	Gruop III -*Dac Malv*	
98-117	4,34	6,58	4,64	8,16	4,58	6,43	9,18	2,72	**5,77**
117-138	3,11	17,54	6,87	11,82	2,47	1,36	4,86	4,54	**6,57**
138-161	9,96	6,58	6,44	9,46	6,6	4,76	6,37	7,37	**7,19**
161-180	4,57	1,38	2,17	4,11	2,21	1,5	4,29	3,22	**2,93**
180-193	0	4,05	1,59	4,91	1,71	2,19	3,14	3,14	**2,59**
193-211	6,04	0	4,58	6,3	9,57	11,9	4,54	4,16	**5,89**
211-218	3,1	0	4,42	5,07	5,66	6,12	4,37	8,76	**4,69**
218-222	27,17	13,15	5,16	7,09	17,95	28,57	7,65	11,9	**14,83**
222-238	9,51	4,93	23,19	2,22	12,06	11,61	7,65	12,33	**10,44**
238-244	14,49	4,37	6,87	0	12,78	7,14	8,5	11,34	**8,19**
244-249	8,69	10,53	0	1,42	5,94	14,28	18,36	12,24	**8,93**
249-253	0	0	0	0	1,24	0	2,55	1,7	**0,69**
253-259	0	0	0	0	0	0	0	0	**0**
259-268	0	0	0	0	0,83	0	1,13	2,27	**0,53**
268-270	0	0	0	0	1,24	0	5,1	0	**0,79**
270-275	0	10,53	0	0	0,99	0	0	6,8	**2,29**

Figure 3. The monetary index (‰/year) of the rural settlements of *Dacia*.

	Military Settlements									Mean
	Alba Iulia	Bumbeşti-Jiu	Căşeiu	Gherla	Ilişua	Moigrad 'Sub Ferice'	Romita	Stolniceni	Veţel	
98-117	2,27	11,82	10	8,04	1,04	6,35	5	10,77	2,32	**6,4**
117-138	5,05	7,79	24,76	9,35	12,9	6,42	7,94	12,45	8,86	**10,61**
138-161	8,21	7,57	4,17	6,7	9,55	7,94	3,47	7,05	13,57	**7,58**
161-180	5,58	5,74	2,11	3,76	3,29	4,59	1,75	2,43	4,89	**3,79**
180-193	4,66	1,4	3,08	2,75	1,6	4,27	6,41	0	7,15	**3,48**
193-211	5,89	3,03	4,44	7,94	12,73	12,35	6,48	6,84	1,29	**6,78**
211-218	4,33	7,79	0	2,55	2,97	5,67	4,76	4,39	3,32	**3,98**
218-222	18,94	0	0	4,46	15,62	7,94	12,5	11,53	11,63	**9,18**
222-238	4,73	2,27	1,25	4,46	3,91	5,95	7,29	2,89	5,81	**4,28**
238-244	7,57	12,12	0	11,9	0	1,32	8,33	10,26	3,88	**6,15**
244-249	15,15	14,54	0	7,14	4,17	1,59	33,33	0	9,3	**9,47**
249-253	0	0	0	0	0	0	0	0	0	**0**
253-259	12,63	0	0	0	0	0	0	0	0	**1,4**
259-268	0	0	0	0	0	0	0	0	0	**0**
268-270	0	0	0	0	0	0	0	0	0	**0**
270-275	0	0	0	3,57	0	0	0	0	0	**0,4**

Figure 4. The monetary index (‰/year) of the military settlements of *Dacia*.

	Military Fortifications														Mean
	Alba Iulia	Bologa	Buciumi	Căşeiu	Drobeta	Gherla	Gilău	Ilişua	Jupa	Moigrad 'Pomet'	Moigrad *Statio*	Răcarii De Jos	Slăveni	Turda	
98-117	4,65	12,06	18,64	17,01	2,54	8,56	9,34	12,57	13,04	9,8	12,8	3,77	0,93	2,04	**9,13**
117-138	8,86	8,21	9,22	13,92	2,29	9,78	13,08	11,41	4,83	8,38	5,81	3,59	0,59	1,94	**7,28**
138-161	1,94	8,62	5,06	3,01	4,02	4,85	5,49	5,42	4,84	7,56	8,54	7,86	2,83	3,46	**5,25**
161-180	3,67	3,62	2,89	2,17	2,39	5,41	2,89	2,49	1,53	3,5	3,21	2,98	2,92	3,58	**3,09**
180-193	1,79	0	0,89	1,59	1,24	1,58	1,69	0,68	1,11	1,79	3,75	1,45	0,47	3,72	**1,55**
193-211	7,75	5,75	5,46	1,72	1,34	9,89	4,88	5,26	4,03	5,87	12,19	6,29	6,52	13,26	**6,44**
211-218	6,64	0	1,65	0	3,83	1,96	1,57	2,11	10,78	2,85	0	10,82	12,35	6,47	**4,36**
218-222	29,07	8,62	8,67	10,31	2,01	8,56	8,24	3,7	3,62	8,3	3,05	4,72	26,23	24,17	**10,66**
222-238	11,63	6,46	3,25	5,15	9,22	5,56	6,18	5,18	6,34	4,54	3,05	7,08	20,45	13,31	**7,67**
238-244	3,88	0	4,82	1,72	12,51	1,[illegible]4	3,66	3,94	4,83	5,54	4,06	28,3	18,52	6,8	**7,12**
244-249	4,65	13,79	3,47	16,49	27,34	10,96	15,38	17,75	11,59	15,28	0	11,32	18,52	12,08	**12,76**
249-253	11,63	0	0,72	0	16,76	0	0	0,74	25,36	4,15	0	9,43	0	3,77	**5,18**
253-259	0	0	0	0	1,79	0	0	0	2,41	1,11	0	0	0	1,26	**0,47**
259-268	0	0	0	0	7,45	0,76	0	0	1,61	0	0	0	0	0	**0,7**
268-270	0	0	0	0	18,77	0	0	0	0	0	0	0	0	0	**1,34**
270-275	0	0	0	0	28,42	0	0	0	0	0	0	0	0	0,3	**2,05**

Figure 5. The monetary index (‰/year) of the military fortifications of *Dacia*.

	Dacia		*Pan Inf*		*Pan Sup*		*Noricum*	*Raetia*		*Germ Sup*		*Agri Decumates*		*Germ Inf*		*Gal Bel*
	Civ	**Mil**	**Civ**	**Mil**	**Civ**	**Mil**	**Civ**	**Civ**	**Mil**	**Civ**	**Mil**	**Civ**	**Mil**	**Civ**	**Mil**	**Civ**
98-117	5,63	9,13	4,25	2,57	2,86	2,72	3,08	10,96	8,94	8,19	5,64	10	6,41	4,84	13,97	2,72
117-138	7,68	7,28	4,45	3,56	3,96	3,94	4,35	7,91	6,65	7,03	6,73	8,53	7,41	6,91	6,03	2,89
138-161	6,73	5,25	2,59	1,76	3,92	4,92	5,79	6,6	5,89	7,58	6,97	7,82	7,78	5,7	1,55	3,17
161-180	3,54	3,09	2,35	2,13	4,24	4,94	5,43	5,57	5,34	7,59	7,32	8,16	7,76	5,99	6,7	3,63
180-193	2,59	1,55	0,98	1,63	1,55	1,87	2,18	2,92	2,68	3,69	3,95	3,94	4,22	5,1	1,6	1,82
193-211	6,34	6,44	3,99	2,44	3,86	3,41	4,26	2,69	7,38	3,4	5,85	3,93	6,49	2,97	1,89	0,71
211-218	4,53	4,36	0,65	1,03	1,99	2,41	1,83	2,98	6,35	2,57	3,19	2,77	3,33	1,77	0,18	0,74
218-222	11,56	10,66	7,01	2,14	7,57	7,83	6,62	4,51	7,8	7,71	9,76	7,76	11,11	6,27	0,92	0,76
222-238	7,62	7,67	4,51	2,97	5,02	4,56	3,58	3,41	3,45	3,42	5,26	3,06	5,91	1,86	0,38	0,83
238-244	8,08	7,12	7,98	5,96	5,42	5,83	5,14	2,28	1,43	2,56	3,55	2,3	3,24	1,92	0,82	1,02
244-249	11,16	12,76	7,36	5,71	6,14	6,35	3,26	3,21	0,8	2,79	3,33	2,2	2,12	1,82	2,37	0,38
249-253	2,26	5,18	4,86	4,43	5,84	8,47	2,97	3,97	0,78	2,37	1,86	1,82	1,3	3,19	0,62	0,47
253-259	1,36	0,47	5,78	1,54	3,36	2,14	2,28	0,73	0,92	0,6	0,41	0,23	0,56	1,32	1,66	0,32
259-268	0,87	0,7	18,56	24,12	16,01	13,76	16,62	4,66	5,25	2,6	1,67	0,94	0,52	6,89	3,89	6,23
268-270	2,16	1,34	53,42	96,67	52,8	51,4	42,42	24,61	20,19	16,67	8,35	4,61	0,78	32,88	59,12	94,3
270-275	2,88	2,05	22,36	31,95	22,45	21,28	20,86	4,55	5,05	9,6	11,39	0,96	0,49	30,25	25,26	85,08

Figure 6. The monetary index (‰/year) of civilian settlements and military fortifications of *Dacia*, *Pannonia Inferior*, *Pannonia Superior*, *Noricum*, *Raetia*, *Germania Superior*, *Agri Decumates*, *Germania Inferior* and *Gallia Belgica* (years AD 98-275).

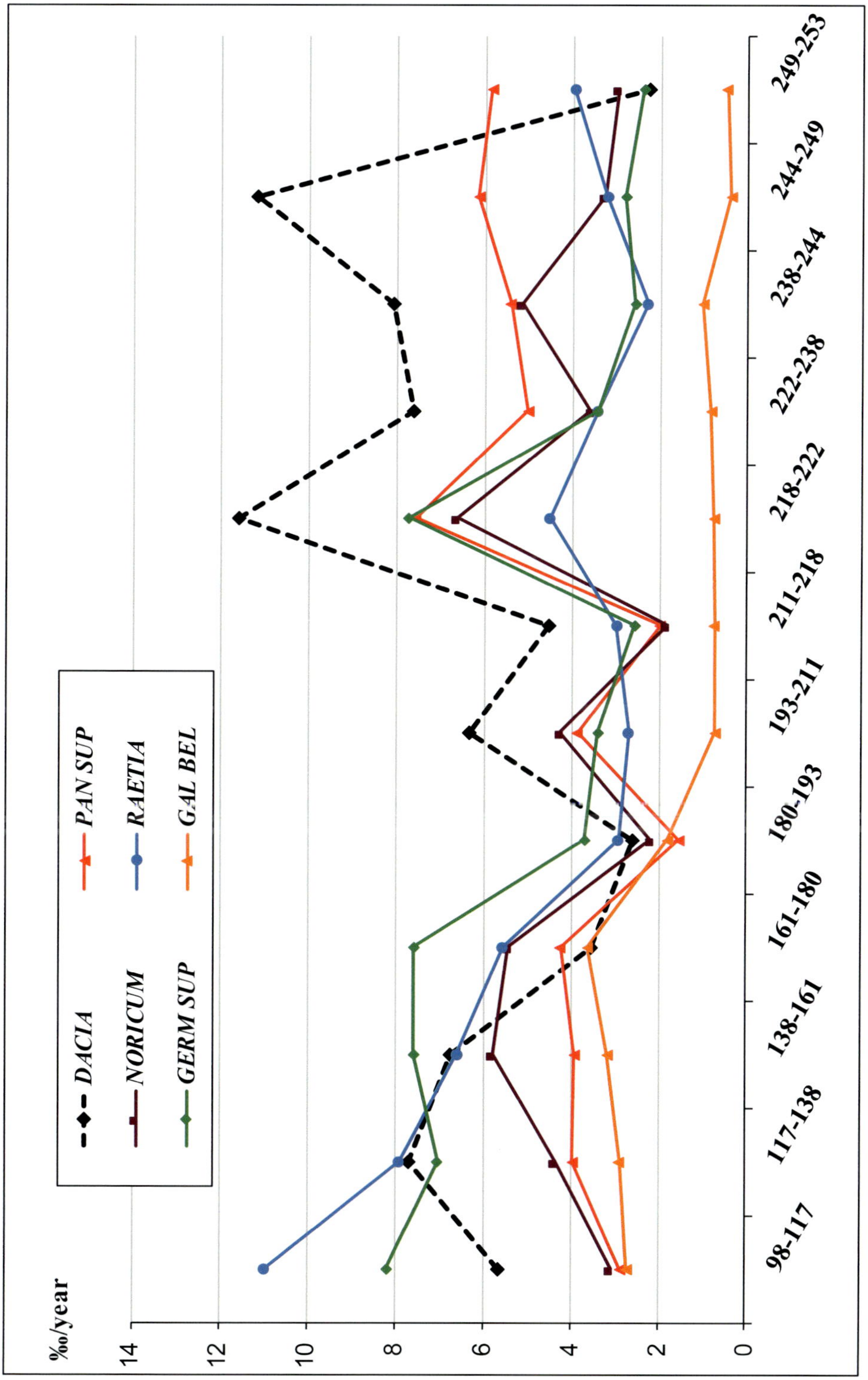

Figure 7. The monetary index (‰/year) of the civilian settlements of *Dacia*, *Pannonia Superior*, *Noricum*, *Raetia*, *Germania Superior* and *Gallia Belgica* (years AD 98-253).

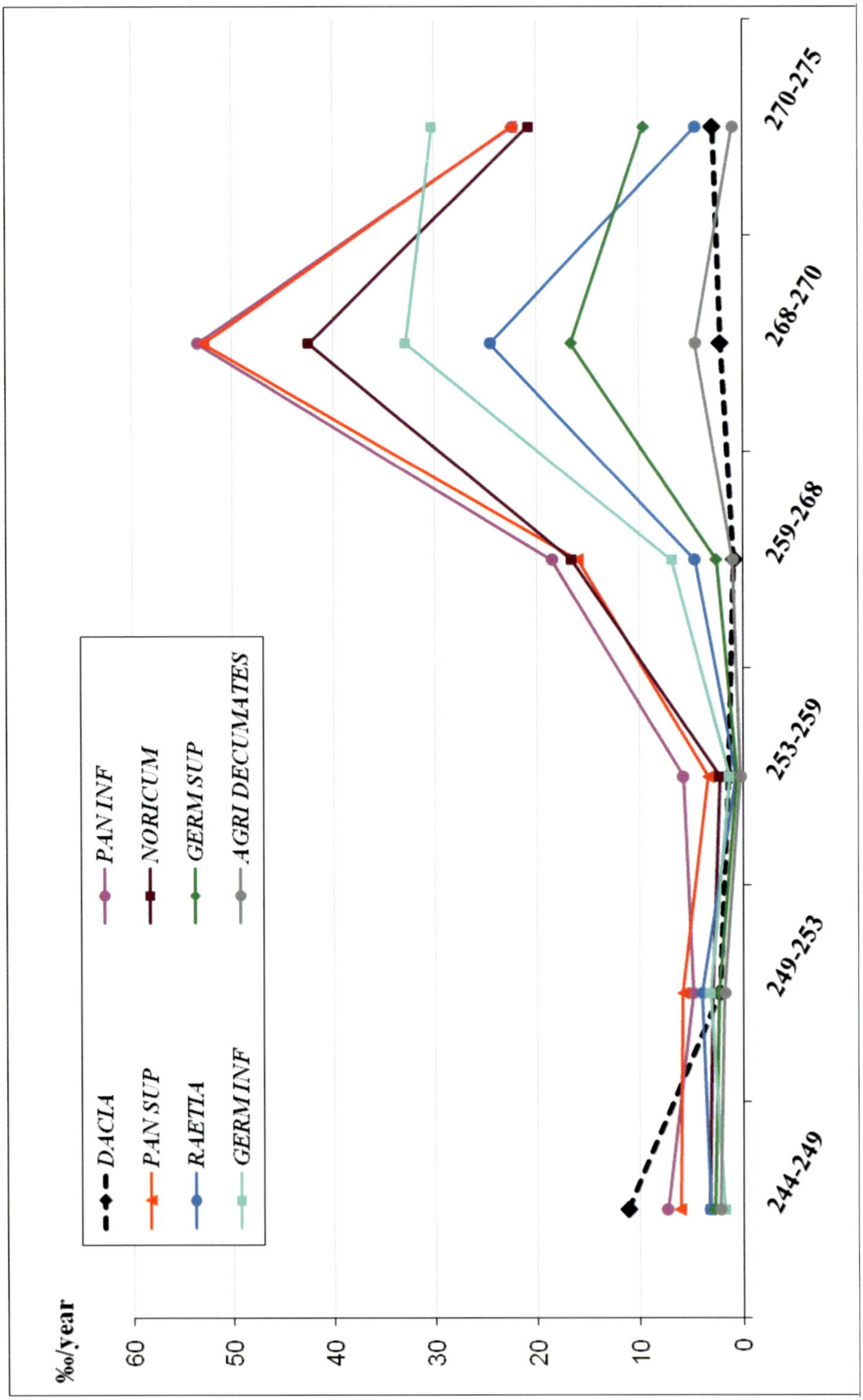

Figure 8. The monetary index (‰/year) of the civilian settlements of *Dacia*, *Pannonia Inferior*, *Pannonia Superior*, *Noricum*, *Raetia*, *Germania Superior*, *Germania Inferior* and *Agri Decumates* (years AD 244-275).

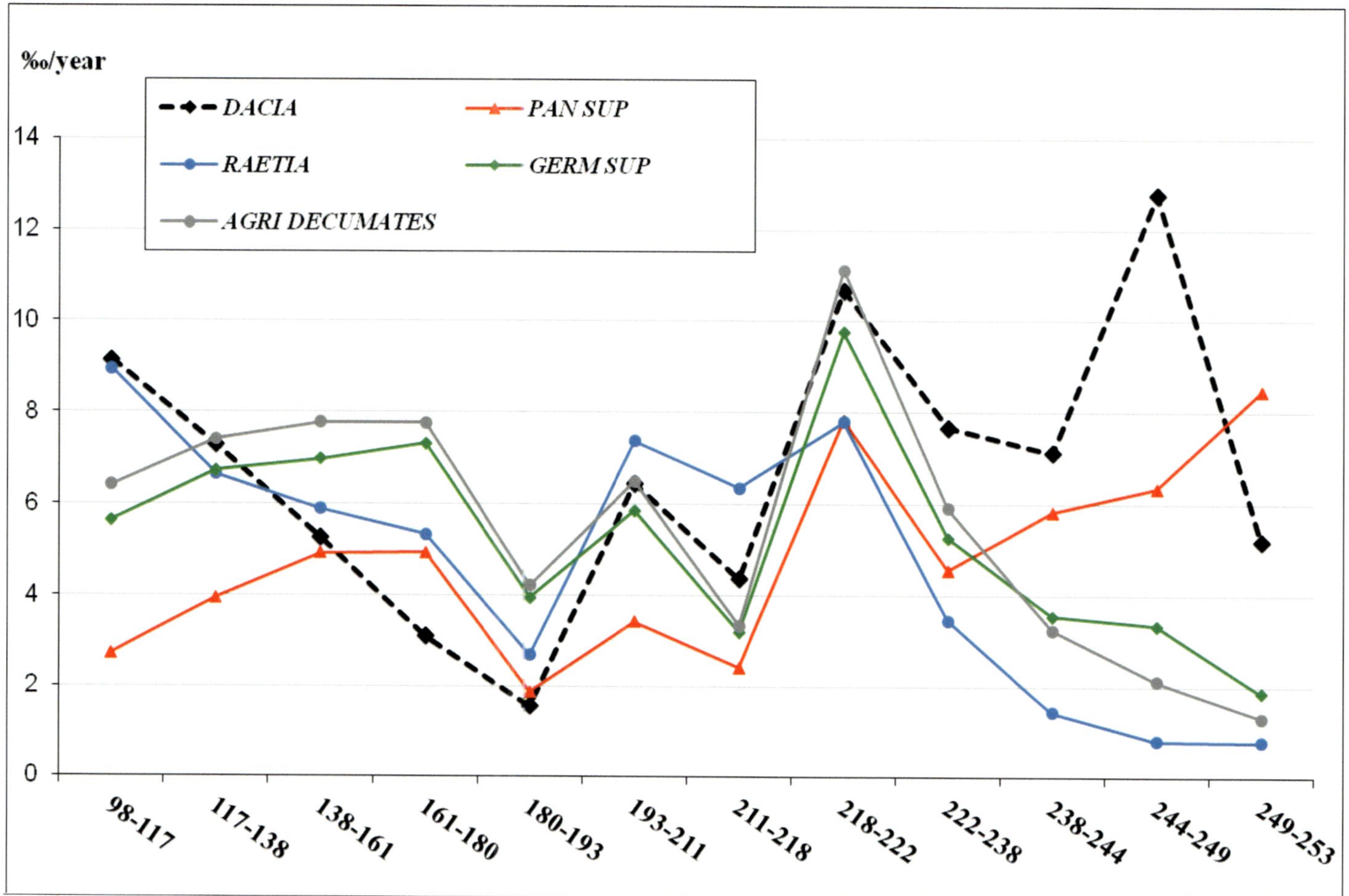

Figure 9. The monetary index (‰/year) of the military fortifications of *Dacia*, *Pannonia Superior*, *Raetia*, *Germania Superior* and *Agri Decumates* (years AD 98-253).

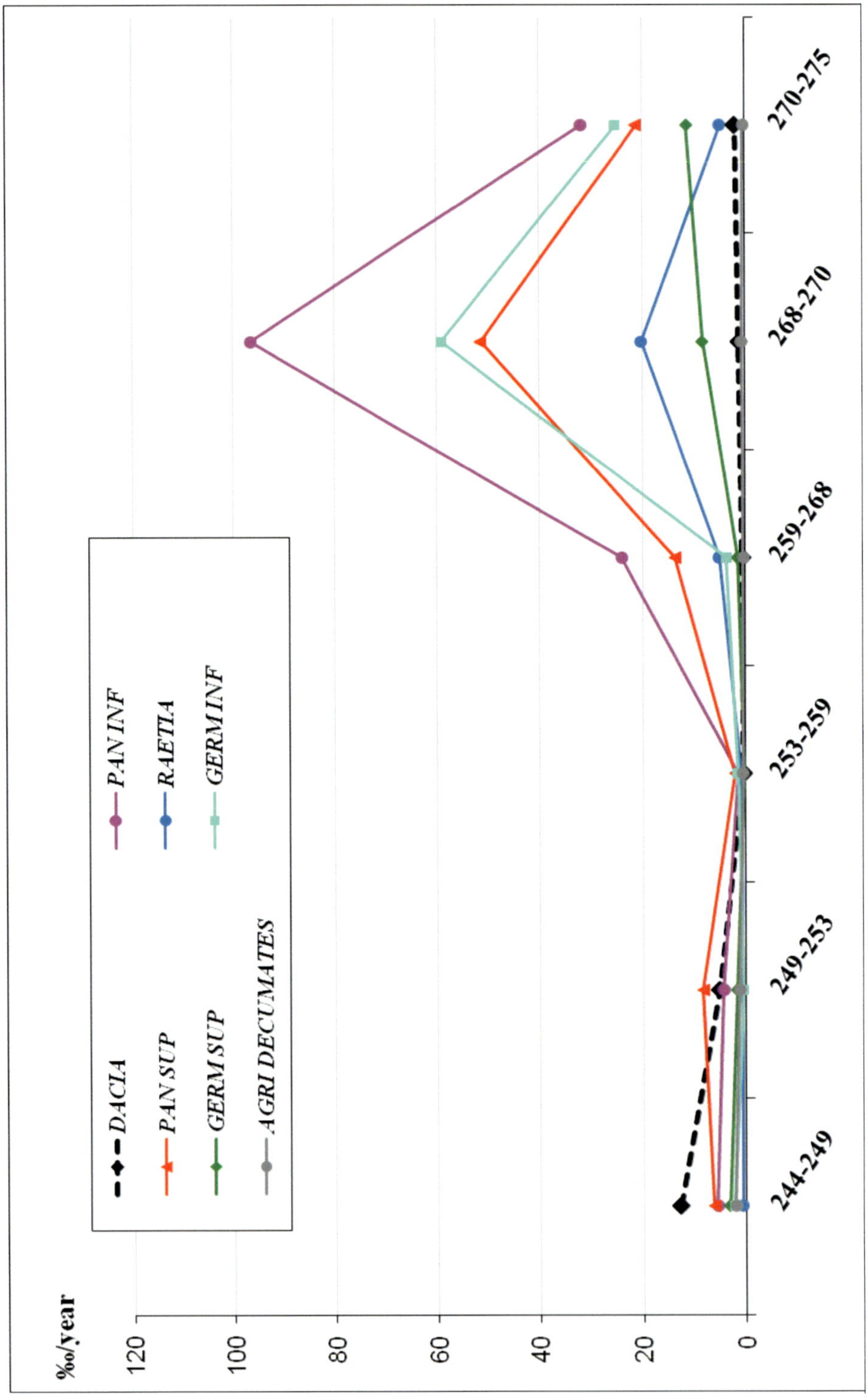

Figure 10. The monetary index (‰/year) of the military fortifications of *Dacia*, *Pannonia Inferior*, *Pannonia Superior*, *Raetia*, *Germania Superior*, *Germania Inferior* and *Agri Decumates* (years AD 244-275).

Überlegungen zur Romanisierung jenseits des dako-moesischen Limes im Spannungsfeld zwischen Schulbuch, Fachwissenschaft und Politik

Alexandru Popa

Muzeul Naţional al Carpaţilor Răsăriteni, Sfântu-Gheorghe

Abstract

The demystification of history is an *en vogue* term used in historical research regarding the post-socialist region. One can ascertain that historical research conducted in many countries of the communist block have revealed and superseded a whole series of historical myths and fabrications of the preceding period. At the same time one can observe that new historical myths, with a clear political influence, have emerged and been promoted in the communist period. In this presentation I intend to discuss the myth of 'The Romanisation of the ancestors of the Romanian people', which is a frequent topic found in Romanian and Moldavian textbooks. I also intend to track the differences between the modern historical discourse with regard to Romanisation and the ways this phenomenon is presented in both older and newer textbooks. As a base for my investigation I have used history textbooks from Moldavia issued after World War II.

Keywords: Romanisation, modern historical discourse

Ausgangssituation

Als Altertumsforscher mit Blick auf das Forschungsgebiet Südosteuropa während der 'Römerzeit' stellte ich in meinem privaten Umfeld fest, dass die moldauischen Schulbücher nur begrenzt Bezug auf die Forschungsergebnisse der letzten Jahrzehnte nehmen. Diese Sachlage veranlasste mich dazu, parallel zu frühgeschichtlichen Arbeiten auch Fragestellungen der Rezeptionsgeschichte und Schulbuchforschung zu formulieren, um die Kollegen dafür zu sensibilisieren, dass der aktuelle Forschungsstand zu manchen Problemen der Frühgeschichte den Schülern nicht mehr konsequent übermittelt wird. In dieser Studie möchte ich mich mit 'Romanisierung in Dakien und jenseits des Limes in den Schulbüchern' beschäftigen bzw. mich grundsätzlich nur auf einen separaten Aspekt der Romanisierung konzentrieren – auf die sog. exogene Romanisierung. Dabei widmet sich diese Studie jedoch keinen schulbuchdidaktischen bzw. pädagogischen Fragestellungen, sondern verfolgt nur einen rezeptionsgeschichtlichen Ansatz. Im Fokus meiner Analyse stehen daher nur solche Fragen ob geschichtliche Zusammenhänge zur Romanisierung in den Schulbüchern wissenschaftlich zeitgemäß und adäquat dargestellt wurden.

Romanisierung in der modernen Forschung

Forschungsgeschichtlich gesehen, ist heute 'Romanisierung' nicht gleich 'Romanisierung' (Woolf 2012. Vgl. auch den Sammelband Rubel 2011). Wie für viele andere Regionen der

Römischen Welt ist auch für das Gebiet nördlich der unteren Donau anzunehmen, dass es sich unter Romanisierung nicht um einen starren, einfach zu definierenden bzw. zu fassenden Prozess handelt[1]. Es geht vielmehr um einen Sammelbegriff, unter welchem sich verschiedene Formen der Akkulturation verbergen. Die Variationsformen sind in Zeit und Raum sehr ausgeprägt (Alföldy 2005). Wie bereits erwähnt möchte ich mich auf die sog. exogene Romanisierung fokussieren[2]. Dabei geht es um eine Romanisierung der von den Römern nie unterworfenen Völkergruppen bzw. um eine Romanisierung vor der eigentlichen römischen Okkupation der jeweiligen Regionen (siehe auch Popa 2013, 141-144). Diese Bevölkerung wird in der rumänischsprachigen Fachliteratur meist unter dem Begriff 'freie Daker' gefasst (siehe dazu Ioniţă 2001, 401-405), mit der Bedeutung 'von den Römern nicht unterworfene Bewohner Dakiens' (Macrea 1968). Dabei handelt es sich um einen wohl nationalistisch geprägten Namen[3], der genauso stark politisiert ist, wie zum Beispiel das '*freie Germanien*' in Mitteleuropa[4]. In der rumänischen und moldauischen Altertumsforschung wird die These vertreten, dass nach der Gründung der Provinz Dakien, nicht nur ihre Gebiete, sondern auch die Völkerschaften und Regionen jenseits des untermösisch-dakischen Limes (im heutigen Moldova und östlichen Walachei) (mit-) romanisiert wurden (Daicoviciu 1940, 24. Siehe auch Berciu 1978, 78). Die Annahme, dass die Romanisierung auch ohne die unmittelbare Anwesenheit des 'Römischen' stattfinden könnte, würde bedeuten, dass der Verhaltenswandel der Bevölkerung allein auf die externen, 'kontaktlosen' Einflüsse aus dem Römischen Reich zurückzuführen ist (Krausse 2006, 51-56). Als Beleg dafür sind oft die sog. 'römischen Importe' überbewertend interpretiert (siehe die Kritik bei Popa 2011). Wie die Untersuchungen aus den letzten Jahren jedoch zeigen, bezeugen die römische Funde im Barbaricum an der unteren Donau keine Romanisierung der Menschen. Man kann höchstens eine Ausbreitung von einigen Elementen provinzial-römischer materieller Kultur feststellen (vgl. Popa 2013, 144). Es handelt sich meines Erachtens um eine Diffusion der Gegenstände provinzial-römischer Herkunft und nicht um eine Akkulturation der Bevölkerung von jenseits des Limes[5].

Romanisierung in den moldauischen Lehrbüchern

Betrachtet man die Darstellung in den einzelnen Schulbüchern, ergeben sich vom Buch zu Buch und Epoche zu Epoche interessante Unterschiede in den uns interessierten Fragestellungen zur Romanisierung der freien Daker. Im Folgenden möchte ich einige Auszüge aus Schulbüchern der Republik Moldau vorstellen, die die Darstellung der Romanisierung illustrieren:

Sowjetische Zeit

- '*Geschichte der moldawischen sowjetischen sozialistischen Republik*', für 7. Klasse[6].

[1] Zur Diskussion über die Überbewertung der Romanisierung in der rumänischen Fachliteratur siehe Rubel 2010.
[2] Vgl. die Diskussion zum 'exogenen Kulturwandel' bei Krausse 2006, 51-56.
[3] Zu den nationalistischen 'Versuchungen' der rumänischen Archäologie und Altertumsforschung siehe Babeş 2007. Vgl. auch Niculescu 2005 sowie Ursprung 2004 / 2005.
[4] Alföldi 1997. In Rumänien wurde auch der Begriff 'Dacia liberă' (Freies Dakien) benutzt – siehe Daicoviciu 1940, 19 sowie Daicoviciu 1964.
[5] Vgl. mit Situation in der *Germania magna* – Meyer 2013, 70-71.
[6] Für die Untersuchung standen drei Buchausgaben aus den Jahren 1973, 1980 und 1983 zur Verfügung. Da die Schulbücher erst auf Russisch verfasst wurden und erst dann ins 'moldawische' übersetz worden sind, habe ich

Ausgabe 1973 (Grosul 1973). Die uns interessierende Thematik wird in diesem Schulbuch innerhalb des Thema zum gesamten ersten nachchristliche Jahrtausend abgehandelt ('*Stammesbünde auf dem Gebiet Moldawiens, 1.-10. Jh., S. 13-19*'). Die Erzählung beginnt mit der Geschichte von Dakien, obwohl diese römische Provinz eigentlich relativ weit entfernt von den damaligen Gebieten der sowjetischen Republik Moldawien lag:

> '*Auch wenn das heutige Territorium Moldawiens nicht als Teil Dakien gewesen ist, sind die römische Einflüsse auch hierher eingedrungen. Dies bezeugen zahlreiche Funde von römischer Münzen, von Geschirrstücken und anderer alltäglichen Sachen.*' (Grosul u.a. 1973, 15).

Bei der Aufzählung der dort lebenden Ethnien kommt für die Autoren neben Sarmaten, Goten, oder Slawen in diesem Gebiet keine dakische Bevölkerung in Frage. Es wird jedoch den Schülern mitgeteilt, dass das ethnische Bild dieser Bevölkerung bunt gemischt gewesen sei. Kein Wort wird auch zur eventuellen Romanisierung dieser Bevölkerungsgruppen verloren. In der nächsten von uns untersuchten Ausgabe dieses Schulbuches (Grosul 1980) wurde auch der für den (rumänischen) Gründungsmythos entscheidende Passus über die Kontinuität der romanischen Bevölkerung nördlich und südlich der unteren Donau integriert:

> '*...die romanisierte Bevölkerung nördlich und südlich der unteren Donau bleibt bis zu heutigen Tagen erhalten*'. Bei der Aufzählung der in den Gebieten der damaligen Republik Moldawien siedelnden Völker kommen in dieser Lehrbuchausgabe die Geten vor (Grosul u.a. 1980, 11).

Eine Veränderung in der Darstellungsweise der Romanisierung findet in der 4. Ausgabe dieses Schulbuches statt[7]. Im Vergleich zu den älteren Editionen wird hier über Romanisierung nicht nur in Dakien berichtet, sondern auch in Untermösien. Dabei findet eine starke Vermischung des geschichtlichen Elementes mit dem politologischen (Stichwort 'Klassengesellschaft'), so dass in vielen Sätzen eine Verbindung zur 'Unterdrückung der Sklaven', zum 'Klassenkampf' oder zur Existenz der 'gehassten Großgrundbesitzer' aufgebaut wird. Zur Romanisierung selbst wird der Schüler wie folgt unterrichtet (Dragnev/Sovetov 1988, 15-17):

> *Neben Geten und Daker siedeln viele Kolonisten aus verschiedenen Gebieten des Reiches. Die ganze römische Administration, die Legionäre und Kolonisten sprachen Latein. Schrittweise begann auch die geto-dakische Bevölkerung aus den besetzten Gebieten diese Sprache zu sprechen. Sie übernahm auch einige römische Bräuche, Werkzeuge und Alltagssachen; einige eigene Sitten wurden jedoch beibehalten. In den römischen Provinzen, sowohl südlich als auch nördlich der unteren Donau fand die Romanisierung statt: die Bevölkerung sprach Latein, ihr Haushalt, das gesellschaftliche Leben und die Kultur waren den römischen ähnlich. Aus diesen Gründen gilt diese Bevölkerung als romanisiert. Im 3. Jh. n. Chr. lebte in der von den Römern eroberten Karpaten-Donau-Region eine bereits romanisierte Bevölkerung. ... Die romanisierte Bevölkerung war eins der entfernten Vorfahren des moldauischen Volkes. ...*

für die Analyse die russischsprachigen Ausgaben benutzt. Alle wurden von Autorenkollektiven geschrieben; der Leiter der Arbeitsgruppe kam aus dem Fachinstitut der Akademie der Wissenschaften in Chişinău.

[7] Mir war die russische Version von 1983 (Dragnev/Sovetov 1983) und 'moldausche' von 1988 (Dragnev/Sovetov 1988) zugänglich.

> *In den nicht eroberten Gebieten der Karpaten-Dnestr-Region (sprich – zwischen den Karpaten Gebirgen und Fluss Dnjestr) lebten weiterhin Thraker, von denen die Karpen den größten Teil stellten. Hierher siedelten*[8] *auch nomadische Sarmaten, später germanische Stämme der Goten und die Slawen über*[9]. *Die römische Kultur hat auf sie einen starken Einfluss ausgeübt, aber diese Stämme haben sich der römischen Macht nicht unterworfen, wurden nicht romanisiert und behielten größtenteils ihre Kultur und Sprache* (Dragnev/Sovetov 1983, 16).

Es lässt sich vermerken, dass im Unterschied zu den letzten beiden angesprochenen Ausgaben verschwinden aus der Erzählung '*die guten Beziehungen dieser Völker mit den Römern*'. Die römischen Funde oder deren lokale Nachahmungen (Münzen, Geschirr, u.a. Fundgattungen) kommen in der Erzählung nicht mehr vor. In den Aufgaben zum Thema kommen in dieser Ausgabe Kontrollfragen vor, die die Romanisierung direkt ansprechen: '*Erklären Sie das: die <Romanisierung>*'; '*Zeigen Sie auf der Karte in welchen Gebieten nördlich der Donau die Romanisierung stattfand*'.

Zu dieser Schulbuchausgabe wurde auch ein Textbuch zusammengestellt (Dragnev 1987). Zu unserem Thema würde ein einziger Textauszug (5 Textzeilen) von Eutropius passen, in dem der antike Autor über die Kolonisation von Dakien spricht. Bemerkenswert sind die Kommentare des Herausgebers dazu (Dragnev 1987, 10): ohne jegliche Erklärung meint der moderne 'Kommentator' des antiken Quelltextes, dass Eutropius mit der Vernichtung der männlichen Bevölkerung Dakiens übertreiben würde. Außerdem kommt der Kommentator zum Schluss, dass aus dem Zitat abzuleiten ist, dass diese gesamte Bevölkerung nur Latein gesprochen hätte. Dies hätte dann zur Romanisierung der Provinzbevölkerung beigetragen. Bei der Einführung in das nachfolgende Thema kommt der Zusammensteller im Kontext der Ethnogenese der Moldawier auch auf die Romanisierung zurück: diese wird von ihm als eine Etappe der Ethnogenese gesehen, deren wichtigste Momente – a) die römischen Eroberungen nördlich der Donau im 2.-3. Jh. n. Chr., b) Entstehung der Provinz Dacia und c) Romanisierung der einheimischen Bevölkerung – hervortreten (Dragnev 1987, 10).

Dies ist ungefähr die Art und Weise wie sich die Darstellung der Romanisierung in den Schulbüchern der 1970-1980iger Jahre veränderte.

Unabhängige Republik Moldau

- 'Istoria Românilor. Epoca veche. Manual experimental pentru clasa a V-a' (Geschichte der Rumänen. Antike. Experimentelles Schulbuch für die 5. Klasse)

1997 wurde vom Verlag Cartdidact die erste Auflage dieses Schulbuches herausgebracht, die die Ur-, Vor- und Frühgeschichte in rumänischen Nationalterritorien abhandelt (Niculiţă 1997). Wenige Jahre danach wurde der Autorentext in einem Schulbuch zum Gesamtfach 'Geschichte' für die 5. Klasse integriert, in dem die Erzählungen sowohl für die Weltgeschichte als auch für Geschichte der Rumänen wiedergegeben waren (Niculiţă

[8] Für diesen Einwanderungsprozess wird im Russischen ein politisch wenig geladener Ausdruck 'pereselit'sja' verwendet – es geht also nicht um eine Einwanderung oder Migration, sondern um Übersiedlung, die sich pazifistischer anhört als beiden anderen Ausdrücke.

[9] Aus dieser Formulierung lässt sich folglich erschließen, dass die Slawen sich hier in der gleichen zeitlichen Dimension wie die Goten befinden.

2000). Da die Texte des zur Diskussion stehenden Problems sich voneinander nicht allzu viel unterscheiden, werden sie hier zusammenfassend abgehandelt.

Der Begriff der 'Romanisierung' kommt zum ersten Mal bei der Erzählung zu den Dakerkriegen vom Kaiser Trajan vor[10]. Dieser wird jedoch nur in der Kapitelüberschrift ('Anfang der Romanisierung. Ursachen der dako-römischen Kriege') bzw. als 'wichtiger Begriff' im didaktischen Teil am Anfang der Lektion erwähnt. Auf eine dedizierte Erklärung des Begriffes oder auf ein Ausfächern der Kapitelüberschrift wird verzichtet. Der Schüler erfährt jedoch, dass

> *... die Bewohner der bereits früher eroberten Dobrudscha und Landesteile in Südmoldau 'sich als erste das Latein eingeeignet haben und die römischen Lebensart akzeptiert haben' und sich schrittweise, dank der zahlreichen kulturellen und Handelsbeziehungen, in die römische Welt integriert haben* (Niculiţă u.a. 2000, 190).

Wahrscheinlich aus didaktischen Gründen bleibt die Erklärung des Begriffes bis zum Ende der Lektion offen. Erst auf der letzten Seite wird die Romanisierung zu einem '*neuen historischen Prozess*', der nach der römischen Eroberung bzw. nach Gründung der römischen Provinz Dakien ansetzt, postuliert.

> *Unter Romanisierung der Geto-Daker und anderer Völkerschaften aus diesem Raum versteht man die Aneignung des Latein, der Kultur und anderer Aspekte der römischen Zivilisation durch die Einheimischen* (Niculiţă u.a. 2000, 195.).

Bemerkenswert erscheint mir die Tatsache, dass in der darauffolgenden Lektion ('*Römische Herrschaft in Dakien*' (Niculiţă u.a. 2000, 196-199)) der Begriff 'Romanisierung' gar nicht vorkommt, obwohl er von der wissenschaftlichen Logik her er dort zu erwarten wäre. Dafür wird er in der Lektion zu den sog. 'freien Dakern' ('*Freie Daker und ihre Beziehungen zum Römischen Reich*') neu erwähnt – wieder einmal nur eine Erwähnung als '*wichtiger Begriff*' im didaktischen Teil, in Form von '*Romanisierung der freien Geto-Daker*' (Niculiţă u.a. 2000, 200-201).

Die nächste Lektion trägt den von uns untersuchten Begriff nicht nur im Titel ('*Romanisierung der Geto-Daker*') und Kapitelüberschriften ('*Romanisierung in den Provinzen Dakien und Moesien*', '*Romanisierung der freien Geto-Daker*') sondern auch im didaktischen Teil als Memo-Feld und zwischen den 'wichtigen Begriffen'.

Zum ersten Kapitel wird auf 1,5 Buchseiten über verschiedene Aspekte der römischen Präsenz in den eroberten Gebieten erzählt (Weiterbestehen der einheimischen Bevölkerung nach der römischen Eroberung; Anzahl und Stärke der dort befindlichen Streitkräften, Kolonisation durch zivile Bevölkerung aus den Provinzen, Urbanisation, römische Verwaltung, Rolle des Latein als Kommunikationssprache zwischen Dakern und Römern) – also alles was traditionsgemäß in der rumänischen Geschichtsschreiben zur Romanisierung beitragen sollte.

[10] In der rumänischsprachigen Literatur werden diese als 'dako-römische Kriege' bezeichnet – original 'Războaiele daco-romane' – Niculiţă u.a. 2000, 190.

Einen eigenen Weg geht der Autor mit der Romanisierung der sog. 'freien Geto-Daker': denen schreibt er eine

> *Romanisierung am meisten im linguistischen Aspekt. Die Aneignung der Sprache fand*
> - *durch zahlreiche christliche Missionare, die auf Latein predigten,*
> - *durch permanente Handelsbeziehungen mit römischen Handelsleuten,*
> - *durch Kriegsgefangene infolge der Überfälle [ins Reich],*
> - *durch den Kontakt mit den römischen Soldaten, die auf den Fortifikationslinien jenseits der Provinzen disloziert waren,*
>
> *statt.*
> *Die Romanisierung, definiert als vollständige Transformation der dakischen Ethnie in die lateinische Ethnie (?!), fand nur in den Städten und Handelsplätzen statt. Bei den freien Dakern beschränkte sich die Romanisierung nur auf die Aneignung/Übernahme des Lateins und einiger Errungenschaften römischer Zivilisation.*

Abschließend wird in einem separaten Memofeld die Romanisierung noch einmal wie folgt definiert:

> *Romanisierung stellt den historischen Prozess dar, bei dem die römische Zivilisation in allen Lebenssphären der lokalen Gemeinden durchdringt.*

Im Aufgabenteil zu dieser Lektion kommt der Begriff Romanisierung in drei (von sechs) Aufgaben wiederum vor: '*Definieren Sie den Begriff Romanisierung*', '*Analysieren Sie die Kräfte und die Mittel der Romanisierung*', '*Wie unterscheidet sich der Romanisierungsprozess in den Provinzen von dem bei den freien Geto-Dakern?*'.

Eigentlich sollte ein Fünftklässler bereits genug von diesem historischen Prozess der Romanisierung gehabt haben!? Nicht aber wenn es um einen moldauischen Fünftklässler geht! Weil die nächste Lektion des hier angesprochenen Schulbuchs diesen Begriff erneut ins Gespräch bringt. Wieder mal in der Überschrift zur Lektion ('*Christentum und seine Rolle im Romanisierungsprozess*' (Niculiţă u.a. 2000, 204-205), auch im didaktischen Teil am Anfang und am Ende der Lektion und dann mehrmals in der Erzählung selbst:

> *Das Christentum spielt eine wichtige Rolle im Romanisierungsprozess.*
> *Die Beziehungen der Geto-Daker zum Römischen Reich bleiben genauso stark [nach Aufgabe Dakiens] wie vorher. Dadurch lässt sich die Tatsache erklären, dass der Romanisierungsprozess sich auch in den folgenden Jahrhunderten fortsetzt.*

Somit wird der Romanisierung der Geto-Daker ein langes Leben vorhergesagt. So wird in der nächsten Lektion ('*Dako-römische Gemeinschaft nördlich der Balkan-Gebirge während des 4.-6. Jhs.*' (Niculiţă u.a. 2000, 206-209) einer der Wege aufgezeichnet, wie die Romanisierung der von den Römern nicht eroberten Gebiete stattfand:

> *Aus den ehemaligen Städten und aus den Zivilsiedlungen bei Militärkastellen gehen Latein sprechende (manche konnten sogar schreiben) Bevölkerungsgruppen über die Karpaten nach Osten und verbreiteten dadurch das Latein.*

Warum und wozu römische Staatsbürger, ehemalige Bewohner der Provinz Dacia die Karpaten nach Osten überqueren sollten(?) – wird in dieser Erzählung nicht erklärt.

> *Einen großen Einfluss auf den Romanisierungsprozess behält weiterhin die Provinz Untermösien, die im Rahmen des Oströmischen Reiches weiter existiert.*

Es sei hier nur kurz darauf hingewiesen, dass nach heutigem Dokumentationsstand die Provinz Untermösien im Jahre 86 n.Chr. entstanden ist und in der Regierungszeit des Kaisers Aurelian aufgelöst wurde. Die östlichen Teile der Provinz wurden damals als *Moesia secunda* reorganisiert und zur Regierungszeit Diokletians – als *Scythia minor*.

Die Romanisierung wird auch bei der Darlegung der diachron angelegten Lektion zu 'Dakorömern und ihren Beziehungen zu Wandervölkern' (Niculiţă u.a. 2000, 210-213) erwähnt. So erfährt der Fünftklässler dass

> *infolge der Romanisierung auf dem ganzen Territorium ein romanisches Gemeinwesen entsteht, wo eine vom Latein abstammende Sprache gesprochen wird und wo ein einziger christlicher Glaube praktiziert wird.*

Auch in der darauffolgenden Lektion ('*Enthnogenese der Rumänen*' [Niculiţă u.a. 2000, 214-215]) spricht der Schulbuchautor die Romanisierung ein weiteres Mal an:

> *Infolge des Romanisierungsprozesses auf dem ganzen Verbreitungsgebiet der Geto-Daker, sprich des historischen Dakiens*[11]*, bildet sich schrittweise ein großer romanisch besiedelter Raum. In diesem Gebiet haben die römischen Elemente zur Entstehung einer gründlichen und notwendigen Basis für das Erlernen der lateinischen Sprache effizient beigetragen.*

Das hier untersuchte Schulbuch beinhaltet neben den in Lektionen gegliederten Narrationen auch eine 'Synthese' (Niculiţă u.a. 2000, 216) und auch hier wird die Romanisierung noch einmal abgehandelt:

> *...In den Provinzen und benachbarten Gebieten findet der Romanisierungsprozess statt, der von dem letzten Jh. v. Chr. bis zum Fall der Grenzen des Oströmischen Reichs andauerte.*
> *Im Prozess der Romanisierung werden sich die Einheimischen mit der römischen Zivilisation vertraut machen, erlernen die lateinische Sprache, die zu dem einzigen Kommunikationsmittel mit den Römern und zusammenlebenden Völkern wird. Dieser Prozess endet mit der Entstehung der Vlachen-Rumänen und der gemeinsamen rumänischen Sprache.*

Und zum letzten Mal wird die Romanisierung im Glossar des Schulbuches (Niculiţă u.a. 2000, 219-222) abgehandelt:

> *Romanisierung – ein Prozess infolge dessen ein Volk die Sprache, die Zivilisation, die Sitten und die Eigenschaften der Römer übernommen hat.*

Ein weiteres Geschichtsschulbuch für die 5. Klasse aus der Republik Moldau wurde 2005 von C. und A. Popovici beim Verlag 'Lumina' in Chişinău veröffentlicht (Popovici/Popovici

[11] Hier ist die Opposition zwischen 'historischen' und 'römischen' Dakien zu beachten.

2005). Es handelt sich dabei um ein Lehrbuch für das Gesamtfach Geschichte. Hier begegnen wir dem Begriff Romanisierung am Anfang der Lektion über '*Römisches Dakien und die freien Daker*' (Popovici/Popovici 2005, 162-165), die als Teil des Kapitels '*Europa zur Zeit des Römischen Reichs*' eingegliedert wurde.

Bereits in der Einführung zur eigentlichen Narration erfährt der Schüler, dass die römische Herrschaft nördlich der Donau zur Romanisierung der autochthonen Bevölkerung führte und somit den Grundstein für die östliche Romanität legte. In der eigentlichen Erzählung kommt der Begriff nur ein einziges Mal vor:

> *Die Städte haben im Großen zur Romanisierung der autochthonen Bevölkerung beigetragen* (Popovici/Popovici 2005, 162).

Sonst begegnet der Schüler dem Begriff noch zwei Mal im didaktischen Teil am Ende der Lektion – als '*Begriff*' und im Aufgabenteil zur Lektion[12].

Das nachträgliche Aufarbeiten des Begriffes Romanisierung findet in einem Zusatz zur o.g. Lektion mit der Überschrift 'Romanisierung der Geto-Daker' statt (Popovici/Popovici 2005, 164-165). Daraus erfährt der Fünftklässler folgendes:

> *...In die Zeit römischer Herrschaft fällt der Prozess einer intensiven Romanisierung der autochthonen Bevölkerung. Dieser wird durch das Eindringen der römischen Zivilisation in alle Lebenssphären der Provinzbewohner charakterisiert und führt zum Ersetzten von deren Sprache durch das Latein.*
> *Die Romanisierung wurde von mehreren Faktoren*[13] *gefördert:*
> *Eroberung und Eingliederung Dakiens in den römische Staat;*
> *das Vorhanden einer römischen Verwaltung, die Latein für die Kontakte mit der autochthonen Bevölkerung nutzte;*
> *die Anwesenheit der römischen Armee, in die auch viele jungen Geto-Daker aufgenommen wurden;*
> *die Anwesenheit der Veteranen und Kolonisten aus allen Teilen des Imperiums;*
> *Attraktivität der von den Römern gebauten Städte, wo Latein gesprochen wurde, für die getodakische Bevölkerung.*
> *Die Romanisierung hat auch die freien Daker erreicht, die nicht unter direkter römischer Herrschaft standen. Die Romanisierung der freien Daker wurde nach dem Abzug der Römer aus der Provinz vertieft, als sie sich mit der Bevölkerung des römischen Dakiens vermischt hat. Nach 275 n. Chr. geht die Romanisierung der autochthonen Bevölkerung weiter, sie sei dabei durch die Kontakte südlich der Donau mit dem Römischen Reich sowie durch die Beziehungen zwischen christlichen Gemeinden beider Donauseiten.*
> *Infolge der Romanisierung akzeptieren Generationen von Geto-Dakern die römische Lebensart und lernen Latein.*

Außerdem wird die Romanisierung in dem Aufgabenteil der Lektion und im Evaluationsteil zum gesamten Kapitel zusätzlich besprochen. Dabei sollen die Schüler:

[12] Es geht um folgende Aufgabe: 'Schreibe ein Essay über das römische Dakien. Benutzte dabei die Worte: Provinz, Romanisierung, freie Daker, Limes.' Es ist mir unverständlich, dass der im Lektionstext noch nicht abgehandelte Begriff der Romanisierung bereits als Stützwort für ein Essay in der 5. Klasse (!) dienen soll.
[13] Die Autoren benutzten das Wort 'Cauza' – Grund, Ursache, was jedoch zu diesem Kontext nicht ganz passt.

die Begriffe und Wortkombinationen aufschreiben, die zum Verständnis des Romanisierungsprozesses der Geto-Daker beigetragen haben;
eine Liste von Problemen zusammenstellen, mit denen sich die geto-dakische Bevölkerung während des Romanisierungsprozesses konfrontiert gesehen hätte;
ein Schemata zusammenstellen, mit der Darstellung von Faktoren, die zur Romanisierung beigetragen haben, sowie von Vorteilen und Nachteilen der Romanisierung.

Wie im Schulbuch von Niculiţă wird die Romanisierung auch in diesem Schulbuch zuletzt im Glossar abgehandelt (Popovici/Popovici 2005, 208):

> *Romanisierung – ein Prozess infolge dessen ein Volk die Sprache, die Zivilisation und die Sitten der Römer übernommen hat*[14].

Soviel zur Romanisierung als Teil der Geschichtsnarration in der 5. Klasse der moldauischen Schulen. Zum Vergleich möchte ich jedoch auch die Darstellung der Romanisierung in einer der älteren Klassen vorstellen.

- 'Geschichte der Rumänen (Antike und Mittelalter)', 10. Klasse.

Die Geschichtssynthese für die 10. Klasse, die Fach 'Nationalgeschichte' vorgestellt wird, wurde von Gh. Postică verfasst und erschien im Verlag Civitas[15]. Beim ersten Blättern der Seiten zur Römerzeit wird man durch das Fehlen des gesuchten Begriffes verwirrend überrascht – weder bei der Narration zu den domitianischen oder trajanischen Dakerkriegen noch bei der Erzählung über die Gründung der römischen Provinz Dakien oder in den didaktischen Teilen dieser Lektionen kommt das Wort Romanisierung (bis auf zwei erst später entdeckte Ausnahmen) überhaupt vor. Die Lösung dieses 'Rätsels' versteckte sich jedoch in einer der nachfolgenden Lektionen ('Etnogeneza Românilor'/ Entstehung der Rumänen), in der ein ganzes Kapitel mit der Überschrift '*Romanisierung der Geto-Daker*' diesem historischen Prozess gewidmet wurde! (Dragnev/Postică 2001, 60-66).

In einer sehr straff strukturierten und systematisierten Narration werden alle denkbaren Aspekte der Romanisierung in einem strengen akademischen Still abgehandelt: Bedeutung, Voraussetzungen, Entfaltungswege, territoriale Schwerpunkte, Faktoren, Etappen, geschichtlicher Vorgang bei den Geto-Dakern. Das ganze akademische Wissen zu diesem Begriff wird dem Schüler auf sechs (A4) Buchseiten vorgestellt. Schauen wir uns jedoch die einzelnen Aspekte dieser Systematik der Romanisierung an:

Bedeutung:
Romanisierung stellt den Prozess der Assimilierung durch das Römische Reich von einigen antiken Völkern aus Europa, dem Nahen Osten und Nordafrika dar.
Romanisierung der Trako-Geto-Daker bedeutete die Zusammensetzung der römischen Zivilisation mit der autochthonen Zivilisation aus der karpaten-balkanischen Region, die Übernahme

[14] Diese Definition sieht der von Niculiţă sehr ähnlich (siehe oben) oder Niculiţă u.a. 2000, 222.
[15] In der ersten Ausgabe wurde diese als Teil des Schulbuches für Geschichte der Rumänen (Antike und Mittelalter) veröffentlicht (Dragnev/Postică 2001). Eine sehr ähnliche Textversion des Kapitels zur Antiken Geschichte im Gebiet des heutigen Rumänien wurde 2010 in einem Schulbuch für (Gesamt-) Geschichte wiedergegeben (Dragnev 2010).

der Kultur vom römischen Typ (? - der römischen Kultur wohl) durch die Einheimischen, der römischen sozialen, wirtschaftlichen, geistigen Strukturen und der lateinischen Sprache als Kommunikationsmittel.
Die Romanisierung hätte zwei aufeinanderfolgende Phasen gehabt: die ökonomisch-kulturelle Assimilierung und die sprachlich-geistige Assimilierung.
Chronologisch lässt sich die Romanisierung in den Zeitraum zwischen 2-1. Jh. v. Chr. und 4-5. Jh. n. Chr. ansetzen. Der geographische Raum der Romanisierung erstreckt sich über das ganze Gebiet des historischen Dakien, einschließlich der Gebiete der freien Daker und die nördliche Hälfte des balkanischen Thrakien. (Dragnev/Postică 2001, 61).

Am Ende der Lektion werden in einem Glossar viele dieser Begriffen noch einmal definiert:

Romanisierung - geschichtliches Phänomen der ethnisch-kulturellen und ethnisch-linguistischen Assimilierung einiger antiken Völkern aus Europa, dem Nahen Osten und Afrika durch die Römer.

Als Pendant dazu ist die folgende Definition zu betrachten:

Ethnisch-linguistische Assimilierung - das Phänomen der kulturellen, ethnischen und linguistischen Integration einer Gemeinschaft im Rahmen einer anderen, in deren Folge die Menschen aus der Ersten ihre alte Identität verlieren und eine neue ethnisch-linguistische erlangen.

Es folgen dann auch weitere Begriffserklärungen:

Sinn der Romanisierung (rumänisch - 'esenţa romanizării') - konzentrierte Daten zur Definition des Romanisierungsprozesses.
Wege der Romanisierung - die Art und Weise der Verbreitung römischer Zivilisation bei den anderen Völkergruppen.
Brennpunkte der Romanisierung - territoriale Zentren mittels deren die römische Zivilisation sich verbreitete.
Faktoren der Romanisierung - Umstände bzw. Elemente die die Assimilation von einigen nicht römischen Völkern durch die Römer ermöglicht haben.
Etappen der Romanisierung - bedeutende zeitliche Abschnitte des Assimilationsprozesses von einigen nicht römischen Völkern durch die Römer.

- 'Din istoria Transnistriei (în contextul istoriei naţionale). Materiale didactice pentru şcoala de cultură generală din Transnistria' (Aus der Geschichte Transnistriens (im Kontext der Nationalgeschichte) Didaktische Materialien für die Allgemeine Schule Transnistriens).

2001 erschein in Chişinău ein Geschichtsschulbuch, das an den Besonderheiten des Faches Nationalgeschichte in der separatistischen Region Transnitria/Pridnestrov'e angepasst sein sollte. Bereits aus der Einführung erfahren wir, dass die Schulbuch-autoren

> *links vom Dnjestr die gleichen Romanisierungsprozesse*[16] *der freien Daker festgestellt haben, die dem Ganzen von den Dakern bewohntem Raum charakteristisch seien und die mit der Entstehung des rumänischen Volkes und der rumänischen Sprache enden sollen* (Dragnev 2001, 5).

Der Romanisierungsprozess wird im Kontext der *dako-römischen* Kriege abgehandelt und in der Lektion- und Kapitelüberschrift unter dem Titel '*Anfang der Romanisierung*' angeführt (Dragnev u.a. 2001, 19). Ohne es weiterhin genauer zu definieren wird hier über die Einflüsse auf die Autochthonen durch Urbanisierung, Kolonisation, römische Heeresrekrutierungen aus der lokalen Bevölkerung, und nicht zuletzt durch das Latein gesprochen. Damit wird hier der Anfang der Romanisierung in den Gebieten südlich der unteren Donau verstanden. Zwei Seiten weiter erfahren wir, dass nach dem Ende der Kriege Trajans gegen dir Daker,

> *'fängt [auch in dieser Region] die Romanisierung an, die eine wichtige Etappe der Entstehung des rumänischen Volkes darstellt'.* (Dragnev u.a. 2001, 21).

Die sprachlichen Ausdrucksformen aus diesem Schulbuch erinnern an die sowjetische Zeit und an die Rolle des Russischen als Kommunikationssprache:

> *In den Werkstätten, auf der Baustellen, in den Minen sprachen die Vorarbeiter und die Meister nur Latein* (Dragnev u.a. 2001, 23).

Auf der gleichen Seite wird es darüber berichtet, dass

> *die Geto-Daker neben Latein auch einige Sitten und Glaubensvorstellungen von den Römern übernahmen. ... Eine wichtige Rolle im Romanisierungsprozess spielte das Christentum.*

Im Text lässt sich auch eine Definition der Romanisierung antreffen:

> *In den Städten und Handelsplätzen der Provinzen findet ein Prozess der totalen Transformation der Ethnie statt, genannt Romanisierung. Infolge dieses Phänomens hat die römische Zivilisation in allen Aktivitätssphären der Einheimischen gewonnen. ...*
> *Bei den freien Dakern beschränkte sich die Romanisierung auf die Aneignung der lateinischen Sprache und auf die Übernahme einiger Erfolge römischer Materialkultur.* (Dragnev u.a. 2001, 24).

Nach der Räumung Dakiens beschreiben die Schulbuchautoren ein interessantes Phänomen, das angeblich stattgefunden hätte:

> *Einige der freien Daker wechseln ihren Wohnsitz im Karpatenbecken neben der romanisierten Bevölkerung, während ein Teil der romanisierten Bevölkerung zu den freien Dakern übersiedelt. ... Die romanisierte Bevölkerung kommuniziert weiterhin mit den freien Dakern in lateinischer Sprache. So haben mehr und mehr Daker das Sprechen, mancher sogar Schreiben in Latein gelernt.* (Dragnev u.a. 2001, 24).
> *In ihrem Kampf mit den Barbaren stützen sich die Reichsbehörden auf ihre Waffenstärke und auf die Unterstützung der romanisierten Bevölkerung von außerhalb des Limes.* (Dragnev u.a. 2001, 25).

[16] Im Originaltext wird über die Romanisierung im Plural diskutiert.

Somit ist die Darstellung in diesem Buch noch nicht zu ihrem Ende angekommen. In der Zusammenfassung zum Kapitel 'Die Antike' wird das Ganze noch einmal rekapituliert[17]:

> *Die Geto-Daker aus der Provinz [Dakien] sowie die, die sich außerhalb befanden (aber stark von der römischen Zivilisation beeinflusst waren), haben sich die Lebensart, die Sprache, die Gesellschaftstraditionen angeeignet. Durch die Romanisierung der Geto-Daker (die auch nach der Räumung Dakiens durch die römische Verwaltung in den Jahren 271-275 fortlief) wurde der Prozess der Entstehung des rumänischen Volks gestartet. Die Romanisierung umfasste auch die Territorien links vom Dnjestr.* (Dragnev u.a. 2001, 26).

Romanisierung der freien Daker – ein Mythos der nationalen Historiographie

Wie dieser schnelle Überblick zeigt, wird die Romanisierung bzw. die Romanisierung der Nicht-Provinzbewohnern in mehreren moldauischen Schulbüchern erwähnt und mit unterschiedlichen Fragestellungen zum besseren Verständnis der Ethnogenese des rumänischen Volkes verknüpft. Gemeinsam ist allen Darstellungen, dass sie einer veralteten und einseitigen Forschungsmeinung aus den überholten oder propagandistisch ausgerichteten Publikationen von Xenopol (Xenopol 1985), Iorga (Iorga 1905), Daicoviciu (siehe Daicoviciu 1940. Vgl. auch die Übersetzung auf Rumänisch – Daicoviciu 1941) oder Berciu (Berciu 1978) folgen. So wie die wissenschaftliche Forschung zum Thema, leidet auch die Darstellungsweise der Romanisierung (darunter auch die der Nicht-Provinzbewohner) in den Schulbüchern an einem starken Einfluss der Tagespolitik. Vergleicht man die ersten Auflagen der untersuchten Lehrbücher, besteht ein klarer Zusammenhang zwischen deren Alter und der Darstellungsart dieses Prozesses. Es geht vor allem um die im Laufe der Zeit veränderbare Rolle sowie um das gegenseitige Verhältnis zwischen den strukturellen Elementen des Romanisierungsprozesses – die (freien) Daker, Römer sowie Dako-Römer.

Eine in den Schulbüchern so definierte und beschriebene Romanisierung jenseits der Grenzen der römischen Provinzen halte ich für nichts anderes als einen politisch motivierten Antikenmythos[18], wie es ihn in vielen Ländern Europas gegeben hat. Sowohl in Frankreich, Deutschland, Großbritannien als auch in der Niederlanden, Belgien oder der Schweiz wurden solche Mythen vor allem im 19. Jh. in die nationalistische Ideologie integriert – '*Ob Autokratie oder Republik, parlamentarische Monarchie oder bürgerlicher Bundesstaat – die unterschiedlichsten Regierungsformen und Staatsideologien haben sich in nationale Mythen gekleidet*' (Löttel 2009, 155). Der Mythos[19] der Romanisierung ist damit ein Teil des Wettbewerbs der europäischen Nationen, wer die ältesten Vorfahren nachweisen kann (siehe dazu Boia 2003 sowie Geary 2002).

Genau wie viele andere Antikenmythen trägt der Mythos 'Romanisierung' die Integrations- und Orientierungsfunktionen sowie die emanzipatorischen und legitimierenden

[17] Im Buchvorwort wird angegeben, dass das Kapitel zur Römerzeit von Dr. habil. Ion Chirtoagă verfasst wurde. Er ist dem letzten Informationsstand zu Folge wissenschaftlicher Mitarbeiter am Institut für Geschichte der Akademie der Wissenschaften in Chişinău. Vgl. http://www.cnaa.md/person/3266/ – Seite zuletzt besucht am 31.1.2016.

[18] Zur Systematik der Antikenmythen siehe Hein 2005. Vgl. auch Hein-Kircher 2009. Eine grundlegende Untersuchung der Relation zwischen 'Geschichte und Mythos' in Rumänien bieten die Arbeiten von Lucian Boia. Auf Deutsch siehe Boia 2003.

[19] Zur Definitionen der Mythen siehe Hein-Kircher 2009, 149. Mit Bezug auf Rumänien siehe Boia 2003, 2-4.

Funktionen in sich (Hein-Kircher 2009, 152-154). Eine Gegenüberstellung und Abgrenzung zu Slawisierung, Germanisierung oder Sarmatisierung des Landes und die Ableitung des Volkes von den glorreichen Römern und autochthonen Dakern gehören zu den Sinneserklärungen dieses propagandistischen Konstrukts. Somit gehört die Romanisierung zur Gruppe der Ursprungs- bzw. Gründungsmythen, die im Zuge des nationalen Erwachens, der Nationswerdung, aber auch bei der Staatsbildung nach dem Zerfall der Vielvölkerreiche und bei der Bildung, Festigung und Legitimierung der neuen politischen Systeme entstanden sind. Dies ist eine typische Eigenschaft der politischen Mythen der 'Staaten bzw. Nationen nach der politischen Wende 1989/90 vor dem Hintergrund des dadurch entstandenen ideologischen Vakuums und der politischen und gesellschaftlichen Entwurzelung' (Hein 2005).

Dies spiegeln auch die Schulbücher der Republik Moldau und Rumänien wider. Ich halte es für gewinnbringend hier die Sichtweise auf die Romanisierung von zwei Seiten des Nationaldiskurses zu präsentieren. Die Gelegenheit dafür gibt die Situation rund um die sog. 'Heimatgeschichte' für die separatistischen Region Transnitria/Pridnestrov'e[20]. Wie es oben gezeigt wurde gibt es für dieses Schulfach sowohl ein von den moldauischen Behörden in Chişinău akzeptiertes Lehrbuch (siehe oben Dragnev u. a. 2001), als auch ein weiteres, das in im Namen der separatistischen Verwaltung aus Tiraspol herausgegeben wurde (Babilunga/Bomeško 2004). Der von uns untersuchte Begriff kommt in der Überschrift zur Lektion '*Romanisierung der Thraker*' und dann auch als Kapitelüberschrift '*Romanisierung Dakiens*' vor. Aus der Romanisierung-Narration lassen sich für unsere Fragestellungen folgende Auszüge aussondern:

> *Ungefähr 200 Jahre wurden die thrakische Gemeinden der Geto-Daker, ...* [im Römischen Reich und in Dakien] *einer verstärkten Romanisierung ausgesetzt, lernten nach römischen Gesetzen und Regeln zu leben. Schrittweise bekamen sie für romanische Völker charakteristische Eigenschaften, erlernten Latein (einen seiner Dialekte), vergaßen die Sprache ihrer Ahnen. Auf der Grundlage der romanisierten Thraker entstanden einige südosteuropäische Völker, darunter die Moldawier.*
> *Die Bevölkerung Transnistriens wurde der brutalen Romanisierung nicht ausgesetzt. ... Die in diesen Gebieten ansässigen Stämme der Thraker, Sarmaten, Germanen, Slawen und anderen Barbaren, erlebten sicherlich die römischen Einflüsse. Aber sie führten ein unabhängiges Leben: sie gehorchen nicht den römischen Gesetzen, sie übernahmen Latein nicht, ihre Kinder gingen in die lateinischen Schulen nicht.* (Babilunga/Bomeško 2004, 36-38.)

Es ist augenscheinlich, dass von den beiden Seiten die Aussagen stark extremisiert wurden: im Lehrbuch aus Chişinău wird die Romanisierung als Teil der rumänischen Ethnogenese anerkannt und auf das heutige Territorium Transnistriens ausgeweitet, seitens der Separatisten wird dieser Prozess dagegen vehement verneint. Die Bevölkerung Transnistriens wird im Schulbuch aus Chişinău zu den 'freien Dakern' gerechnet, im Schulbuch aus Tiraspol werden dafür alle mögliche historische Namen wie Slawen, Sarmaten, Germanen, Thraker verwenden, aber nie (romanisierte) Daker. Die Aneignung der lateinischen Sprache durch die Bevölkerung Transnistriens wird

[20] Zu dieser separatistischen Region der Republik Moldau siehe z. B. Ihrig 2008, 38-39 mit der Bibliographie.

im Schulbuch aus Chişinău postuliert, in dem aus Tiraspol wird diese mit Vehemenz negiert. Da in den politischen Diskursen beiderseits vom Dnjestr solche Begriffe wie Daker, Römer oder Latinität verzerrt mit den heutigen Rumänen und Rumänien assoziiert werden (Ihrig 2008, 29-36), versucht jede Seite deren Größe und Bedeutung für sich zu nutzen.

Zeitliche Entwicklung des Mythos

Im Laufe der Untersuchung habe ich mich gefragt, ob sich eine zeitliche Abfolge der grundlegenden Aussagen des Mythos 'exogener Romanisierung' ablesen lässt? Die Analyse der Schulbücher zeigt, dass in Moldawien die Romanisierung auch in den sowjetischen Zeiten Teil des Geschichtsunterrichts war, aber mit einer deutlich geringeren bemessenen Bedeutung. Nach der Neuausrichtung des Schulfaches im Zuge der Emanzipationsbewegung und nach der anschließenden Unabhängigkeitserklärung des Landes am Anfang der 1990er Jahre (vgl. dazu Ihrig 2008, 29-36) entfaltet sich der Mythos 'Romanisierung' in den moldauischen Schulbüchern prächtig. Diese Entwicklung steht unter starkem Einfluss der rumänischen Geschichtsschreibung. In Rumänien ist die Geschichte dieses Herkunftsmythos deutlich länger. Wie Boia es aufzeichnen konnte, wird seine Dynamik von den außen- und innenpolitischen Entwicklungen des Landes bestimmt (Boia 2003). Die bisherigen Untersuchungen lassen die Annahme zu, dass der Mythos 'Romanisierung' gleich nach der Bildung des Nationalstaates im 19. Jh. in die rumänischen Schulbücher Eingang findet. Dieser entwickelt sich nicht aus einer Fragestellung der Geschichtsforschung, sondern aus den politischen Auseinandersetzungen im Nationaldiskurs mit den benachbarten Nationalstaaten. Rumänien kommt zu dieser Diskussion seit der Geburt als moderner Staat. Eine Herausforderung der Geschichtsschreibung bezüglich des hier untersuchten Begriffes beginnt in den ersten Jahrzehnten des 20. Jhs., als in Rumänien, wie in vielen anderen Ländern, die Nationalgeschichte neu geschrieben werden sollte, weil zu Rumänien im Zuge der politischen Veränderungen nach dem Ende des 1. Weltkrieges Banat, Crisana, Maramures, Bukowina, Siebenbürgen, Bessarabien und Dobrudscha hinzugekommen sind. Es sollte dabei auch eine Umorientierung der rumänischen Geschichtslehrbücher in Bezug auf die Römerzeit stattfinden: die sog. Dako-Römer (Dako-Romanen) werden geboren und ab jetzt ist deren Romanisierung ein fester Bestandteil der rumänischen Geschichte. Die Dako-Römer stellen meines Erachtens ein forschungspolitisches pseudo-ethnisches Konstrukt der rumänischen Historiographie dar. Von seiner Struktur scheint der Begriff eine Übernahme aus der französischen Historiographie zu sein, wo zur Mitte des 19. Jhs. die 'Gallo-Römer' als Bezeichnung für die Bevölkerung in den Gallischen Provinzen erfunden wurde (Brather 2007, 123 und Anm. 9). Inhaltlich werden unter Dako-Römer romanisierte Daker verstanden, aber nicht nur aus der römischen Provinz Dakien, sondern auch von außerhalb.

Da das römische Dakien in seiner Ausdehnung nicht die Grenzen Grossrumäniens nach dem 1. Weltkrieg vollständig umschließt, werden zu den Dako-Römern auch die 'romanisierten freien Daker' aus den anliegenden Gebieten gezählt[21]. Es ist augenscheinlich, dass diese

[21] Noch gegen die Mitte des 19. Jhs. taucht der Name Dakien als Bezeichnung für die von Rumänen bewohnten Gebiete auf – Boia 2003, 43.

Drehung in der Darstellung der Vergangenheit geschah, nicht weil neue Forschungsquellen erschlossen wurden oder neue Forschungsmethoden Anwendung fanden, sondern wohl um die von den nachkriegszeitlichen Friedensverträgen vorgegebenen Landesgrenzen zu rechtfertigen. Der Aufbau des Nationalstaates aller Rumänen förderte das Identitätsgefühl und das Bewusstsein eines gemeinsamen und einzigartigen Schicksals (Boia 2003, 74). Somit war der hier behandelte Mythos geboren und über die Schule bzw. Geschichtslehrbücher an die Bevölkerung weitergegeben. So wie Boia feststellte, '*ein Geschichtslehrbuch erreicht viel größere Kreise, als ein historiographisches Meisterwerk, das für eine Elite geschrieben wurde*' (Boia 2003, 2).

Das Ende des 2.Weltkrieges brachte einen deutlichen Paradigmenwechsel in der Forschungsgeschichte des untersuchten Geschichtsmythos mit sich. Die Debatte zwischen den römerzentristischen und dakerzentristischen Tendenzen der Zwischenkriegszeit (vgl. dazu 76-84) – wurde durch die Machtübernahme den Kommunisten gestoppt: das sowjetische stalinistische Model der Historiographie wurde zwangsimportiert und die Forschungen gerieten in eine sog. 'antinationale Phase' (Boia 2003, 85-88). Die vorherigen Wahrzeichen der rumänischen Geschichtsschreibung wurden auf den Kopf gestellt: aus der 'Rumänischen Geschichte' wurde 'Geschichte der RPR'[22]. '*Eine neue Geschichte begann, die nicht nur anders, sondern der alten auch völlig entgegengesetzt war. Auch eine neue Kultur entstand, die rumänische Variante der Sowjetkultur*' (Boia 2003, 85). Die rumänische Historiographie orientiert sich ihrerseits an die alleinherrschende Dominanz des slawischen Elements und, *last but not least*, die Nationalidee wurde durch Klassenkampf und durch einen uneingeschränkten Internationalismus ersetzt[23].

Die Phase der starken Sowjetisierung und des übermächtig gewordenen Panslawismus dauerte nicht lange Zeit. Die politischen Divergenzen und der anschließende Bruch mit der UdSSR führten spätestens seit der Mitte der 1960 Jahren zu Veränderungen auch in der Orientierung der rumänischen Geschichtsschreibung (Boia 2003, 89-93). Es wurden die vorherigen Mythen über die starken Daker und über die langlebigen Dako-Römer aus der Schublade zurückgeholt. Einige Jahre danach wurden auch die Römer von offizieller Propaganda nun als Eindringlinge auf dem Gebiet der Daker betrachtet, als die sog. Phase des 'Hemmungslosen Nationalismus' begann (Boia 2003, 93-100). Als Hintergrund dafür gilt der vom Regime verfolgte Kurs der außenpolitischen Unabhängigkeit und Autarkie, sowie der Wunsch, die autochthonen und damit seit Urzeiten auf dem Gebiet des heutigen Rumänien ansässigen Geto-Daker als die ausschließlichen Vorfahren der Rumänen zu präsentieren (Ursprung 2004/2005, 412). Im Lande findet eine Aneignung der Vergangenheit der romanisierten Daker bzw. Dako-Römer durch die moderne Nation statt. Diese Situation verzerrte das von den Schülern rezipierte Bild der Antike: in deren Bewusstsein wurden die romanisierten Daker – die ersten Rumänen. Diese Situation findet ihre Erklärung in den Bemühungen der krisenerschütterten kommunistischen Regime um eine historische Legitimierung ihrer Herrschaft. Zu diesem Zweck wurden die traditionellen Mythen der

[22] Die Abbreviation 'RPR' steht für '*Republica Populară Română*' (auf Deutsch – Volksrepublik Rumänien) und liegt im Wortklang und in der Struktur den Namensabkürzungen sowjetischer Republiken sehr nah. Vgl. die Kritik bei Boia 2003, 86.

[23] Eine sehr gute Darstellung der Prozesse im rumänischen Forschungsmilieu dieser Zeit gibt in Bezug auf die Problematik der Provinz Dakien die Arbeit von Florian Matei-Popescu zum Bild vom Römischen Dakien in der rumänischen Geschichtsschreibung zwischen 1945-1960: – Matei-Popescu 2007.

nationalen Historiographie ausgedehnt um die Geschichte der eigenen Nation möglichst weit in die Vergangenheit zu verlagern. Die Propaganda des Ceauşescu-Regimes war der unübertroffene Führer der Instrumentalisierung der Geschichtsforschung in den Ländern des damaligen Ostblocks (Babeş 2007).

Die politische Wende brachte Ende der 1980iger Jahre fundamentale Veränderungen in den Ländern des Ostblocks. Für die Wissenschaftler erfüllten sich dabei zwei wichtige Voraussetzungen für die fachliche Weiterentwicklung: die Zensur der Publikationen wurde aufgehoben und es bestand die Möglichkeit des wissenschaftlichen Austausches durch Reisen und durch nicht mehr überwachte Korrespondenz. Dazu kommen die digitale Revolution und das Internet, die die Informationsbeschaffung deutlich erleichtert haben. Es ist jedoch äußerst merkwürdig festzustellen, dass sich die Struktur der Schulbücher, trotz dieser Veränderungen, nur wenig geändert hat. Wie die am Anfang vorgeführten Beispiele aus den heutigen Geschichtsschulbüchern zeigen, sind die Fragestellungen zu der von uns untersuchten Romanisierung meist im Sinne der nationalistischen Rhetorik formuliert und in den Antworten fehlt nur selten das nationalistische Element. Man gewinnt den Eindruck, dass der militante Nationalismus aus der sozialistischen Zeit ein pseudo-demokratisches Gewand übergezogen bekommen hat (Babeş 2007).

Für die Zeit des kommunistischen Regimes hört man häufig die Rechtfertigung, dass die Kompromisse die Überlebensstrategie des Wissenschaftlers und des Schulbuchautors bzw. ein Mittel zum Umgehen der staatlichen Zensur darstellten. Welche Gründe für das Weiterbestehen der überholten Fragestellungen mit einem ausdrücklichen nationalistischen Hintergrund gibt es heute noch? Eine ausführliche Antwort darauf wurde von Niculescu in Form einer Rezension zum Akademie-Werk 'Geschichte der Rumänen', an dem viele der heutigen Schulbuchautoren sich orientieren, formuliert. So hält er fest, dass

> 'The low quality of the interpretation stems mostly from the subordination of archaeological knowledge to political goals: many interpretations are not meant to lead to a better understanding of the past, nor are they made for colleagues to read and critique. Rather, they are for politicians to appreciate and reward, based on their interests and their common knowledge. Such constructions are not evaluated against validity criteria made by the archaeologist, but are matched to the perceived imperatives of the political present, with 'the national interest' to which normative, ritualized discourses about the nation, disguised in professional knowledge about the past, are offered.' (Niculescu 2005, 123).

Die Realität der historischen Forschung und des Schulbuchschreiben in der Republik Moldau und zum Teil auch in Rumänien wird nach der politischen Wende der 1990iger Jahre von einigen Aspekten bestimmt, die meines Erachtens zu beachten und baldmöglichst zu verändern sind. Erstens, es gibt in der rumänischen und moldauischen Altertumsforschung bestimmte Themenbereiche, die von der offiziellen Propaganda und dann von den Meinungsbildnern so stark instrumentalisiert wurden, dass deren Infragestellung oder nur eine Abweichung davon gleichsam als Verrat an der nationalen Sache galt und noch immer gilt (vgl. dazu Ursprung 2004/2005, 417). Zu diesen Themenbereichen gehört 'die durchgreifende

Romanisierung dakischer Bevölkerung in allen heute rumänischen Nationalterritorien'. Infolge, wird jeder Versuch, die Romanisierung mancher Teile der dakischen Bevölkerung zu verneinen, scharf – und selbstverständlich negativ – apostrophiert und politisiert. Aus einem wissenschaftlichen Zweifel eines Historikers wird es dann zu einem Problem der politischen Positionierung desselben in der Gesellschaft (siehe dazu auch Babeş 2007).

Ein weiteres methodisches Problem, das ich hier ansprechen möchte, ist die Art, wie man in Südosteuropa allgemein, und in Moldawien speziell, Geschichte schreibt. Ich meine damit die sog. 'Hegemonie der historischen Fakten': man versucht die Daten und Fakten als weitgehend geschlossene Informationsblöcke darzustellen. Diese erscheinen den Autoren aus sich selbst heraus verständlich, so dass deren Anordnung, Strukturierung, Analyse oder Interpretation kaum noch problematisiert werden (vgl. Ursprung 2010/2011, 366 und Anm. 26). Diese Art 'Pseudo-Positivismus' lässt die Methodik der historischen Forschung, angefangen bei der Quellenkritik, in den Hintergrund treten. Die analytische Aneinanderreihung von Einzelfakten anstelle einer synthetischen Zusammenstellung und Wertung war während der Sozialismus-Zeit eine Methode, um die Zensur zu umgehen (Ursprung 2010/2011, 366). Leider wird diese Art der Geschichtsschreibung heute immer noch angewendet, obwohl die staatliche, politisch motivierte Zensur nicht mehr existiert. Nach 1989 verzichten viele Autoren auf den marxistischen bzw. stalinistischen Jargon der vorangegangenen Zeit (Boia 2003, 272), die Methoden ihrer Forschungen bleiben jedoch sehr oft unverändert. Das ganze Problem spiegelt sich dann in der Denkweise und den Schreibaktivitäten einiger unserer Zeitgenossen, die auch als Schulbuchautoren tätig sind.

Schlussfolgerungen

Der hier vorgelegte Überblick besteht zum Teil aus Kritik an den älteren Forschungsmeinungen, die in den heutigen Schulbüchern immer noch Platz haben. Die Darstellungen von Widersprüchlichkeiten aus Schulbüchern konnten den großen Abstand zwischen Wirklichkeiten und Wahrnehmungen mancher Schulbuchautoren verdeutlichen. Wir stellen dabei fest, dass die tatsächliche Darstellung der Romanisierung in manchen Schulbüchern nicht zeitgemäß und wissenschaftlich inadäquat vorkommt. Die Kluft zwischen Wissenschaft und Schulbüchern ist im Fall der Romanisierung der sog. 'freien Daker' ziemlich groß geworden. Diese kritische Sichtweise und die dekonstruktive Haltung alleine wären allerdings recht unbefriedigend, wenn nicht Hoffnung bestehen würde, in der Zukunft neue Ansätze zu diesem Problem entwickeln zu können. Diese Situation erfordert meines Erachtens ein energisches Handeln von Seite der Altertumsforscher, vor allem in die Richtung der viel engeren Kontakten zu den Schulbuchautoren bzw. zu den Curricula bestimmenden Institutionen des jeweiligen Landes. Nicht zuletzt sollen meines Erachtens neue publikumsnähere Publikationen entstehen, die den Weg zwischen den neuesten Ergebnissen der Altertumsforschungen und Schülern in den beiden Ländern deutlich verkürzen.

Ich möchte diesen Beitrag mit einem Zitat aus dem bekannten Büchlein von Patrick Geary 'Europäische Völker im frühen Mittelalter' beenden – ein Zitat, das unsere Aufgaben in Bezug auf die ethnischen Deutungen allgemein und auf die Romanisierung speziell auf den Punkt bringt:

'Die Geschichte der europäischen Nationen leistete der nationalistischen Ideologie hervorragende Dienste, hatte aber zur Folge, dass unser Verständnis der Vergangenheit eine Mülldeponie für das Gift des ethnischen Nationalismus darstellt, das tief ins allgemeine Bewusstsein eingesickert ist. Die Entsorgung dieses Abfalls ist die wohl bedrückendste Aufgabe, die sich heutigen Historikern stellt.' (Geary 2002, 25).

Acknowledgement

Dieser Beitrag entstand mit einer Finanzierung von der Nationalen Behörde für Wissenschaftliche Forschung Rumäniens, im Rahmen des Forschungsprojektes CNCS – UEFISCDI PN-II-ID-PCE-2011-3-0652.

Bibliographie

Alföldi, M. R. 1997. Germania magna, nicht libera. Notizen zum römischen Wortgebrauch. *Germania* 75, 1: 45-52.

Alföldy, G. 2005. Romanisation – Grundbegriff oder Fehlgriff? Überlegungen zum gegenwärtigen Stand der Erforschung von Integrationsprozessen im römischen Weltreich. In Z. Visy (Hrsg.), *Limes XIX. Proceedings of the XIXth International Congress of Roman Frontier Studies held in Pécs, Hungary, September 2003*: 25-56. Pécs.

Babeş, M. 2007. Die rumänische Archäologie und die Versuchung des Nationalismus vor und nach der Wende. In S. Rieckhoff/U. Sommer (Hrsg.), *Auf der Suche nach Identitäten: Volk – Stamm – Kultur – Ethnos. Internationale Tagung der Universität Leipzig vom 8.-9. Dezember 2000*: 193-195. British Archaeological Reports International Series 1705. Oxford, Archaeopress.

Babilunga, N. V. and Bomeško, B. G. 2004. *Istorija Rodnogo Kraja. Učebnik dlja obščeobrazovatel'nych učebnych zavedenij*. Tiraspol.

Berciu, D. 1978. *Daco-Romania. Archaeologia mundi*. München.

Boia, L. 2003. Geschichte und Mythos: über die Gegenwart des Vergangenen in der rumänischen Gesellschaft. Studia Transylvanica. Köln [u.a.].

Brather, S. 2007. Ethnische Identität und frühgeschichtliche Archäologie. Das Beispiel der Franken. In S. Rieckhoff and U. Sommer (Hrsg.), *Auf der Suche nach Identitäten. Volk, Stamm, Kultur, Ethnos. Internationale Tagung der Universität Leipzig vom 8.-9. Dezember 2000*: 120-133. British Archaeological Reports International Series 1705. Oxford, Archaeopress.

Daicoviciu, C. 1940. *Le problème de la continuité en Dacie. Observations et précisions d'ordre historique et archéologique*. Bucharest.

Daicoviciu, C. 1941. Problema continuităţii în Dacia. Câteva observaţii şi precizări de ordin istorico-arheologic. *Anuarul Institutului de Studii Clasice* III (1936-1940): 200-270.

Daicoviciu, C. 1964. *Dacia liberă şi Dacia romană*. Bucureşti, Editura Didactică şi Pedagogică.

Dragnev, D. (Hrsg.). 1987. *Istorija RSS Moldovenešt'. Krestomacie. Partea I, pentru klasele 7-8*. Kišineu.

Dragnev, D., Chirtoagă, I. Jarcuţchi, I. Negru, E. 2001. *Din istoria Transnistriei (în contextul istoriei naţionale) I. Materiale didactice pentru şcoala de cultură generală din Transnistria*. Chişinău.

Dragnev, D., Postică, G. 2001. *Istoria Românilor. Epoca Antică şi Medievală. Manual pentur clasa a X-a de liceu*. Chişinău.

Dragnev, D. M. and Sovetov, P. V. 1983. *Istorija Moldavskoj SSR. Učebnik dlja 7 – 8 klassov*. Kišinev.

Dragnev, D. M. and Sovetov, P. V. 1988. *Istorija RSS Moldovenešt'. Manual pentru klasele 7-84.* Kišineu.

Dragnev, E., Dragnev, D., Mistreanu, T., Pâslariuc, V., Postică, G. 2010. *Istorie. Epoca Antică şi Medievală. Manual pentur clasa a X-a de liceu.* Chişinău.

Geary, P. J. 2002. *Europäische Völker im frühen Mittelalter. Zur Legende vom Werden der Nationen.* Aufl. Frankfurt am Main: Fischer-Taschenbücher 2.

Grosul, J. S., Mochov, N. A. and Russev, E. M. 1973. *Istorija Moldavskoj SSR. Učebnoe posobie dlja ... klassov srednej školy 7 - 8 3. izd.* Kišinev.

Grosul, J. S., Mochov, N. A. and Russev, E. M. 1980. *Istorija Moldavskoj SSR. Učebnoe posobie dlja 7 - 8 klassov srednej školy 7. izd.* Kišinev.

Hein-Kircher, H. 2009. Zur Definition, Vermittlung und Funktion von politischen Mythen. In S. Berke (Hrsg.), *2000 Jahre Varusschlacht. Mythos*: 149-154. Stuttgart.

Hein, H. 2005. *Historische Mythosforschung.* In *Digitales Handbuch zur Geschichte und Kultur Russlands und Osteuropas.* (http://www.vifaost.de/texte-materialien/digitale-reihen-und-sammlungen/handbuch/2005).

Ihrig, S. 2008. *Wer sind die Moldawier? : Rumänismus versus Moldowanismus in Historiographie und Schulbüchern der Republik Moldova, 1991 - 2006. Soviet and post-Soviet politics and society.* Stuttgart: Ibidem Verlag.

Ioniţă, I. 2001. Dacii liberi. In D. Protase and A. Suceveanu (Hrsg.), *Istoria Românilor. 2. Daco-romani, romanici, alogeni*: 401-437. Bucureşti, Editura Academiei.

Iorga, N. 1905. *Geschichte des rumänischen Volkes im Rahmen seiner Staatsbildungen.* Gotha, F. A. Perthes.

Krausse, D. 2006. *Eisenzeitlicher Kulturwandel und Romanisierung im Mosel-Eifel-Raum. Die keltisch-römische Siedlung von Wallendorf und ihr archäologisches Umfeld.* Römisch-Germanische Forschungen 63. Mainz, Philipp von Zabern.

Löttel, H. 2009. 'Märtyrer der Freiheit'. Antikenmythen in den europäischen Nationalstaaten des 19. Jahrhunderts. In S. Berke (Hrsg.), *2000 Jahre Varusschlacht. Mythos*: 155-163. Stuttgart.

Macrea, M. 1968. Dacii liberi în epoca romană. *Apulum* VII, 1: 171-200.

Matei-Popescu, F. 2007. Imaginea Daciei Romane în istoriografia românească între 1945 şi 1960. *Studii şi cercetări de istorie veche şi arheologie* 58, 3-4: 265-288.

Meyer, M. 2013. Romanisierung? Überlegungen zum römischen Einfluss auf die kaiserzeitliche Germania Magna. In A. Rubel (Hrsg.), *Imperium und Romanisierung. Neue Forschungsansätze aus Ost und West zu Ausübung, Transformation und Akzeptanz von Herrschaft im Römischen Reich.* SAGA Studien zu Archäologie und Geschichte des Altertums: 57-72. Konstanz, Hartung-Gorre Verlag.

Niculescu, G. A. 2005. Archaeology, Nationalism and 'The History of the Romanians' (2001). *Dacia* N.S.: 58-59; 99-124.

Niculiţă, I. 1997. *Istoria Românilor. Epoca veche. Manual experimental pentru clasa a V-a.* Chişinău.

Niculiţă, I., Potlog, V. and Arnăut, T. 2000. *Istorie. Epoca străveche şi antică. Manual pentru clasa a V-a.* Chişinău.

Popa, A. 2011. 'Importuri' provincial-romane şi romanizare în hinterlandul provinciilor romane Dacia şi Moesia Inferior In A. Rubel (Hrsg.), *Romanizarea: impunere si adeziune în Imperiul Roman*: 201-221. Iaşi, Editura Universităţii 'Alexandru Ioan Cuza' din Iaşi.

Popa, A. 2013. Provinzial-römische Importfunde als Anzeichen der Romanisierung jenseits der römischen Reichsgrenze? Fallbeispiel Karpaten-Dnestr-Raum. In A. Rubel (Hrsg.),

Imperium und Romanisierung. Neue Forschungsansätze aus Ost und West zu Ausübung, Transformation und Akzeptanz von Herrschaft im Römischen Reich. SAGA Studien zu Archäologie und Geschichte des Altertums: 127-144. Konstanz, Hartung-Gorre Verlag.

Popovici, C. and Popovici, C. 2005. *Istorie. Manual experimental pentru clasa a V-a.* Chişinău.

Rubel, A. 2010. Romanisierung als theoretisches Forschungsproblem. Vorüberlegungen zu einer rumänischen Romanisiserungsdebatte. *Arheologia Moldovei* 32: 57-71.

Rubel, A. (Hrsg.) 2011. *Romanizarea: impunere si adeziune în Imperiul Roman.* Iaşi, Editura Universității 'Alexandru Ioan Cuza' din Iași.

Ursprung, D. 2004/2005. Historiographie im Zeichen der Beharrung: Kritische Anmerkungen zur umfangreichsten Gesamtdarstellung der rumänischen Geschichte. Südost-Forschungen. *Internationale Zeitschrift Für Geschichte, Kultur und Landeskunde Südosteuropas* 63/64: 408-421.

Ursprung, D. 2010/2011. Geschichtsschreibung und Vergangenheitsbewältigung in Rumänien. Von den Mühen des Umgangs mit zeitgeschichtlichen Themen. Südost-Forschungen. *Internationale Zeitschrift Für Geschichte, Kultur und Landeskunde Südosteuropas* 69/70: 358-388.

Woolf, G. 02 February 2012. Romanisierung. In H. Cancik, H. Schneider and M. Landfester (Hrsg.), *Der Neue Pauly.* Brill Online. Universitaetsbibliothek Giessen.

Xenopol, A. D. 1985. *Istoria românilor din Dacia Traiană. 1 Dacia anteromană, Dacia romană şi năvălirile barbare, 513 înainte de Hr. - 1290* Ed. 4. Bucureşti, Editura ştiinţifică şi enciclopedică.

Constructing identities within the periphery of the Roman Empire: north-west Hispania

Manuela Martins, Cristina Braga, Fernanda Magalhães, Jorge Ribeiro

Department of History, Archaeology, Lab2PT research unit. Unit of Archaeology, Braga, Portugal

Abstract

This paper aims to analyse the interaction and process of change that took place in the north-west of the Iberian Peninsula as the area came under the control of the Tarraconensis province during the administrative reorganisation of Hispania by Augustus. Following a general cultural description of the region, further detail will be offered of its integration into the bracarensis conventus. The unique characteristics of the local pre-Roman communities and their systems of power led to a particular evolutional process in the region. After describing the main changes in the cities and the territories, we will highlight the negotiation processes underlying the adaptation to the Roman way of life, through which new places, new symbols and new narratives related to identity emerged.

Keywords: north-west Hispania, *bracarensis conventus*, Iron Age, cultural identity, acculturation

Introduction

Based upon archaeological research conducted over recent decades that has been cross-referenced with the epigraphic record, this paper aims to assess the interaction and processes of change that impacted the north-western region of the peninsula between the late 2nd century BC and the late 1st century AD.

This region encompasses several areas of differing size. First, we will look at the entire north-west of the peninsula in order to highlight the cultural diversity that pre-dated the Roman conquest and identify the limits of the various territorial identities mentioned by Roman officials during the process of conquest. At a second stage, our analysis will focus on the region referred to as the *bracaraugustanus conventus*, so that we can then narrow our focus to the *Bracari* territory and the site where the city of *Bracara Augusta* was later established.

The period chosen is key to understanding the evolution of the indigenous communities starting at the moment when they first came into contact with Roman troops, around 138-136 BC, until the Flavian dynasty when Augustus's vision of organisational structure of Roman Hispania was fully consolidated.

We will analyse the changes that took place in the territorial and settlement organisation, the identity of both communities and individuals and the negotiations between the indigenous elites and the new Roman authorities. In order to fully understand these events, we need to describe the peculiar geographical features of the region, as well as the pre-Roman cultural entities at the end of the 1st millennium BC. We intend to point out the way indigenous communities structured different types of organisation and power, while mapping the various territorial identities. In reality, the gradual contact of the Roman authorities with the Iberian north-western communities created conditions conducive for change that emerged at variable rates of time and included several groups of participants. This transformation led to new habits, new needs and new prerogatives intimately connected to the leadership patterns of the various local regional elites as well as the Roman interests within the different north-western peninsular territories.

Considering the extent of the geographical area under study and the cultural diversity of Iberian north-western pre-Roman communities before the Cantabrian Wars, we will seek to individualise the territories, the indigenous identities and powers aiming to better understand the way the conquest and integration processes impacted upon the creation of new cultural identities. Ultimately, we are dealing with a period when the geographical area comprising the Iberian north-west was gradually included under Roman domain until its definitive administrative integration, as a consequence of the Augustan reforms that were only fully consolidated during the Flavian dynasty.

Territories and identities

Natural and cultural landscapes

The north-west of the Iberian Peninsula has particular geographical attributes that distinguish it from other parts of the peninsula. It has a series of characteristic features (i.e. high mountains, plateaus, river valleys, lowlands, alluvial and coastal plains) that make up a fairly varied collection of landscapes and resources. This multiplicity reinforced the cultural and economic diversity of its pre- and proto-historic communities. Thus, the Iberian north-west displays a more fragmented and idiosyncratic geography than the more homogenous coastal regions, and the proximity of the ocean, which has played an important role within the overall development of the region, has favoured communications and has served as the easiest axis for the circulation of people, artefacts and ideas.

The archaeological record shows that the western coastline of Asturias exhibited more cultural similarities with the Galician *bracarensis* region than with the inner Pontevedra province. Equally, coastline regions have always shared common features that are markedly distinct from inland mountainous areas (González Ruibal 2008: 907). On the other hand, the peninsular north-west played a strategic role as the link between the Mediterranean and the Atlantic regions. It was an important step on the ancient 'Atlantic Route' which had been active since the Bronze Age, long before the Romans made it the main supply route of the armies settled in the Germanic *limes* and *Britania* (Fabião 2005: 83-84).

This contrasting and fragmented geography also contrasts with a highly diversified human and cultural landscape, which was, however, unified by two major ethnic groups,

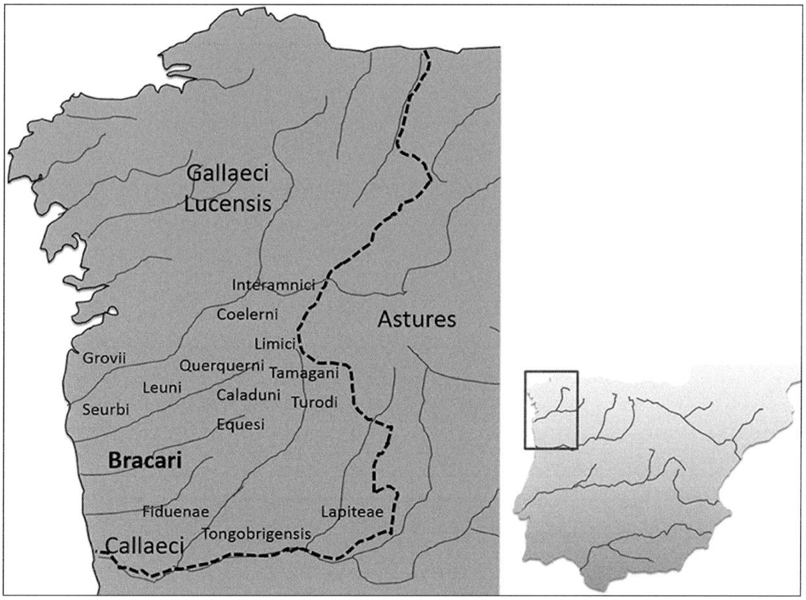

Figure 1. Pre-Roman political geography of the north-west of Iberia according to written and epigraphic sources.

the Galicians and the Asturians, both of which were made up of several *populi* (Bravo Castañeda 2007: 50). Some of these peoples had been mentioned by ancient geographers and historians while others only appeared in epigraphic sources (Figure 1). Nevertheless, the discovery of new inscriptions has contributed to a greater understanding of the north-western territory's pre-Roman human geography.

Despite the ethnic diversity of the Iberian north west, the pre Roman settlements were traditionally categorised as examples of the 'Castro Culture', with its characteristic hill forts and round, stone houses (Silva 1986; 1995: 505-546). However, archaeological research over recent decades has pointed toward greater heterogeneity in terms of topography, size and internal organisation, as well as in chronology (Martins 1997: 150-151). We are aware that the hill forts of the southern *bracarensis* region were older than those of Galicia and Asturias, often dating back to the Late Bronze Age. They were also more common along the coastline and surrounding valleys than those in the inland mountain areas. The peninsular north-west was marked by greater cultural variety over time.

The material culture, specifically domestic architecture, ceramics and items of prestige, attests to the increase in cultural diversity during the second Iron Age. These features serve as meaningful indicators of the social variability that existed at this time and point to the different manners in which power was organised in proto-historic communities (Aýan 2008: 903-1003; Carballo Arceo and Fábregas Valcarce 2006).

Based upon this elaborate material culture several researchers have argued that the peninsular north-west can be divided into three socio-political regions: the 'heroic societies' of the north (Parcero Oubiña 2002); the 'house societies' that were typical of the southern and western areas (Gonzalez Ruibal 2006: 144-177); and the 'segmentary societies' of inland Galicia territory and the Asturian mountains (Sastre 2002: 213-248). In the first, warrior status, cattle and jewellery provided the main ways to acquire and sustain power. The second category, arising mostly in the 2nd century BC, used the home as the prime symbol in the overall competition for power, as the house was where most of the material and immaterial social capital was invested in the form of jewellery, imported prestige goods and architectural ornaments, but also lands, positions and even genealogies (Gonzálel Ruibal 2008: 909). Finally, the 'segmentary societies' are characterised by a lack of prestige goods and fairly homogeneous domestic architecture. No investment has been identified in marking social differentiation for these societies.

The geographical diversity and fragmentation of the peninsular north-west does in fact correspond to different cultural landscapes organised during the 1st millennium BC, particularly those from the Late Iron Age period, when the formation of distinct identities was identified and recognised by the Romans who distinguished clearly between the Galicians and the Asturians.

Regional cultural identity: the **Galician bracarensis** *region*

Extant archaeological data from the southern and western region of the Iberian north-west, nowadays encompassed within Portuguese territory between the Douro and the Minho Rivers, as well as the southern and western part of Galicia, clearly demonstrate the cultural differences that distinguished this region from the inner mountainous ones. This regional identity had been developed since the Late Bronze Age and it was characterised by continuous maritime contacts with the Mediterranean that favoured Atlantic navigation throughout the 1st millennium BC. This contact intensified during the second Iron Age (González Ruibal 2004: 289-290) and is confirmed by Punic and Greek wares which have been found alongside other artefacts of prestige, such as Republican and neo-Punic Roman ceramics uncovered in several coastline hill forts (Gonzalez Ruibal *et al.* 2007: 43-74; Silva and Pinto 2001: 232-233). The regular contact between this region and the Mediterranean seems to have influenced its historical evolution and favoured its transformation into a unique socio-political organisation that González Ruibal (2006-2007: 144-177) has termed the 'house societies'.

This is precisely the region where large hill forts, generally between seven and 24 hectares, would be later constructed, although even larger settlements have been identified (Lemos 2009: 128-131). The location of these hill forts corresponds to the Augustan *bracaraugustanus conventus*, in particular its western area.

We are dealing with real urban settlements (*oppida*) developed during the 2nd century BC and reaching their peak during the following century. Although some authors argue that this type of settlement already represented a consequence of Romanisation (Sastre 2004: 99-110), others hold that that process only began with the *Decimus Junius Brutus* campaigns (Queiroga 2007: 169-179). Nevertheless, it is important to point out that their development occurred within an eminently indigenous context and clearly preceded Roman administrative control over the region, which only began to be felt from the year 19 BC onwards, following the end of the Cantabrian Wars. It seems inappropriate to

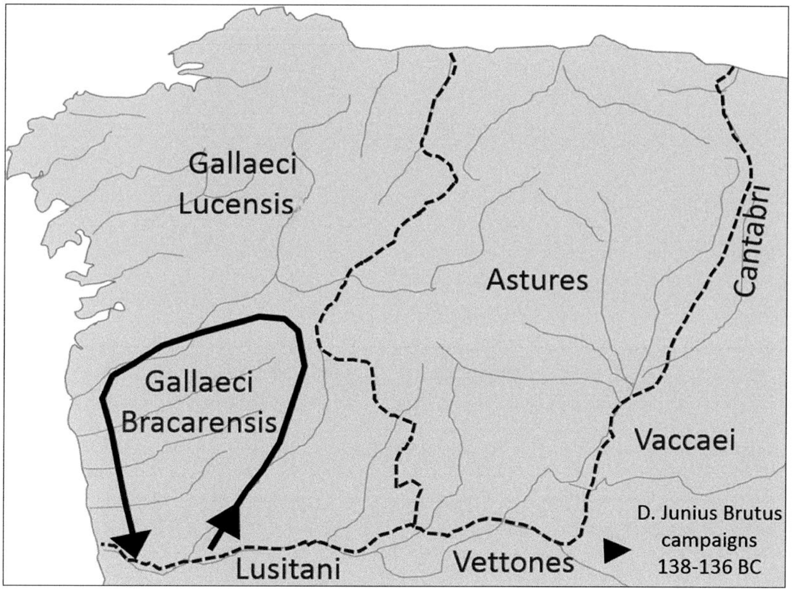

Figure 2. *D. Junius Brutus'* campaign itinerary (138-136 BC).

speak about Romanisation before the Augustan period, as it marked the beginning of the moulding of a true imperial identity, as has been argued regarding other regions of the Roman world (Woolf 1998: 176).

The characteristics of the pre-Roman settlements located in the Galician *bracarensis* area during its administrative integration into the Roman empire seemed to have been linked to social and economic processes of territorial reorganisation that occurred from the 2nd century BC onwards, perhaps following the *D. Junius Brutus* expedition to the region between 138-136 BC (Figure 2), which failed to cross the Minho River (Alarcão 1988: 8-9; Fabião 1993: 217-218). There are remarkable overlaps between the area pacified by *Brutus* and that where the *oppida* settlements were found. However, the changes in the *Callaeci Bracarensis* region during the 1st century BC need to be explained in terms of the wider organisational framework and the cultural traits of the regional communities which were distinct from those of other north-west peninsular peoples during the Late Bronze Age and whose identity was forged during the Iron Age (Silva 1999). On the other hand, the high population density in the Galician *oppida* seems to have resulted from synoecism processes that existed in other Iberian regions in the last two Republican centuries, which were clearly influenced by Mediterranean organisational models (Curchin 2004: 81). The rise of such large settlements, which served as central places, seems equally related to a hierarchical settlement pattern, with the *oppida* controlling smaller hill forts in valleys mainly dedicated to agriculture and livestock (Martins *et al.* 2005: 284). We highlight the similarity between these Galician *oppida* and similar sites from around the same period and in other parts of the peninsula, namely the Meseta, historically known as the Vettones land (Alvarez-Sanchis 1997), in the Rhine basin (Fernández Götz 2011; Woolf 1993), or in southern England (Pitts 2010: 32-63; Pitts and Perring 2006: 189-212). These were large hill forts whose urban features arose as a consequence of rising population density resulting from the development

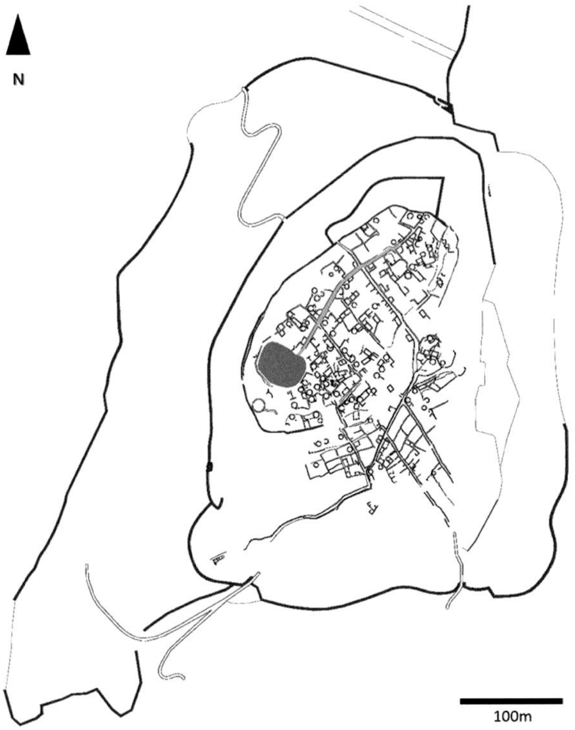

Figure 3. Plan of 'Citânia de Briteiros' (Guimarães).

of trade, as well as the intensification of agriculture and manufacturing, together with growing social complexity and undeniable cultural landscape hierarchy (Collis 1996: 227; Woolf 1993: 224).

The *oppida* benefitted from great visibility over their surroundings and invariably included complex defensive systems, normally comprising several lines of walls (3 to 5). Internally, they were organised into a roughly orthogonal road structure with residential quarters occupied by family units (Lemos 2009: 130-131). These domestic areas were frequently interconnected by slab pavements unifying buildings with different functions. Some of them had vestibules, others served as granaries and others were dedicated to manufacturing (Figure 3).

These *oppida* included several public infrastructures. Public buildings for ritual bathing were one of the most common buildings in the *bracarensis* region. They often were comprised of an oven, a steam chamber, an antechamber and a patio (Lemos *et al.* 2008: 319-328; Silva and Machado 2007: 20-60). Another public building type, the round council house with bench seats along the walls, was described by Strabo. The best-known example is the council house of 'Citânia de Briteiros' which measured 11m in diameter (Lemos 2009: 131).

These were commonly encountered features of the *oppida* of the *bracarensis* region, although the 'Citânia de Briteiros' in Guimarães (Cruz 2015: 403-414; Lemos 2009: 131) and 'Citânia de Sanfins' in Paços de Ferreira, with an area over 15 ha (Silva 1999), are thought to be the prime examples, as they have been the most extensively excavated (Figure 3). These hill forts with their complex internal organisation, large size, high population density, and developed manufacturing, as well as the concentration of political, economic and ritual functions, can be considered as true 'indigenous cities' that were included within hierarchised social formations and persisted up until the Roman conquest. They stand in obvious contrast to the segmentary social structure common in the Asturias region (Sastre 2001; 2004: 99-110).

Another cultural characteristic of the *bracarensis* territory are the warrior statues which were distinct from artwork of the inland north-western peninsula (Calo Lourido 1994: 75-100). These sculptures, presumably associated with figures of the local elite (Silva 2003: 41-50), would most likely have been placed in the walls of the hill forts and may have represented heroic figures intended to protect the settlements (Silva 1999: 16). Some decorative elements on these statues appear in pre-Roman jewellery that was representative of the power of the local elite, as in the case of the *viriae* or the torcs, or even the round shields, the *caetra*, in front of the statues (Figure 4).

Figure 4. S. Julião Galician warrior (Archaeological Museum D. Diogo de Sousa, Braga).

Equally, there was a close correlation between the motifs decorating the warriors' clothing, namely their tunics (Martins and Silva 1984: 34-35), and those decorating the sculpted slabs ('pedras formosas') of ritual bath buildings (Queiroga 1992: 25). The unique nature of Galician *bracarensis* regional art is also represented in the decoration of the house doors (Calo Lourido 1994: 70-80, 141-148; Silva 1986: 48-51), which attests to the significant investment the local communities made in the symbolic capital of their houses, as a way of highlighting social differences (Figure 5) (González Ruibal 2006-07: 383-401).

Today, it is commonly accepted that territories within the Galician *bracarensis* region were already pacified at the beginning of the Cantabrian Wars, between 29 and 19 BC, probably after the *Decimus Junius Brutus* expedition in 138-136 BC. Between that particular expedition and the Cantabrian Wars, a century passed during which the hill forts grew in size and population and were substantially reorganised, sometimes with an orthogonal plan that is thought to have been promoted by the Romans themselves (Queiroga 2007: 169-179).

Given the possibility that the territory between the Douro and Minho rivers remained under the control of the *Hispania Ulterior* province, due to the 138-136 BC military campaign, it does not seem credible that all the transformations until the end of the Cantabrian Wars can be explained without reference to a strong dynamism on the part of the indigenous communities. In reality, the campaigns of *Decinus Junius Brutus*, the pro-consul of the *Hispania Ulterior* province, together with the forthcoming expeditions of *Crassus* and *Julius Caesar*, both holders of identical provincial positions, failed to establish either any military

Figure 5. Decorated door at Sabroso hill fort (Martins Sarmento Museum, Guimarães).

occupation of the territory or a Roman administrative structure. These events only took place following the Cantabrian Wars a century later. It was precisely throughout the 1st century BC that profound changes in the Galician *bracarensis* region were registered, including a profound reorganisation of settlements and significant economic intensification, all of which created favourable conditions for the development of more complex and diversified architecture and original artistic development. This resulted in the consolidation of the indigenous elites' political and the military power.

The conception of the *oppida*, including the complexity of their defensive systems (i.e. wall lines, trenches, turrets, and monumental doors), the hierarchical structure of the street network, the existence of statues on the walls, the public spaces and architecture and the decoration of some of the houses all stand as clear evidence of an affirmation and display of the power of the governing elite (Figure 5). These features further demonstrate the stark differences that existed between these communities and those of other interior and northern areas.

The original organisation of the *bracarensis* region, represented by the *Bracari* territory, contributed towards the original transformation that this region would undergo in consequence of Roman rule and that was in full effect by the end of the Cantabrian Wars in 19 BC.

New powers and identities

A new political and administrative context

Between 19 and 15/13 BC a new political reality emerged in Hispania. Three administrative provinces were subdivided into several juridical *conventus*, each one with their own capital (Figure 6). The same period witnessed the establishment of cities, with new ones emerging whenever necessary. This was a period of intense reform presided over by Augustus and

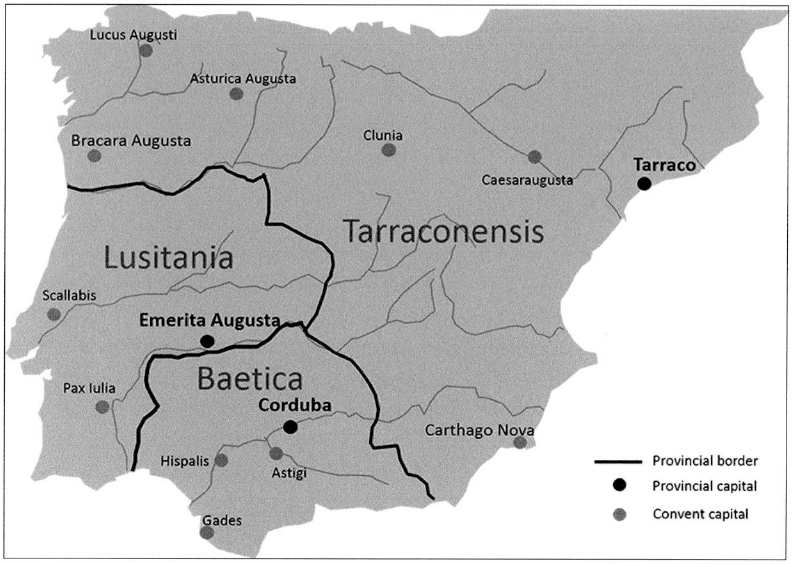

Figure 6. The administrative division of Hispania as implemented by Augustus.

focused on finding the best solutions for managing the wide and heterogeneous territory of the Iberian Peninsula, consolidating Roman power and ensuring the full integration of indigenous communities that were ethnically and culturally distinct. Surely this situation required extensive negotiation between the indigenous elites, the Imperial agents and the Emperor himself, as demonstrated by the 'Bierzo' Edict, or the 'Bembibre' *tabula*, dated to 15 BC (Grau and Hoyas (eds) 2001; Sánchez Palencia and Mangas 2000). It explicitly mentioned that the north-west region was included in the Transdurian province and governed by the *legatus* Lucio Sestio Quirinal, before its definitive merging with the Citerior province at an unknown time, which is believed to be placed between 16 and 13 BC (Syme 1970: 79; Tranoy 1981: 146), or between 12 and 7 BC (Alföldy 1969: 207).

This Edict of Augustus, signed in *Narbo Martius* (Narbona), reveals some hesitations regarding the organisation of the peninsular north-western region that also reflect an acknowledgement on behalf of Rome of the unique nature of this territory, in particular when compared to the regions included in the Lusitania and Citerior provinces. Equally, it shed some light on the provincial reorganisation of Hispania and the foundation of the Augustan cities. These dynamic processes inevitably involved compromises between the Roman authorities and the indigenous elites, as corroborated by the available epigraphic record (Dopico Caínzos 2009: 35). On the other hand, the 'Bierzo' Edict revealed that Augustus himself was directly involved in rewarding the *castellani Paemeiobrigensis*, going so far as to provide them with access to lands and perpetual immunity. This suggests Rome's great interest in clearly defining the territories, which would be subject to taxes through negotiation processes between the local elites and the imperial representatives.

Epigraphic sources have shown that the creation of the Hispanic juridical convents was an Augustan initiative (Alföldy 2000: 177-205; Dopico Caínzos 2009: 31-35), rather than a result of a Flavian reform, as traditionally suggested (Tranoy 1981: 153). The *tabula Lougeiorum*

(Dopico Cainzos 1988) dating back to the year AD 1 supports this thesis. This document states that the *civitas* of the *Lougeiosex gente Asturum* established a hospitality pact with Caio Asinio Galo, belonged to the *Ara Augusta conventus* in the Asturias region, probably referring to an early division of the *Conventus Asturum* and corresponding to an acknowledgment of the differences existing between the *Astures augustanus* and the *transmontanus* (Alföldy 2007).

According to Pliny the Elder (HN. 3, 3, 18) the peninsular north-west was divided into three convents during Vespasianic times (*Bracaraugustanus*, *Lucensis* and *Asturum*). They were smaller than the other provincial *conventus*, including the Citerior, and their territories seemed to have been established according with the areas occupied by the three main pre-Roman ethnic groups of the north-western peninsula: *Gallaeci bracarensis*, *Gallaeci lucensis* and *Astures*. The capitals were represented by the three cities founded by Augustus: *Bracara Augusta*, *Lucus Augusti* and *Asturica Augusta*. Within the *Tarraconensis province* the *conventus* represented both juridical and religious divisions focused on the Imperial cult. They also carried out census-taking and taxation functions (Ozcáriz Gil 2009: 333-334) and were instrumental in organising the northern Hispanic territories, supporting Roman control and the urbanisation of the north-western region that had been initiated by Augustus.

The epigraphic record of the north-west refers mostly to either individual or collective pacts of hospitality established between the local people and the Roman citizens. These writings provide us with a dynamic vision of the processes of reorganization of the northern Hispanic region and the power negotiations at the early stages of its integration within the Roman Empire. We highlight the 'Monte Murado' *tabulae*, one from the year AD 7 and the other from the year AD 9, that signalled the establishment of client relationships between a Roman citizen and local people living at the hill fort (Silva 1983: 9-26). We are dealing with evidence of the early immigration of Roman citizens into the newly integrated territories, a fact which most likely encouraged the adaptation to new traditions as local people and Roman citizens started to enter into close patron-client bonds. Later, yet not less important, was the Astorga *tabula*, a juridical text referring to a hospitality pact established between two tribal groups (*gentilitas*) from the *Zoelae* people, the *Desoncos* and the *Tridiavos*, with the subsequent amendments highlighted and dating back to the year AD 27, in *Curunda,* and AD 152, in Astorga (CIL II: 2633).

The period between 19 BC and the first years of our era witnessed profound changes in the overall organisation of communities across the different sub-regions of the peninsular north-west. The territory was still mainly populated with hill forts, although some had begun to be abandoned (Carvalho 2016: 181-183). Other areas saw new settlements established that were either dedicated to mining or to intensive agricultural production, as took place both in the inner Trás-os-Montes (Lemos 1993) and Asturias (Sastre 1998: 34). The western area of the *bracarensis conventus* witnessed the abandonment of the small and medium hill forts at low altitudes and the emergence of new forms of land use. In a first stage, villas and *vici* were constructed, tied to the road network system established in the Augustan period (Carvalho 2012: 151-153). The new secondary settlements (*vici*) mainly developed in the Flavian dynasty, in conjunction with new forms of agriculture and livestock management in the villa sites. They made significant contributions towards the alteration of the rural landscape in the region.

In recent decades archaeology has revealed that cultural diversity in the north-western peninsula remained even after the region's integration into the Roman Empire. In general terms, we believe that the Iberian north-west was quickly and fully integrated within a new administrative structure created by Augustus and supported by the urban centres, the road network system and the intensive exploitation of resources (Martins and Carvalho 2011: 281-298). This political and administrative integration mainly favoured the elites, particularly in those areas lacking either military installations or imperial mining as, for example, in the Asturias.

The cities founded by Augustus on a classic model (*Bracara Augusta*, *Lucus Augusti* and *Asturica Augusta*) and that undertook political, religious and economic functions became the new centres of power (Martins *et al.* 2012; Rodríguez Colmenero and Covadonga Carreño 1999; Sevillano Fuertes and Vidal Encinas 2002). Despite having similar functions, equipment and monumental architecture, these cities displayed substantial differences in their structure and evolution as a consequence of the role they played in their regions and their social make up, which was rather diverse, as suggested by the epigraphic sources (Tranoy 1981).

We are aware that the new urban centres provided a setting for the promotion of the indigenous elites, whose leading role was greater in *Bracara Augusta* than it was in *Lucus Augusti* or *Asturica Augusta*. This has been suggested by epigraphy, but also by the data emerging from urban archaeological studies carried out in all three cities in recent decades. The combined research has enabled us to better understand the different urban cultural contexts, in which identity changes were taking place alongside the emergence of new powers.

The specific characteristics of the bracarensis region

Within the *Callaeci Bracarensis*, there was an important pre-Roman ethnic entity, known as the *Bracari* settled in the region between the Lima and Ave rivers, where dozens of hill forts have been identified, several of which are of large dimensions (Lemos 2009: 128-131). The Roman city of *Bracara Augusta* was set up at the very centre of this region (Martins 2006: 213-222; 2009: 181-221).

Bracara Augusta was the only civilian city founded in the peninsular north-west, while *Lucus Augusti* and *Asturica Augusta* were built from military camps (García Marcos and Vidal Encinas 1996; Rodríguez Colmenero 1995). *Bracara Augusta* is a city where the role of the local elites is best recognised and illustrated by the epigraphic monuments.

Archaeological research and systematic excavations conducted over the past four decades in Braga have demonstrated that the Roman city was an *ex novo* foundation, with an orthogonal layout aligned 19º N/NW with square city blocks measuring 156 ft on each side. This model was identified based on street remains and city porticos, but also by way of the orientation of buildings (Martins 2009: 190-192). Among the most important public

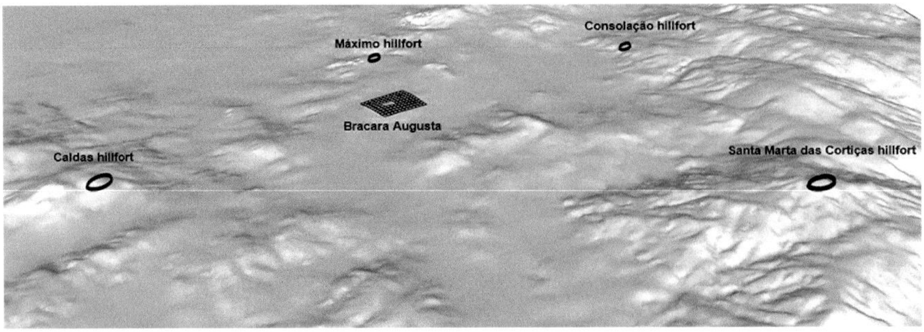

Figure 7. Pre-Roman hill forts around *Bracara Augusta.*

buildings are several baths (Martins 2005; Martins *et al.* 2011), a theatre (Martins *et al.* 2013: 29-68; Martins *et al.* 2014), and an amphitheatre (Morais 2001: 55-76).

The rural territory registered changes that accentuated the unique nature of the *bracarensis* region. The foundation of the city led directly to the early abandonment of several hill forts (Figure 7). However, some remained occupied throughout the 1st century AD, probably due to their strategic control over the road network, whose construction began in the Augustan period. Their continued usage, alternatively, may be due to the fact that they were associated with particular functions inherent to the new political, economic and social order (Carvalho 2016). Nevertheless, the survival of the pre-Roman hill forts owes very little to the pre-Roman social organisation, as they were gradually integrated into the *civitates* territories and became dependent on the new political power located in the *conventus* capital (Martins *et al.* 2005: 281-282).

Other than the surviving hill forts, new open sites of the *vici* type emerged mostly along the road network but also nearby mining and thermal water resources (Carvalho 2016), representing real secondary cities. New farming settlements following upon the Italian model (villas) also emerged and they were numerous in the outskirts of *Bracara Augusta*, alongside the roads and across the valleys (Carvalho 2016).

Studies in the surrounding rural region have revealed the profound changes that impacted upon the agrarian landscape, linked to the implantation of a Roman cadastre that indicates the land divisions and boundaries that were laid out to control land use and subsequent taxable income. Important evidence of this practice was provided by two *cippi* land markers found near Braga that provided the boundaries of one *centuria* with around 20 *actus,* 16º N/NW, coinciding with the orthogonal layout of the Roman city (Carvalho 2016; 2012: 154).

Bracara Augusta *and the construction of new identities*

Based upon available archaeological data, we can state that the development of *Bracara Augusta* followed the urban and architectonic patterns of any Roman city. It adopted a classical language that established the context where the local residents were able to develop their new cultural identity. Roman models in the cities and the territories demonstrate the population's conformity with new forms of power and the adoption of cultural elements of Roman origin. Nevertheless, it is important to highlight the negotiation that focused on establishing new identities for the indigenous communities living in the city.

One of the privileged spaces where new identities could be displayed was the Roman style house which commonly including a peristyle (Magalhães 2010; Martins *et al.* 2012). The *domus* offers us fertile evidence regarding the processes of representation and social emulation. The structures included colonnades, porticos for circulation and peristyles that served as settings for both living and presentation, where conversation and debates took place. They were also linked to nature by way of gardens, while human activity was represented by dining rooms and reception areas (Magalhães, 2010; 2013: 13-30). Equally, the house was the main space of articulation between the public and private domains, the former represented by reception areas, while the private areas were exclusively for family use.

The vast majority of *domus* known to have existed in *Bracara Augusta* date to the mid 1st century AD and the Flavian dynasty. We are certain that several *domus* owners were of indigenous origin. They had acquired, throughout at least two generations, the ability to understand the language of their new residential areas of clear Hellenistic influence, a circumstance that enabled them to take full advantage of the spaces. The urban epigraphic record (Tranoy and Le Roux 1989-90: 224-225) has documented that the vast majority of city residents were of indigenous origin, some of whom had come from the regional hill forts, as noted in several inscriptions exhibiting an inverted C, indicating *castellum* or *castrum* (hill fort) (Pereira Menault 1983: 169-192).

This predominance of indigenous residents within the city, as well as their roles as political and religious leaders, well documented by epigraphic record, differentiated *Bracara Augusta* from *Lucus Augusti* and *Asturica Augusta*, where the key social players were linked with the military and the administrative sectors. However, it is important to point out that the indigenous elites represented in the honorific, votive or funerary inscriptions of Braga, corresponded to a privileged segment of the hill fort population who were able to negotiate their relocation to the city. This appears to have taken place before the years 4 and 3 BC, when, on the birthday of *Paulus Fabius Maximus*, Augustus received the gift of a statue, of which only the pedestal remains (Le Roux 1975: 155; Tranoy 1981: 328). This is the first known monument dedicated to the Emperor by the *bracaraugustanus*, the new civic community settled in *Bracara Augusta* that was already using the city name.

The early date of the Augustan statue pedestal, as well as the two other missing statues, contribute to our understanding of the importance that monuments and writing had acquired as representations of the power of the new indigenous elite (Woolf 1994: 84-98). Writing made reference to a certain type of privileged knowledge that formed the basis of a powerful narrative, the (re)negotiation of identities, showing off the power of families and individuals and displaying positions of status.

The process of constructing a new identity was especially visible in the funerary world, where new rituals, symbols and narratives emerged. Both monuments and writing were used by the indigenous elites not only as symbols of their newly emerging power but also

Figure 8. Funerary monument of an indigenous family (*Caturus* son of *Camalus*, *Meditia* daughter of *Medamus* and *Medamus* son of *Caturus*, *Culaeciensis*) (Archaeological Museum D. Diogo de Sousa, Braga).

as a way to negotiate their identities and their status. The necropolises at *Bracara Augusta* included monuments evocative of the identity of the dead, representing an ideal setting for analysing the cultural changes emerging between the end of the 1st century BC and mid 1st century AD (Braga 2010; Braga 2014).

It is known that the pre-Roman population of peninsular north-west cremated their dead, as did the Romans. However, the indigenous funerary rites were carried out privately as opposed to the habit of the Romans, who publically marked the identity of the deceased with *arae*, *stelae* or tombstones that were placed near the graves with the names inscribed. These practices, which can be translated into a newfound visibility for the dead, were adopted and the funerary spaces were monumentalised through the presence of buildings and epigraphic elements representing new narratives supported by the written word alluding to the indigenous elite's genealogies (Figure 9).

In this sense, there was an important identity shift when the indigenous population adopted the Roman funerary practices and began to mark graves with epigraphic monuments both in urban and rural areas (González Ruibal 2006-2007; Sastre 2007). However, the nature of the inscriptions in Braga revealed that these did not refer to undifferentiated sectors of the population, but rather to people of indigenous origin who had become fully integrated into the urban elite and who sought recognition through their funerary practices. Part of that recognition came from the presence of *stelae* but also through the re-creation of the rich iconography of the *bracarensis* region in the pre-Roman period represented by *lunulae*, circles and cords (Figures 9 and 10). These symbols allowed those indigenous elites of *Bracara Augusta* who had already merged with the urban aristocracy to reaffirm their relationship with their past, while simultaneously transmitting their new identity and status via the use of Roman funerary monuments and

Figure 9. Statue pedestal honouring Augustus (Martins Sarmento Museum, Guimarães).

Figure 10. Funerary monument honouring a descendant of *Bloena* with indigenous origin (Archaeological Museum D. Diogo de Sousa, Braga).

writing (Woolf 1994). In this sense, the necropolis served as a new context for representing and negotiating identities.

It is worth pointing out the uniqueness of the funerary and the symbolic worlds of *Bracara Augusta* that were marked by monuments like *stelae* and how they differed from those in other peninsular north-western cities where plaques and *arae* dominated (Tranoy and Le Roux 1989-90). These types of monuments, much more common in the Italian universe, were rather used by the vast majority of prosecutors and senior officials who managed the gold mining at 'Bierzo' living in *Lucus Augusti* and *Asturica Augusta.* Contrary to what took place in *Bracara Augusta*, those northern cities failed to witness the rise of a powerful indigenous group. For that reason, funerary inscriptions in Braga served as first-hand testimonies to the overall understanding of identity changes occurring among the urbanised pre-Roman and indigenous population, who had adopted the Roman way of life.

Funerary inscriptions of Braga give testimony to the progressive affirmation of the private and singular character of death in Roman society, and the necropolises became the new narrative spaces, replacing the previous spaces represented by the houses and hill forts where the symbolic capital of indigenous communities was traditionally accumulated (González Ruibal 2006-2007). While the indigenous houses had often demonstrated the differentiated power of its residents, through its exceptional decorative motifs, this role was now taken over by decorated funerary monuments and texts (Woolf 1994).

Special mention should be given to the extraordinary changes in mentality registered in the indigenous community's way of life that resulted from the integration of the peninsular north-west into the Roman world (Sastre 2007). This process affected perceptions of space and time, turning identity negotiation into a need that seemed to clearly give priority to the funerary spaces. In the case of *Bracara Augusta*, this process took place between the Augustan and Flavian periods.

Conclusions

In recent decades archaeology has demonstrated that the peninsular north-western territory remained culturally diverse after its integration into the Roman Empire. This was a natural consequence of the social organization of pre-Roman communities and of the expression and nature of the different sub-regional cultural identities. As we reject the existence of a single 'castreja' identity during the Iron Age we also refute the idea of a monolithic 'Roman cultural identity' which might serve as a benchmark against which to measure the greater or lesser degree of change of the local populations. In fact, the Roman acculturation of this region, i.e. the process of creating a provincial culture, was neither peripheral nor incipient, as some have argued, nor was it the mere result of the imposition of macro-economic policies that determined the forced transformation of segmentary or heroic societies into a tax-based society.

The archaeological record has revealed the assimilation of a set of technological changes associated with cities, while the road network system, the new settlement patterns and the new forms of land and resource usage dismantled the previous organizational structure and indigenous powers. In some regions, and in a similar way as the western part of the *bracarensis conventus*, the pre-Roman elites perpetuated their power by inserting themselves into the new Roman political and social order, adopting Roman culture and its living standards. On the other hand, the archaeological record elucidated the negotiation processes inherent to the construction of new identities, initially linked with funerary spaces and writing adopted in the creation of new genealogical narratives. Nevertheless, we are not dealing with the construction of a Roman identity but rather with a newly miscegenated one combining both Roman and indigenous elements and reinterpreting them in a new political, social and economic context.

Available data suggests that indigenous societies endured substantive cultural changes with their integration in the Roman Empire that were processed at different rates. These alterations were fully dependent on the regional cultural traditions and were mainly determined by the use of a distinct material culture that was gradually imposed and negotiated, reinterpreted and integrated into the daily life of the indigenous communities. This is a polymorphous process, in which indigenous communities took on a leading role. The archaeological record, more expressive when it comes to the practices and traditions of the urban elites, has demonstrated that the indigenous population was not limited to the assimilation of the Latin culture or the Roman technologies and way of life. It underwent cultural transformations that changed its vision of landscape, society, economics, religion and death. The understanding of a new social and cultural order that put its imprint not only on the concept and use of space but also on the meaning and use of time, demanded the construction of new genealogies and new narratives which can be clearly seen in the funerary contexts, although further research is still needed to fully understand this complex process.

References

Alvarez-Sanchis, J. 1997. *Los Vettones. Arqueología de un pueblo protohistórico.* Unpublished PHD thesis, Universidad Complutense de Madrid.

Ayán Vila, X. M. A. 2008. Round Iron Age: The Circular House in the Hillfort of the Northwestern Iberian Peninsula. *E-Keltoi. Journal of Interdisciplinary Celtic Studies* 6: 903-1003 (online).

Alarcão, J. 1988. *Roman Portugal.* Warminster, Aries & Philips Ltd.

Alföldy, G. 1969. *Fasti Hispanienses. Senatorische Reichsbeamte und Offiziere in den spanischen provinzen des römischen Reiches von Augustus bis Diokletian.* Wiesbaden, F. Steiner.

Alföldy, G. 2000. Das neue Edikt des Augustus aus El Bierzo. *Zeitschrift für Papyrologie und Epigraphik* 131: 177-205.

Alföldy, G. 2007. Fasti und Verwaltung der hispanishen Provinzen: zumheutigen Stand der Forschung. In R. Haensch and J. Heinrich (eds), *Herrschen und Verwalten: Der Alltag der römischen Administration in der Hohen Kaiserzeit.* Colonia-Weimar-Viena, Böhlau.

Braga, C. 2010. *Rituais funerários em Bracara Augusta: o novo núcleo de necrópole da Via XVII.* Unpublished Master's thesis, Universidade do Minho.

Braga, C. 2014. A new sector of the via XVII necropolis in Bracara Augusta: the high empire phase. In *Atas XVIII International Congress of Classical Archaeology - Centre and periphery in the ancient world*: 1253-1257. Mérida, Museu Nacional de Arte Romano.

Bravo Castañeda, G. 2007. *Hispânia. La epopeya de los romanos en la Península.* Madrid, La Esfera de los Livros.

Calo Lourido, F. A. 1994. *Plástica da Cultura Castrexa Galego-Portuguesa.* La Coruña, Fundación Pedro Barrié de la Maza.

Carballo Arceo, L. X. and Fábregas Valcarce, R. 2006. Variaciónes rexionais nas sociedades pre e protohistóricas galaicas. In R. Álvarez, F. Dubertand and X. Sousa (eds), *Lingua e territorio*: 66-92. Santiago de Compostela, Universidade de Santiago de Compostela.

Carvalho, H. 2012. Marcadores da paisagen e intervenção cadastral no território da cidade de Bracara Augusta. *Archivo Español de Arqueología* 85: 149-166.

Carvalho, H. 2016. *The Roman Settlement Patterns in the Western Façade of the* Conventus Bracarensis. British Archaeological Reports International Series 2789. Oxford, British Archaeological Reports.

Collis, J. 1996. Urbanisation in Atlantic Europe in the Iron Age. *Gallaecia* 14-15: 223-239.

Cruz, G. 2015. O surgimento do espaço urbano no Noroeste da Ibéria. Uma reflexão sobre os *oppida* pré-Romanos. In R. Martinez Peñin and G. Cavero Domínguez (eds), *Evolución de los espácios urbanos y sus territórios en el Noroeste de la Peninsula Ibérica*: 403-414. Léon, Ediciones El Forastero S.A.

Curchin, L. A. 2004. *Roman Spain, Conquest and Assimilation.* London, Routledge.

Dopico Caínzos, M. D. 1988. *La Tabula Lougeiorum. Estudios sobre la implantación romana en Hispania.* Vitoria, Universidad del País Vasco.

Dopico Caínzos, M. D. 2009. A transformação dos pobos do noroeste Hispánico na época de Augusto: a evidencia epigráfica. In M. D. Dopico Caínzos, M. Villanueva Acuña and

P. Rodríguez Alvarez (eds), *Do Castro á Cidade. A romanización na Gallaecia e na Hispânia indoeuropea*: 31-53. Lugo, Disputación de Lugo.

Fabião, C. 1993. O povoamento proto-histórico e romano. In J. Matoso (dir.) *História de Portugal* 1: 76-299. Lisboa, Círculo dos Leitores.

Fabião, C. 2005. Caminhos do atlântico romano: evidências e perplexidades. In C. Fernández Ochoa and P. Garcia Diaz (ed.). *Unidad y Diversidaden el Arco Atlanticoen época romana*. 83-85. Gijon, British Archaeological Reports IS1371.

Fernández Götz, M. 2011. Cultos, Ferias y Asambleas: los santuarios protohistóricos del Rin Medio – Mosela como espacios de agregación. *Palaeohispanica* 11: 127-154.

García Marcos, V. and Vidal Encinas, J. M. 1996. Asturica Augusta: De asentamiento militar a urbs magnífica. In A. Rodríguez Colmenero (coord.), *Los orígenes de la ciudaden el noroeste hispánico. Actas del Congreso Internacional*: 911-944. Lugo, Disputación de Lugo.

Grau, L. and Hoyas, J. L. (eds) 2001. *El bronce de Bembibre: un edicto del emperador Augusto delaño 15 a.C.* León, Consejería de Educación y Cultura.

González Ruibal, A. 2004. Facing two seas: Mediterranean and Atlantic contacts in the NW of Iberia. *Oxford Journal of Archaeology* 23 (3): 287-317.

González Ruibal, A. 2006. House societies vs. kindship-based societies: an archaeological case from Iron Age Europe. *Journal of Anthropological Archaeology* 25 (1): 144-173.

González Ruibal, A. 2006-2007. *Galaicos. Poder y Comunidad en el Noroeste de la Península Ibérica (1200 a.C - 50 d.C.)*. Brigantium 18-19. La Coruña, Museu de San Antón.

González Ruibal, A. 2008. Los pueblos del Noroeste. In F. Gracia Alonso (coord.), *De Iberia a Hispania*: 899-930. Barcelona, Ariel.

González Ruibal, A., Rodríguez Martínez, R., Aboal Fernández, R. and Castro Hierro, V. 2007. Comercio mediterráneoen el castro de Montealegre (Pontevedra, Galicia. Siglo II a.C.-inicios del siglo Id.C. *Archivo Español de Arqueología* 80: 43-74.

Lemos, F. S. 1993. *Povoamento romano de Trás-os-Montes Oriental*. Unpublished PhD dissertation. Braga, Universidade do Minho.

Lemos, F. S. 2009. A transformação do habitat e da paisagem castreja no contexto da romanização: o exemplo dos grandes castros. In D. Dopico Caínzos, M. Villanueva Acuña and P. Rodríguez Alvarez (eds), *Do Castro á Cidade. A romanización na Gallaecia e na Hispânia indoeuropea*: 109-141. Lugo, Disputación de Lugo.

Lemos, F. S., Cruz, G. and Fonte, J. 2008. Estruturas de banhos do território do Bracari: os casos de Briteiros e de Braga. *Fervédes* 5: 319-328.

LeRoux, P. 1975. Aux Origines de Braga (Bracara Augusta). *Bracara Augusta* 9 (67-68): 155-157.

Magalhães, F. 2010. *Arquitectura doméstica em Bracara Augusta*. Unpublished Master's thesis. Braga, Universidade do Minho.

Magalhães, F. 2013. Arquitetura doméstica em *Bracara Augusta*. *Interconexões* 1: 13-30.

Martins, M. 1990. *O povoamento proto-histórico e a romanização da bacia do curso médio do Cávado*. Cadernos de Arqueologia. Monografias 5. Braga, UAUM.

Martins, M. 1997. The Dynamics of change in North-west Portugal during the first millennium BC. In M. Diaz-Andreu and S. Keay (eds), *The Archaeology of Iberia*: 1143-157. London/New York, Routledge.

Martins, M. 2005. *As termas romanas do Alto da Cividade. Um exemplo de arquitectura pública em Bracara Augusta*. Bracara Augusta. Escavações Arqueológicas 1. Braga, UAUM/NARQ.

Martins, M. 2006. *Bracara Augusta*: a Roman town in Altantic area. In L. Abal Casal, S. Keay and S. Ramallo Arensio (eds), *Early Roman towns in Hispania Tarraconensis*: 213-222. *Journal of Roman Archaeology* Supplementary Series 62. Portsmouth, Rhode Island.

Martins, M. 2009. *Bracara Augusta*. Panorama e estado da questão sobre o seu urbanismo. In M. D. Dopico Caínzos, M. Villanueva Acuña and P. Rodríguez Alvarez (eds), *Do Castro á Cidade. A romanización na Gallaecia e na Hispânia indoeuropea*: 181-211. Lugo, Disputación de Lugo.

Martins, M. and Silva, A. C. F. 1984. A estátua de guerreiro de S. Julião (Vila Verde). *Cadernos de Arqueologia* 1: 29-47.

Martins, M., Lemos, F. S. and Pérez Losada, F. 2005. O povoamento romano no território dos galaicos bracarenses. In C. Fernández Ochoa and P. Garcia Díaz (eds), *Unidad y Diversidaden el Arco Atlantico en época romana*, 279-296. British Archaeological Reports International Series 1371. Oxford, Archaeopress.

Martins, M. and Carvalho, H. 2010. Bracara Augusta and the changing of rural landscape. In C. Corsi and F. Vermeulen (eds), *Changing Landscapes: The impact of Roman towns in the Western Mediterranean, Proceedings of the International Colloquium*: 281-298. Ammaia, Antequem.

Martins, M., Meireles, J. and Ribeiro, M. C. 2011. As termas públicas de *Bracara Augusta* e o abastecimento de água da cidade romana. In *Atas do Seminário Internacional Aquae Sacrae. Agua e sacralidad en época antigua*: 69-102. Girona, Universidade de Girona.

Martins, M., Ribeiro, R., Magalhães, F. and Braga, C. 2012. Urbanismo e arquitetura de *Bracara Augusta*. Sociedade, economia e lazer. In M. C. Ribeiro and A. Melo (coord. de), *Evolução da Paisagem Urbana: Economia e Sociedade*: 29-68. Braga, CITCEM.

Martins, M., Mar, R., Ribeiro, J. and Magalhães, F. 2013. A construção do teatro romano de *Bracara Augusta*. In A. Melo and M. C. Ribeiro (coord.), *História da Construção. Arquiteturas e técnicas Construtivas*: 41-76. Braga, CITCEM.

Martins, M., Mar, R., Ribeiro, J. and Magalhães, F. 2014. The Roman theatre of Bracara Augusta. In *Atas XVIII International Congress of Classical Archaeology - Centre and periphery in the ancient world*: 861-864. Mérida, Museu Nacional de Arte Romano.

Morais, R. 2001. Breve ensaio sobre o anfiteatro de Bracara Augusta. *Forum* 30: 55-76.

Ozcáriz Gil, P. 2009. Organización administrativa y territorial de las províncias hispanas durante el Alto Império. In J. Andreu Pintado, J. Cabrero Piquero and I. Rodá de Llanza, I. (eds), *Hispania. Las províncias hispanas en el mundo romano*: 333-334. Tarragona, Institut Català d'Arqueologia Clàssica.

Parcero Oubiña, C. 2002. *La construcción del paisaje social en la Edad del Hierro del noroeste ibérico*. Ortigueira, Fundación Federico Maciñeira.

Pereira Menault, G. 1983. Los castella y las comunidades de Gallaecia. In *Actas do II Seminario de Arqueologia del Noroeste*: 169-192. Madrid, CSIC.

Pitts, M. 2010. Re-thinking the southern British Oppida: Networks, Kingdoms and material culture. *European Journal of Archaeology* 13: 32-63.

Pitts, M. and Perring, D. 2006. The making of Britain's first urban landscapes: The case of Late Iron Age and Roman Essex. *Britannia* 37: 189-212.

Queiroga, F. 1992. *War and Castros: New Approaches to the Northwestern Portuguese Iron Age*. Unpublished PhD thesis, Oxford University.

Queiroga, F. 2007. The Late Castro Culture of North-west Portugal: Dynamics of Change. In C. Gosden, H. Hamerow, P. Jersey and G. Lock (eds), *Communities and connections. Essays in Honour of Barry Cunliffe*: 169-179. Oxford, Oxford University Press.

Rodríguez Colmenero, A. 1995. *Lucus Augusti. Urbs Romana. Los Orígenes de La Ciudad de Lugo.* Lugo, Ayuntamiento de Lugo.

Rodriguez Colmenero, A. and Covadonga Carreño, M. 1999. *LucusAugusti*, Capital romana del finisterre hispânico. In *Actas da Mesa Redonda, Emergência e Desenvolvimento das cidades romanas no norte da Península Ibérica*: 115-132. Tongobriga.

Sánchez Palencia, F. J. and Mangas, J. 2000. *El Edicto del Bierzo: Augusto y el NO de Hispania.* Léon, Fundación Las Médulas-Fenosa.

Sastre, I. 1998. *Formas de dependencia social en el Noroeste peninsular (Transición del mundo Preromano al Romano y Época Altoimperial).* Ponferrada, Instituto de Estudios Bercianos.

Sastre, I. 2001. *Las formaciones sociales rurales de la Asturia romana.* Madrid, Ediciones Clásicas.

Sastre, I. 2002. Forms of social inequality in the Castro Culture. *European Journal of Archaeology* 5 (2): 213-248.

Sastre, I. 2004. Los procesos de la Complejidad social en el Noroeste Peninsular: Arqueologia y Fuentes Literárias. *Trabajos de Prehistoria* 61 (2): 99-110.

Sastre, I. 2007. Campesinado, escritura y paisaje: algunas cuestiones sobre el mundo provincial romano occidental. *Gerion vol. extra: 375-381.*

Sevillano Fuertes, A. and Vidal Encinas, J. M. 2002. *Urbs Magnífica. Una aproximación a la Arqueología de Asturica Augusta.* Astorga. León, Museo Romano.

Silva, A. C. F. 1986. *A cultura Castreja no Noroeste de Portugal.* Paços de Ferreira, Museu arqueológico da Citânia de Sanfins.

Silva, A. C. F. 1995. A evolução do habitat castrejo e o processo de proto-urbanização no noroeste de Portugal durante o I milénio a.C. *Revista da Faculdade de Letras* 12: 505-546.

Silva, A. C. F. 1983. As *tesserae hospitales* do Castro da Senhora da Saúde ou Monte Murado (Pedroso, Vila Nova de Gaia). Contributo para o estudo das instituições e povoamento da Hispânia Antiga. *Gaya* 1: 9-26.

Silva, A. C. F. 1999. *Citânia de Sanfins. Catálogo Museu da Citânia de Sanfins.* Paços de Ferreira, Câmara Municipal.

Silva, A. C. F. 2003. As expressões guerreiras da sociedade castreja. *Madrider Mitteilungen* 44: 41-50.

Silva, A. C. F. and Pinto, J. M. M. 2001. Comércio púnico com o Noroeste. In A. A. Tavares (ed.), *Os púnicos no Extremo Ocidente*: 229-238. Lisboa, Universidade Aberta.

Silva, A. C. F. and Machado, J. 2007. Banhos castrejos do Norte de Portugal. In *Pedra Formosa-Arqueologia Experimental*: 20-60. Vila Nova de Famalicão, Câmara Municipal de Vila Nova de Famalicão/Museu Nacional de Arqueologia.

Syme, R. 1970. The conquest of North-West Spain, in *Legio VII Gemina*: 79-108. Leon, León Inst. Leones de Estud. Romano-visigoticos.

Tranoy, A. 1981. *La Galice romaine. Recherches sur le Nord Ouest de la Péninsule Ibérique dans l'Antiquité.* Paris, Diffusion du Boccard.

Tranoy, A. and Le Roux, P. 1989-1990. As necrópoles romanas de *Bracara Augusta* – Les inscriptions funéraires. *Cadernos de Arqueologia* 6-7: 183-230.

Woolf, G. 1993. Rethinking the oppida. *Oxford Journal of Archaeology* 12 (2): 223-234.

Woolf, G. 1994. Power and the spread of writing in the West. In A. K. Bowman and G. Woolf (eds), *Literacy and Power in the Ancient world*: 84-98. Cambridge, Cambridge University Press.

Woolf, G. 1998. *Becoming Roman. The Origins of Provincial Civilization in Gaul.* Cambridge, Cambridge University Press.